15¢

D1511501

M.N.RAWSON

MARION NICHOLL RAWSON
has also written

HANDWROUGHT ANCESTORS

"For years she has been reproducing the pattern of an earlier American life, and with a great deal of success. The results are delightful for many reasons, . . . they serve to enlighten the newest generations . . . and they bring back vivid memories of the dying days of skilled craftsmanship . . ."— Herschel Brickell, *New York Post*.

"The book adds one more to the series. . . . The Rawson books are by far the most popular of their kind in general circulation . . ."— *Boston Evening Transcript*

LITTLE OLD MILLS

"It is a volume to thrill all who are devoted to Americana and especially all who would get close to the beginnings of our great industrial enterprises of today."
— John Clair Minot, *The Boston Herald*

SING OLD HOUSE

"A woman who seems to know more about how early Americans lived than the most profound historians."
— Harry Hansen, *The New York World-Telegram*

"Mrs. Rawson continues to explore old America through the medium of America's old houses and—in this instance —their 'fittings.' She has become the foremost authority in this pleasantly specialized field . . . the illustrations are joys themselves."— *Providence Sunday Journal*

FROM HERE TO YENDER

"The whole book is abundantly conceived and keeps well the unhurried measure and observational tone of old journeys throughout the country." — *The New Republic*

WHEN ANTIQUES WERE YOUNG

"A charming exposition of the social customs of old New England."— *The American Mercury*

COUNTRY AUCTION

"To the lover of the antiques of the early American style, the book may act as a guide, but to the lover of real American home life the book is a treasure."
— *The Buffalo Evening News*

CANDLE DAYS

OF THE EARTH EARTHY

The "Old Forge" in Virginia's Iron Gate,
built in 1794.

MARION NICHOLL RAWSON

OF THE EARTH
EARTHY

HOW OUR FATHERS
DWELT UPON
AND
WOOED THE EARTH

ILLUSTRATED BY THE AUTHOR

E. P. DUTTON & COMPANY, INC.

S. A. Jacobs, The Golden Eagle Press
Mount Vernon, N. Y.

"For the master spirit of
the earth shall not sleep
peacefully upon the wind
till the needs of the least
of you are satisfied."

To D. B. C.
the
Compleat Delver

CONTENTS

CONTENTS

OF THE EARTH EARTHY

Come with us to the field, or go with our brothers
to the sea and cast your net;
For the land and the sea shall be bountiful to you
even as to us.

— *Kahlil Gibran*

*Separate kitchen at old "Crows" tavern, Midland
Trail, Virginia, with original irons and brasses in
chimney place*

Being Bridges

"EVERY time the old man came to visit Grandfather he
would take me on his knee and ask, 'What kind of cedar can
be used for shingles ? ' I was a very small child and a girl at
that, and in all probability should never need to know the
niceties of shingles, yet I must always winsomely reply,
'Only that cut from trees whose grain turned toward the
sun.' "

"Precept on precept," was the old rule for raising children,
and along with memorized facts went little slices of philoso-

11

T: U.S.

ra

phy adroitly slipped in by the old folks who yearned to be bridges for their descendants, bridges which would span the morasses of much that was hard to learn, bridges that would serve as short cuts to bear them safely across the Jordan to success.

Who of us has not seen gnarled old trees stripped of their bark and showing a perfect spiral in the twisting of their trunk, and wondered why it was so. To make a perfect shingle? Perhaps. And again, perhaps because in cedar nature there is a reaching out for warmth and sunlight as intense as that of the sunflower which turns on its god, the sun, when he sets, "the same face that it turned when he rose," marking the round of the cardinal points every twenty-four hours. A mighty textural weave such a sunwise-turning trunk must have, and it were well that a child should know it, and incidentally the ceaseless straining toward a great light, the resultant power — the perfect shingle.

Outside of above chimney

EARLY EXPEDIENCES

Scattered throughout the country there still remain marks of the wise knowings of old men, the wheel-ruts worn in the rocks of convenient Southern brook beds where carts once went back and forth into the mountains on some now forgotten errands; those drooping but persisting structures which were neither house nor barn, mill nor shop, but shelters of some work which brought the worker even closer to the Earth than did that of the miller and the tinkerer, and made them the theatres of the embryonic beginnings of to-day's great industries. Out of shipyard, quarry, paint mine, pine forest, rope walk, and a score of other old work spots still come the rememberings of old men from the premachine age, of individual ingenuity and resourcefulness.

"I remember a man that had his horse living on a merry-go-round. There wasn't any brook handy for water power, so he had a flat disk wheel in the cellar of the mill — a treadmill, you know — and when he wanted to work the mill he just slipped back the brake and the horse had to start walking whether he wanted to or not. He was always there, right handy."

A mountain man whose work was gathering an expensive herb near a rattlesnake cliff, passed on his knowing thus: "When the snake's tooth strikes your leg, it pushes back against the bellows and the poison runs out through the hollow in the tooth"; he remembered too that when he had to hollow out a section of a tree trunk to form a trough for toting newly found honey out of the woods, he controlled the slow-burning fire used in the gouging, with lumps of wet clay. Another man who knew his earth and its earthiness and rivers, had to cross the Hudson on the ice one midnight to reach his farm. He had crossed in the morning but the ice had begun to break up under a noon thaw, and slush warned

13

him that there would be danger spots and might be holes. Out in the middle of the river the black spots became places of potential death, but there was no turning back. Suddenly he reached in his coat pocket and drew out some hard candy he had bought at the store for a little treat, and began stoning those black spots as he approached them, for "if they could stand one of those rock candies they could surely hold me."

Old Root cellar, Low Moor, Virginia

As one old man puts it: "They's tricks you got to get on Nature. You send a greenhorn aboard to tie a knot, or make a bight, and let him work never so long, you'd never get tight. A man can go in a quarry but if he aint a good quarryman, he won't get the stuff out. You got to learn the tricks." Somewhere in us lies a need for useful physical work and the one who feeds this need and learns the tricks, finds his peace. The brain worker must just so often touch the earth, or the body sinks and the brain itself atrophies. We complain that in the old days there were so many ways of delving for a livelihood in the earth, which are gone today. But the earth is still with us, one of the few unchangeables in a world of change. There are still mountain springs and their wheel-turning waterways, there are still minerals awaiting their resurrection in mountains whose beauty alone is health and wealth, there are the same growing plants whose fibers give birth to rope, and ancient paint rocks offering their age-old colors if we but stretch out a hand for them. Standing before a long pier-glass we see ourselves with the room apparently stretching away on before us like a vista, and not behind us at all. Prophecy must be like this, the background forming the foreground, and the future simply a reflection of the past. What has been done, can be done again.

The passing on of an industry from father to son through four or five generations of the same family, meant adding knowledge to knowledge in an unbroken line until the sum of these additions ran into high figures, and we are apt to deplore a world which has outgrown this tendency and left many an old shop locked with nail and cobweb after the passing of a father whose sons had all left home, because so much was laid away in the grave besides the man's body. Yet, hope is not all lost even here. In 1724 a charter was granted by the English Crown to the master carpenters and builders of Philadelphia, for what was really an English workingman's guild, and future membership was to be limited to those descendants of the charter members who followed their fathers' trades. The membership in old CARPENTERS HALL was never over fifty-seven, even in its balmiest days, and today there is a membership of forty-nine. While it might have grown to rather vast proportions if many sons had come to each member and all had followed their fathers' trades, it still shows a considerable amount of handing-down of family interests in one city, and we shall find many families doing likewise. Our brooks are still flowing on though their sources may be forgotten.

Our Oldest Industry

Little is known of our first real land industry but if only to mention it, it must have first place here. In 1528 the Spanish found the sassafras tree in the New World but already the English were saying that "the roote of Sassafras hath power to comfort the liuer," and it was not long before several European countries were sending their ships across the great waste to get this humble root. Along the shores of the future Massachusetts Colony, and where Egg Harbor was one day to form a part of New Jersey's shore line, men found the shrub or tree and took it back to London in great shiploads. Even the bark had its uses medicinally as an "alterative," and sassafras tea became a drink on both sides of the water. In 1622 John Smith called it "saxefras," and in the mountains of Virginia some diggers of the root today call it Sassafruit." Sassafras was, barring fish, the greatest lodestone which the New World possessed during the 1500s and the first decade of the 1600s. Ships carrying it to Holland, one of its big markets, went "north about" to avoid its falling into greedy English hands, and when it had arrived, it was made into a beverage called "sloop."

The Spring House

Often among the most artistic of our old landmarks of early industries are those common, half-forgotten outbuildings which stand never far off from the old farm home, or the "buckra house" of the Southern plantation, and are so individual that they should never be allowed to slip into

16

oblivion. Domestic they are, to be sure, but most of our early industries had their beginnings at home.

The spring-house was the old-time dairy.

Dwelling and spring house in one. Pennsylvania

Deep in a ravine over a flowing brook or running spring, a spring-house might have no inducements to offer as a home, but by the side road, or part way down a meadow, it might be a likely place to settle, and Pennsylvania combined her dairy with her house in many cases, building strong stone houses with a big central room with a fireplace on the first floor off the slanting meadow, sleeping quarters above, and using the basement for the kitchen with the running water close at hand and one section walled off for refrigeration. Here was a structure, of the earth earthy, the icehouse and dwelling under one roof and all a part with the brook bed. The usual spring-house was little more than the milk-house where the stone milk pans were set in the flowing stream, but they could be of stone, timber, clay, or log; the upper part might be a smoke-house with the ceiling pierced with hooks for holding the smoked meats. Today, if there be anything left of a milk-house, it is a thing of loveliness.

Pennsylvania spring house with its brick arch for cooking swill

The Smoke House

The smoke-house was the early butcher shop.

"We smoke our hams with corncobs. They make the best smoke, flavor them best. Just be sure there's a smudge burning all the time they're curing." So speaks New York from her smoke-house.

"Mighty sure there's no likelier way to smoke hams than save your tobacco stems and get a good smoke going." North Carolina.

18

Exterior of above spring house

"Be sure your smoke-house is airtight, then make a fire in the pit or in an iron vessel, of good hickory wood. Let it smoke away like I tell you until the ham is sure smoked through and then you'll taste that special flavor that only old hickory can give." Virginia has spoken.

"You better put your killin' in brine for about six weeks; the shoulders and hind quarters for ham, the flat pieces along side for bacon. The rest you can use for sausage and spare-ribs and pork chops. You'll have been eating so much beef up to killin' time that they'll taste uncommon good if you do 'em right. After they come out of the brine you hang 'em in the smoke-house for about ten days. Each mornin' you start a fire in the ash kettle down in one corner, cover it well to make a smudge-fire of corn cobs. You got to be sure you build a good smoke, though." New England.

Naturally these smoke-houses were built of stone or brick as a safeguard against fire. They followed the earlier smoke-closets which were built into many of the houses of the first century, and were connected with the great chimney, and generally on the second floor where they caught the escaping smoke from the hearth below and used it to cure the meats hanging from iron rod and hook, Certainly these must be allowed room among the important industrial structures of the past.

1. *Old Van Lear smoke house of 1700s, Marple County, Pennsylvania*
11. *Smoke-holes in upper walls, four to six inches*

New Hampshire smoke house

The Loom House

The loom-house was the later "drygoods store."

EARLY EXPEDIENCES

*Southern loom house with shingles curling because
they were rived in the light of the moon*

As with food in the smoke-house so it was with clothes in
the loom-house, they grew by the yard under the hands of
men, before the Revolution, and those of the women afterwards. They were as a rule a part of the farmhouse itself in
the Northern parts of the country, where the cold weather
drove all sorts of work under one roof for warmth. In the
Southern colonies they stood apart, a place in which some of
the slaves spent their days carding and hatcheling, spinning
and reeling, weaving and perhaps even preparing the cloth
for its fulling, and drying out in the open fields. They stand
today, low and compact, or on their raised foundations,
furnished with a large chimneyplace and a stone floor, sometimes ornamented with alternating rows of curved and un-
curved cypress shingles, and inadequately lighted with small
windows. The one in the illustration has a veritable feather-
bed of curled but still faithful handcut and shaved shingles.
A rare collection of odds and ends is their fare today for the
"old loom-house" is a fine storage place.

OF THE EARTH EARTHY

The Sugar House

The sugar-house was the candy store and the sweet shop.

This center of sugar-making was generally off in the sugar-orchard, or "bush" or "grove," or "lot," away from the usual haunts of men, for great sugar trees and their soil were left undisturbed by the plow and allowed to run their own lives in peace. Sometimes a New Hampshire sugar-lot, with trees of great age and height growing up from among mica-glistening rocks, became a fairyland of a fall evening when the moon was rising. It was only when spring's cold nights and warm days brought the first run of sap that the trees were tapped, little hollowed spiles made from the sumach set in the tiny holes, the sap buckets set beneath to catch the slow drip, drip of the sap—and the sugar-house door opened. Like a tobacco-house a sugar-house must have always a generous woodpile close by, for the sugar fire is a gourmand and in a fortnight's time will claim a heavy toll from the near-by woods. A door and a window or two, a hole in the roof through which the steam of boiling may pass off, or a part of the roof raised and set with transoms. Down in the pans the evaporation will go on through hours and days of watching until the sap has become syrup and is carried out for the "sugaring off." Much sugar was made with no shelter above it but in a kettle hung from a lugpole between crotched poles over a blazing fire; but roof or no roof there must still be thirty gallons of sap to produce one gallon of syrup. Two thousand metal buckets make a pretty frieze among the sugar-maples today, but more interesting were the old-fashioned sap buckets made like the old wooden milking pigins, with unbulged staves and one left longer than the others to serve as handle with a hole in it. Before these, came the gouged-out tree-trunk trough, a yard long and set at the foot of the tree beneath the spile. There might be three or even four active weeks of sugaring, another when all was made sweet and clean again, but then, months of utter rest for the sugar-house while it did nothing but store the equipment for the next spring's run.

"Krout" cutter of Lewisburg, West Virginia

Bakehouse and Kitchen

These were the bakery and the delicatessen shops.

The New Englander had his kitchen within his house. The New Yorker along the Mohawk and the New Jerseyite sometimes had a kitchen apart from the house, as late as the end of the 1700s, which seems strange since they too felt the cold of winter. The South was glad to keep its cooking areas at arm's length from the living quarters. The Pennsylvanians had both attached and unattached kitchens, with

Old Crows, Alleghany County, Virginia

an occasional oven built into the kitchen but with its door on the outside. At Crows Tavern on the old Midland Trail through Virginia — its log "square" built before 1800 but its great length growing quickly thereafter — the "rough cooking" was done in the kitchen back of the tavern, and here today we find the massive chimneyplace with its lovely curved crane and pothooks, pots and brass kettles still in place. Because this tavern was a popular resort it is probable that most of the cooking was done here. Here kitchen, wood-shed, and loom-house stood in a long row under one roof.

So did precept on precept and hard bodily labor make the world go round for our forefathers who delved in the earth for their livelihood. Artless little shelters arose where the wool of the sheep, sap from the trees, ripe heads of grain, and many another product of the earth's surface or the creatures which roamed upon it, were brought to be made useful to man and his family. Beneath the surface there were yet other floors where the equal though varying riches could be found for the delving and the taking. It is these floors of riches above and below, so definitely of the earth earthy, and the shelters which they brought into form, the excitement of discovery

24

and the native ingenuity which was constantly called for, which have seemed crying out for expression and a chance to tell their own tales.

Original "square" of Old Crows built of logs before 1800, showing steps up to door from a porch of later date. Benches with hinged covers at each side of door

"As the hart panteth after the water brooks."
— *Psalm xlii*

Florida drinking gourd

Bridging It

AMONG the gifts of the earth water holds a first place, and it is impossible to consider the early industries without listing it and touching upon those things which were the direct outcome of its being pressed into universal service. Its intimate comings and goings and the way these were met by the colonists makes simple but interesting reading. Met on the journey to settlement, it had often to be crossed, and we have our various bridges, each one a manifestation of the mind of

26

"Kissing Bridge," Chatham Square,
New York City, 1730s

Collierstown, "two and a half miles long and
eighteen inches wide" has a bridge every
hundred feet or so

the builder, the need of the locality, the strength and width
of the stream which it spanned, but not the period in which
it was built because no matter what the century, early comers
used early ways. The log foot-bridge is still in place across

isolated mountain streams, the toll-bridge is also still with us, and even the swinging wire bridge swoops across our rivers, writhing like a serpent at the first step of the oncomer and continuing to writhe and undulate until the stream has been passed over, trying like a bronco to loosen its rider's hold.

Probably the most beloved bridge is the "Covered Bridge," the "Old X Bridge" as it is called in New Hampshire because of its crisscross framework structure. An outstanding covered bridge spans the Dunlap Creek in western Virginia, and is known as the "Humpback Bridge" because of its arched design. Built in 1842 of hewn oak pinned with locust, it has carried the covered-wagons which went west on the old Midland Trail through the Alleghanies, and the modern trucks, and is still as strong as an ox. It stands detoured now just west of Covington but will be preserved as a unique antique.

Old Warm Springs, Virginia

Healing Springs

As far back as 1772 the white man had started making money from the healing waters which bubbled up here and there through the country, having learned from their Indian friends — who hated a bath above everything — that to bathe in certain spots was to be healed of disease. White Sulphur Springs in West Virginia was probably the pioneer commercial water, for at that time it could boast of a gouged-out log bath tub whose waters were quickly heated with hot rocks. A certain Mrs. Anderson was the first patient and arrived on a stretcher, but was so soon able to walk that the story spread around. Soon tents were set up and little rows of log cabins. These Cottage Rows gave the Springs their real impetus, and became variously famous. They bore the names of neighboring states; there was Paradise Row to which newly weds were assigned; there was also Wolf Row spoken of with bated breath: "Unless you are young and foolish, and love noise and nonsense, frolic and fun, wine and wassail and a Hell of a time, sleepless nights and headache, avoid Wolf Row." Apparently one needed to be near a healing spring at White Sulphur. Because of the great mineral wealth of some of these Southern counties the variety of springs was numerous. One county today has five springs within sixty feet of each other and each one pouring out a different kind of mineral water.

Water to Drink

Lying on your stomach was the surest way of getting refreshment, but wooden noggin and dried gourd and even the leather "blackjack" came to lessen this custom. Hollow logs stood at the side of the road beneath a spring brook's fall, and small hollow logs led water from springs on the hillsides or meadows into homestead water barrels. In 1793 New Orleans buried red cypress logs under the city streets and had a water system; in 1799 Aaron Burr did likewise in New

York City and tucked little lead or iron spouts into wedge-like borings to lead the water to the different homes which had signed up. These old wooden logs have been their own testimony to their longevity within the last few years, when they have come to light again in fine condition.

i. & ii. Wooden waterpipes in Philadelphia and New Orleans. iii. House taps in New York City water-system, of same type, late 1700s

The village or town pump was an established institution for many generations. New York City's famous Teawater Pump was a center of social gathering for years, with the less famous pumps splashing their drippings and muddying the streets elsewhere but no less attractive in their neighbor-

Almshouse porch pump, Ephrata, Pennsylvania

hoods. A sort of king among old pumps is one which stands on the back porch of the old almshouse at Ephrata, Pennsylvania. It is quite towerlike in construction and octagonal, ending in a finely wrought eight-sided pyramid. A wooden spout still protrudes from one side, its ancient gouged hollowness strengthened by a handwrought band of iron close to the mouth. For a handle it has a sort of king's sceptre floating out at one side.

For well-curbs and well-houses, with their frequent square buckets, there were designs without number, another chance for both the ingenious and the uningenious to use his hands and his wits. Along country roads, in addition to the water-trough already mentioned, were sunken casks — the tax-payer getting a rebate if he kept the water running — and

Well-curbs of the Carolinas

"spout-springs" which jetted out from a rock through a wooden spout. Remembering its sun, some of the Southern waterplaces for man and beast were sheltered with wooden awnings whacked up to throw a shade.

Florida shades her drinks

The Mountain Sled

Surely no leftover from the ingenuity of the past can top the "mountain sled" which grew up in West Virginia and is still in use, or was until 1932. The mountaineers in some localities had no other roads than the streams which they fished and drank from, and winter snows and fall rains and spring mud made travel along them and the rockbound earth beside them, a difficult proposition. A way out of having to "hoof it" was the invention of the mountain sled, which could manage snow and rain and mud. An eight or nine foot log of ash was well peeled of its bark, and had a series of three legs on each side stuck up into it from below. These wooden legs, somewhat over a yard long but slanting out at the bottom to a spread of about a yard, brought the sled to less than this height, and were fastened into a pair of oak or hickory runners made by splitting a young tree in half and peeling the bark from the lower surface. The front ends of these runners curved up to the line of the seat log and met at a

33

point to which the mule was hooked. Thus, this mountain sled could override ordinary rocks with little difficulty. Half-way up the legs a footbar ran from front to rear. To make the equipage comfortable for the riders who straddled it and hooked their feet into the footbar, the top was stuffed and covered with sheep pelts. When the mule was hooked in, those who were going to town climbed aboard, and six could go in comfort and leave room for the bags of groceries and meal which would be traded for down below. These bags were double-ended and slung across the sled like saddlebags, but the riders at the rear must watch out for their safety. In the old days of great gentility, the women and girls rode side-saddle, but now they go astride.

Mountain Sled for West Virginia's mud, snow and summer brooks

The Sociable Brook

Many of us think of brooks as places of heavenly beauty and peace, or as streams which catch our hearts up in their ripples and bear them along with a song, or as dappled ways of shadow which no man can paint nor kodak capture. It is only when the brooks which still range the distant mountain fast-nesses are found and explored, that any adequate conception can be had of their practical usefulness and highway advan-tages. Many a half-hidden brook has its great flat rocks well wheel-worn close to the brookside brush, worn through years of travel when this water-way was the only road in the whole farflung neighborhood. Once a brook has become a road, it seems to grow immune to overhanging branches, even though travel fall off and new growth come in, but keeps on its way squarely clipped on either side, as though still awaiting the coming of the old carts by which their width was once measured and determined.

Where the departed foot-log was chained to its tree

Floodgate for a pasture stream

Then there is the sociable "footlog" which lies across the stream near the place where mule and horse make the ford, often chained to some great tree against the coming of the spring floods. The "floodgate" is still in place and doing duty where cattle range, swinging easily on its long log stretched from shore to shore, riding the waters both high and low, as at the time of the "cold sheep rain" in May, indifferent to their force since it will rise and float with them or settle down to rest at their subsidence.

Close to one of these old streams grows Virginia's lovely tree-bush, that garden nosegay, "Sharos of Silver."

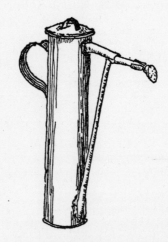

Early New England watering pot

III. THE WAMPUM MINT

"This belt preserves my words."
—*The Iroquois*

A White Man's Trade

PERHAPS there was no stranger industry carried on by our forebears than the making of wampum money for the American Indians. Those who know Indian lore tell us that strings and belts of wampum had their place in the business transactions of the red man not only as money but also as a polite symbol and encouragement while the deal was being put through. Here is a pretty ceremony recorded as having been performed at Burlington, New Jersey, by His Excellency, Francis Bernard, Esquire, with the Minisink or Munsey Indians.

> Brethren: As you have come from a long journey, through a wood full of briars, with this string I anoint your feet, and take away their soreness. With this string I wipe the sweat from your bodies; with this string I cleanse your eyes, ears and mouths, that you may see, hear and speak clearly, and I particularly anoint your throat, that every word you say may have a free passage from your heart, and with this string I bid you heartily welcome.

All four strings of wampum were handed to the Indians who thanked the Governor for bidding them welcome in the custom of their fathers. Certainly Francis Bernard must have had help in producing such a masterpiece of prose, for words used in such simple yet beautiful rhythm are found generally only among primitive peoples.

37

OF THE EARTH EARTHY

Wampum was a medium of exchange made from shells, and so well established in its values when the white men came, that they began to use it themselves and accept it as legal tender from the Indians along the Hudson and the Delaware. There was a ferry between Communipaw and New Netherlands in 1669 and the fare across was "in wampum 6 stivers," which was equal to our six cents. The standard unit was the "fathem," a length of twelve inches, and this obtained in both the black and white wampums, although the latter was worth but half the former.

Francis A. Westervelt, to whose article on wampum making we are indebted for many points, tells us that "Ye Town on the Pesayak," or the modern Newark, was purchased in 1667 by settlers from Connecticut from the Hackensack Indians for various articles, among them being eight hundred and fifty fathems of wampum. Wampum was also made for ornamental purposes, each however having its standard value.

Wampum Mill on Pasack Creek, New Jersey,
1860 to 1889

THE WAMPUM MINT

The Family of Campbells

White men began making wampum at so early a date that it was not set down, but by 1750 both men and women were busy at the strange new work. New Jersey seems to have done more than her share, and this was largely because she could claim the Campbell family as her own. William Campbell, who came from Ireland in 1735, was the patriarch of the family, and settled in Schraalenburgh, New Jersey, and the same year made Elizabeth Demarest his wife. It was his son John who established the Campbell homestead of the wampum makers at Pasack — now Woodcliff Lake — before 1775, and began the business which was to last until 1899, roughly one hundred and twenty-five years. Sons followed fathers in the work until several members running through four generations of Campbells had acquired fame as wampum makers.

Materials

Many of our local industries sprang up because the raw materials had been found close at hand and offered an evident invitation to be seized upon and used. The Campbells, however, had to travel far for their raw materials and one wonders how the idea of making wampum ever started with them. Their overhanging Dutch house — made in the style of that Dutch-settled neighborhood — was of dark red stone and stood on the Pasack Creek, a tributary of the Hackensack river, and twenty-five miles from New York City. The hard shell clams for the making of black wampum lay far away at Rockaway on Long Island, which meant that in order to keep a supply of material on hand, a long and tedious trip must be made every so often in a row boat from New Milford down the Hackensack and across great Newark Bay, and even out

39

through New York Harbor. Arrived at Rockaway, the Atlantic sea clams were obtained, and as much of the fine beach sand as could be loaded into the boat along with them.

It is interesting that the Campbells made their own work a means of livelihood to their neighbors as well, for the clams were dumped under some trees and the neighbors invited to come and gorge themselves with the delicacy, so only that they left the shell intact, and then, if they chose, could take the shells home with them to work into wampum. This was not wholesale charity for the wampum made in the homes by the women was used as barter at the neighborhood store, and later bought by the Campbells to be added to their own store.

When old Washington Market was started in New York City, the Campbells used their brains and arranged to buy all of the clam shells thrown away after clams on-the-half-shell had been served over the wooden counters. This cut their trip to Rockaway out of the picture, and brought their supply much nearer home. They could pull up at the west shoreline of the city, get out their hammers and break out the "black hearts" of the shells and fill their barrels with them and be home again in much shorter time than previously. New Milford was the last landing place on the Hackensack, but they wagoned the shells across country to Pasack.

The Campbell Mints

The homestead of John Campbell in time was finally out-grown as a shop for wampum making. Here he and his family had ground out the odd coinage, having no machinery except his grinding and polishing stones run by foot power, until it appeared that the farming of the land was less pro-ductive and his trade must take first place. An old wool mill standing near by was rented and turned into a real wampum mint. Here it was possible to have water-power for turning the stones, and in time thousands of dollars worth of wampum was turned out, to be used both for money and ornament. It was not until 1860, when the peak of the industry had been reached that the new mint or wampum shop was built on home land at the banks of the Pasack Creek. In this building the lower floor saw the hard work done and the upper loft was held sacred to secret processes and machinery which none but a Campbell of the blood might know. Today New Jersey has little left to mark this famous old industry, and this little is an occasional pile of long forgotten shell bits near some old farm home, and the refuse heaps near the old mint where pieces of broken and imperfect wampum have been found.

The Wampum Market

The market for Indian money lasted for two hundred and fifty years after the coming of the Pilgrims. In the vicinity of the Campbells' county there were no markets, but out among the western tribes of Indians there was an active one for all of the genuine wampum which could be procured. "Genuine" meant wampum made from shells in the good old Indian way and not from colored glass and imitation substances. The great fortune built up by John Jacob Astor had its foundation partly upon the work of the Campbell family, for soon after he came to this country in 1783 and went into the fur business he contacted them and arranged for his necessary supply of wampum if he was to do business with the Indian fur traders. From 1811 until 1848 when he died, he was the largest customer of the Campbell family, the two sons Abraham and William, and finally of the four grandsons. In fact it is said that the third generation formed itself into the more widely known firm, only because of his urgings and his offer to teach them some of the business processes which he had learned from their fathers, and they had never bothered to learn. In time the Campbell wampum was under order in Philadelphia, New York, Chicago, Texas, as well as with Government agents in the West.

Thanks to the work of the Bergen County Historical Society of New Jersey, which has gone deeply into a study of this old industry and made their findings available to others, we have the remembrance of a Campbell descendant who as a boy used to drive about Bergen County with his father on his regular wampum gatherings. All of the wampum made in the homes of the neighborhood was used as barter in the nearest store, as we have already seen, and so had been used as money before it started out to the Indians. "My father went often to the general store at Schraalenburgh which was kept by a man named Conklin. Sometimes he would pay him in cash as high as $500 for wampum which he had taken in trade." As Conklin was only one storekeeper we can judge somewhat of the work carried on in different homes. "Certain women, like Jane Ann Bell, became proficient in the work," while others simply "worked out the blanks" ready for finishing by the Campbells.

The finished black wampum beads were sold for five dollars a thousand, and this thousand was made up of twenty strings twelve inches long, holding fifty beads.

Shop Equipment and Tools

Fortunately "Barber and Howe" undertook in 1844 to describe the actual processes of this industry, so that we have the details nicely presented to us. In substance they said:

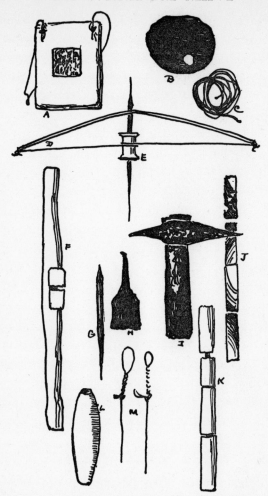

Wampum tools: *A. Wooden breast plate with iron inset; B. Cowhide form for moon; C. Wire 12 inches to hold wampum beads against fluted grindstone for polishing; D. Bow and string; E. Drill and spool; F. Hickory Vise; G. Drill; H. Handleless chisel; I. Pick; J. Black wampum; K. White wampum; L. Wampum pipe; M. Wire picks for removing powdered shell from pipes.*

43

Black wampum is made from the thick and blue part of the sea clam shells, and the white wampum from the conch shell. Intense hardness and brittleness of the material necessitates handwork as well as machinery. The article is produced by wearing and grinding the shell. First, split off the thin part with a slight hammer stroke. Clamp this into the sawed crevice of a slender stick, hold in both hands and grind smooth on a grindstone, until an eight-sided figure nearly an inch in length and nearly half an inch in diameter is produced. It is now ready for boring. Shell is inserted into another piece of wood, sawed similarly to the other, but fastened firmly to a bench. One part of the wood projects over the bench, at the end of which hangs a weight, causing the sawed orifice to close firmly as in a vise, ready for drilling. Drill is made from an untempered handsaw, ground to a proper shape and tempered in a candle flame. A rude ring with a groove on its circumference is put on it, "around which the operator (seated in front of the fastened shell) curls the string of a common bow." Adjust drill point to center of shell, and the other end against the operator's chest protected by a wooden board with a plate of stone or steel inserted in it. When the boring has commenced "about every other sweep of the bow, the drill is dexterously drawn out, cleaned of the shelly particles by thumb and finger, above which drops of water fall to cool the drill, which is still kept revolving by the use of the bow with the other hand, the same as though it were in the shell." This boring is hard work, the peculiar motion of the drill bearing hard against the breast, yet is done with great swiftness and skill and with care against bursting from friction. When the drill has passed half-way down the shell length, the wampum is reversed so that the same process may be worked through the other end. The finishing comes next. This calls for a wire about a foot long to be fastened at one end of the bench. "Under and parallel to the wire is a grindstone fluted on its circumference, hung a little out of the center so as to be turned by a treadle. The left hand grasps the end of the wire on which is strung the wampum, and as it were, wraps the beads around the hollow circumference of the stone. While the grindstone is revolving, the beads are held down to it and turned round by a flat piece of wood held in the right hand, and by the grinding soon become round and smooth. A female could make from five to ten strings a day, and these are sold to the country merchants for twelve and a half cents a string, cash, and constitute the support of many a poor and worthy family."

Moons in the rough, and finished

Wampum Moons

The concave disks or "moons" were made from the conic centers of the conch shells, grouped or laid one upon another in sets of from three to five disks, and tied together with red worsted yarn ending in a tassel, which was drawn through the two holes bored at each center. These ranged in size from an inch and a half to five inches in diameter, the largest placed at the bottom, and the glazed and pinkish upper parts showing in the light. Much as the white woman wore her

old-fashioned breastpin, did the Indians wear these ornamental moons to designate individual, tribal, or ceremonial
distinctions. A wealthy chief wore a set of five moons, while
the Poor Lo might have to get along with but one small disk.
Although these moons were worn as ornaments, they too
had their standard values, and a set of five meant a value of
three dollars, a set of three, two dollars, and the single disk
one dollar and a half.

Among the Campbell products were: the "chief's buttons," a smaller disk; the "Iroquois" a conical white shell
almost uniformly an inch and a half long, and at the flare,
about the thickness of wampum; there was also a lozenge-
shape bead with a large hole in the center; the "popular
charmed necklace" built up of twenty sections of wampum,
alternating with twenty shells chosen for their unusual form
or coloring; mussel shells were also polished for ornaments
but were not liked by the red men.

Wampum Pipes

We have already read the description of drilling by hand but
now come to the Campbell invention which made "pipes"
possible with less labor. Once more we find the conch shell
turned to, this time for its large ridges or ribs on its lips which
were broken out with a pick and chisel and made into the
pipe which was both for beautification and bodily protection.
The larger the shell the better for this purpose, and a five
pound specimen was a joy to the shell grinder because of the
large-sized pieces which it yielded, and the large amount left
over for beads.

These very beautifully shaped slender pipes measured anywhere from an inch and a half to six inches in length, tapering at each end, and in the middle being a little larger around

than a lead pencil. It seems rather a pity that ornaments so
good to look upon should often be worn next the skin as
breast plates, but such was the case; other chiefs wore their
pipes lying horizontally and one above the other over their
outer garments; again they sometimes called them "hair
pipes" and slid them up the strands of hair where it fell
over their shoulders, and tied them into place with bright-
colored thongs or strings. They too had a set value.

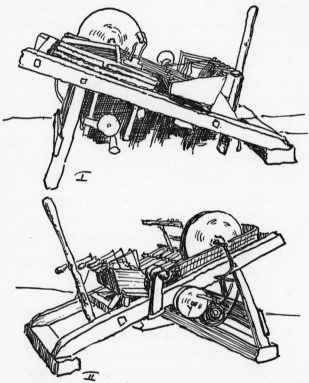

*Secret wampum pipe-drilling invention of David
and James Campbell, in active condition and after
abandonment*

The third generation of Campbells produced David and

James, who became the inventors of the family, making a machine — never patented because they feared to let the secret out even to the patent office — which became the family's most guarded possession and was kept in the upper part of the mint under lock and key. Here was a long jump from the old breast-drill or bow-drill, for this new machine would not only drill through six inches of shell but do six shells at the same time. So crude was it that the flywheel was nothing more than the heavy grindstone, set in a cumbersome but strong wooden frame, turned by hand with the help of a thick leather belt. "Six spools were arranged to hold the handmade drills of fine steel, like a medium size knitting needle, tempered in a candle flame to a cherry heat, then dropped in sheep's tallow that had been melted." Opposite the drills were six spiderlike, angular clamps which held the pipes already ground to their required form, and the task was to surface them to a perfect smoothness and polish. A lever brought the opposing forces together and it was necessary that the drill be kept always exactly in the center of the shell length lest the latter be shattered. Now comes a nice arrangement, a lever which lowers the pipes and drills down into a tank of water directly below. The hand power was applied and continued until half of the length had been bored through. Once more the lever is pushed, the drills and pipes go into reverse, the combination made and lowered into the tank again, and the remainder of the boring completed until a hole runs from end to end of the new pipes.

The art of drilling under water and the use of buttermilk for both softening and bleaching the shell, were guarded secrets along with the machine itself, and brought the inventors a business which was among the most outstanding in Bergen County.

IV. THE LIME-KILN

~~~~~~

Lime-Stone, of which Store of Lime is made, for stone
and brick houses.

— *Delaware 1724*

~~~~~~

Shell Beds

THAT there should be usefulness or even romantic interest
in a pile of ancient and forgotten shells under water, would
seem improbable to many, but down along that aged River
May, the modern St. Johns of Florida, romance is so thickly
laid upon palm-tree and shell-bed, coquina hut, and
thousand-year-old live-oak, drifting sand dune and lapping
tide, that even a bed of shells waxes romantic for the lover
of history. Our knowledge of shells in this locality runs back
only about four hundred years to the 1500s and 1600s
when the Spanish began to use tiny coquina shells solidified
through the ages into rock formation, for the building of those
mission houses, some of which remain for us in ruins. Other
shell gathering in deep beds was going on for eons of time
before any Europeans arrived here, that of the cast-off oyster
shells, slenderly formed and beautifully colored in mother-of-
pearl and blues and tawny purples.

At the head of the St. Johns River, at Mayport — one of
the first ports of stop for the French Huguenot leader, Jean
Ribault, in 1562 — there are today deposits of oyster shells
which go down under the surface of the sea for sixty-five
feet. They are assigned to "some previous era" and while
there are many conjectures as to their mass formation — one
of which is a colossal man appetite for oysters in past ages —

guesses are the only answer. While Maine has her vast shell deposits which mount into great cones upon whose sides an earlier people are believed to have lived because of the bonfire craters still found there and within their formation, there is no other shell deposit throughout the world to equal the one at Mayport. Of course, one always makes such claims with the understanding that some new discovery may disprove them at any time.

Ancient Shells for Modern Fruitfulness

In the Fairfield section of Jacksonville, Florida, an outstanding building of purest white stands boldly silhouetted against the blue of the sky and sea. Sometimes it is seen through a snow-white veil which shifts with the wind, now south, now north, softening the fine outlines and making them melt softly into the seascape. With the yellow sand burning under a hot sun as a foreground, one can imagine it a scene in some Eastern country where such whiteness sometimes dares to show itself. Here in America we are seldom so lavish with purity. A nearer approach brings one to the tiny door of the white building which bears upon its lintel a humble and disappointing sign, for one sees that no Maharajah lives here, and that it is only the "White Shell Factory." No ancient place of industry, either, is this place, but, dealing with an ancient material, it becomes one of this book's interests. What goes on here is best told by the manager:

"We bring the shells up the river on large lighters from the great sixty-five-foot deposit of oyster shells at Mayport, where they are dredging for them. We wash and grind them with one process." This process is such a noisy one, with furnace doors opening and shutting, great hollow cylinders turning, and the grinding up of the age-old shell, that his words are hardly audible, but through the roar comes: "The ground shell is piled up out of doors to bleach. That's the white you saw blowing through the air, and thought was smoke. All day long if there's any breeze at all, the lime keeps swirling about, covering everything. It finally bleaches snow-white. Oyster shell you know is $99\frac{1}{2}$ per cent calcium carbonate, and the other half per-cent magnesia. When we bring it in again it's put into the furnaces and dried at a temperature of 325° Fahrenheit." We had walked over to the furnaces and the great door was thrown open. Inside there was a raging fire, a tumultuous one which burned for perhaps ten feet back in the cylindrical firebox, and reminded one of the sparklers of a Fourth of July twilight, as they throw their stars of sudden light in sparkling blossoms and then pass into the night to make room for their other lights which follow. "That's the oil dropping into the flame which makes those sparkles. Quite a little heat, isn't it?"

From the furnaces the lime passes through shutes which carry it above to be screened and where too the lacy white clouds go billowing off in the out of doors. "After this we pack it in bags. There's a steamer there now at the wharf loaded with 65,000 bags we're sending to Liverpool—the whole cargo will be shell fertilizer." So, the old shells from the "River May" down yonder will soon be lying over English fields to make them bloom and bear.

"There are plastic mills, too, you know, where instead of bleaching and drying the oyster shells, they are ground and burned at a heat of about 1200 degrees, and then when it is put into water it makes plaster or cement."

Why Lime

We read of "wattles and daub" being applied to houses of

rough or square hewn logs to chink their intervening cracks, and of "catted chimneys." Together these obsolete terms mean simply smearing some earthy substance over broken branches or switches or cane-growths, to keep the air out, lead the smoke up, keep the heat in, the woody pieces forming the modern "re-inforced concrete" of whatever "daub" was made of mud or clay. Better and more permanent houses could be made of brick or stone, or of frame with a brick chinking, but these needed lime. For many of the settlers there was no lime in the ground but plenty of shells in the sea, and so it was used for the building of homes, the coating of brick ovens which stuck like warts from the early houses, the finishing of porch ceilings and those parts of the house wall which came beneath the porch's shelter. An old Hudson River house has carried its outdoor plaster for over a hundred years without too great cracks, but this plaster was made and buried for nine months before it was considered ready for use.

Three doors to the Earth

Another reason for lime was to sweeten and fertilize the land, and just as England is needing our lime now, we needed it on our fields when the first flush of virgin richness had begun to pass. Middleport, New York, has a famous chicken house of massive gray stone, which until a few years ago was a great stone plaster mill turning out plaster from limestone brought from Oriskany Falls some miles away. Avondale, Pennsylvania, still has an old six-foot millstone by the roadside, which was cut and used for grinding oyster shells for fertilizing lime.

Lime's uses were many but among the important ones was that of acting as a flux in the making of glass and iron.

Where Lime

It has been said that Massachusetts made her first houses of wood because she had no lime for building with brick or stone "but what is burnt of oyster-shells." It has also been shown that she found limestone in her eastern parts as early as 1629. The burning of lime is one of Vermont's oldest industries. In 1766 there was no importing of lime into North Carolina because she had her own supply. New Amsterdam could have her brick corbel-roofed houses because she too could produce lime. Roger Williams on his Providence Plantations found limestone ready to hand and soon had a flourishing trade in lime which enabled his people to build huge chimneys at once; Thomas Hackelton was granted the right to burn lime at certain places on the Providence Common. We would say today that to install a lime-kiln in one of our public "commons" was a questionable blessing but probably we too would make sacrifices to a need upon which depended a cozy chimney and a heart-warming hearth. Tidewater Virgina depended upon her sea-shells, and her oldest house still standing, built about 1640 of brick, proves that her native lime had holding qualities; in 1680 her shell lime was finer and more enduring than the chalk lime of the mother country. The Swedes and English Quakers who settled along the Schuylkill found an abundance of lime to burn, which was used to hold its fine ledge stone or rough field stone in house and barn, spring-house and outdoor oven.

OF THE EARTH EARTHY

Lime Stone

To drive through some of our mountainous limestone country, is to become excited over the constant finding of caves and pockets, high and low and where one would least expect to find them. Limestone is not like granite or even sandstone, but full of layers and ledges which can be readily induced to fall apart. Another characteristic of limestone country is its shameless way of dropping out of sight in spots, without warning, and leaving a deep sink-hole to mark the spot where perhaps a house once stood. Within a year a man looked out of his kitchen window and saw his barn disappearing and his truck ready to follow. A little later he looked in his sink-hole and found that eighteen feet below the surface a pleasant little lake had come to him.

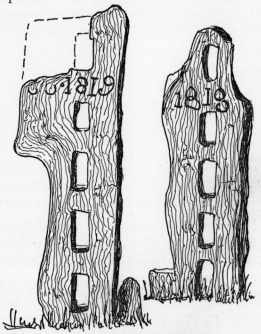

Limestone barway posts, Brattleboro, Vermont

THE LIME-KILN

Perhaps there is no better illustration of the yielding quality of some limestone than the six old barway stone posts which stand today along the highway at Brattleboro, Vermont. They bear the dates 1818 and 1819 and were originally barway posts between outlying fields. They are still standing by, to be sure, but parts here and there have succumbed to the New England winters and dropped or been worn away, leaving a most artistic contour behind them. They were cut with five oblong holes to accommodate five rows of wooden rails, and it is interesting to remember that while Southern snake fences have generally ten rails in their height, five rails in Vermont was rather a generous number, — although one old barway in New Hampshire had seven-hole posts, and fences were much higher in their original state than we generally give them credit for being. See the section of old wall which stands unshaken on a base of rock and compare it with its neighbor which has had only the ground for support.

Along with the cut-able and burn-able qualities of limestone we must remember that it had its staying qualities as well, and statistics show that limestone is the most widely used building stone quarried in the country. There is an old limestone quarry at Low Moor, Virginia, some three hundred feet across the entrance face and fifty feet from floor to ceiling, which is a magnificent hillside amphitheater, supported by its great columns or pillars which have been left for strength. Twenty minutes after it was visited for the accompanying sketch, a hundred feet along the front surface fell, the first to drop in many years.

Lime quarry, Low Moor, Virginia

THE LIME-KILN

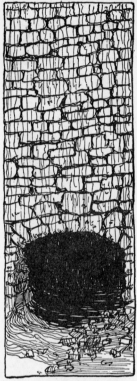

*Lime kiln in use for 125 years, at Pepack,
New Jersey*

Lime Kilns

Like all of our great industries today, that of lime burning
began in a simple way. One could build up a pile of the
rough limestone, leaving a sort of arch underneath for a firebox, and set the mound burning with charcoal or wood, then
begin to cover it with sod to make it smoulder slowly and
after three or four days have rough pale grey lime in small
chunks which could be crushed, and bleached if necessary.
If a farmer had any amount of limestone on his farm it would
pay him to build a solid base of stone or brick and on this

erect a cone-shaped structure of rock—lined with brick pref-
erably, and leave an arch at the bottom and a hole at the top
for dumping the limestone through into the rough hopper.
It is no uncommon thing to come across an abandoned lime
kiln while driving through the country. There will be what
looks like a walled-up front to a vault, close at the side of the
road, and at its base one or two nice stone arches. If the kiln
be an old one like one at Peapack, New Jersey, which was
built over a century and a quarter ago, the face of the wall will
be smoothly and well built, the rocks cut and placed closely
together as the old stone mason knew so well how to do when
he was building for a good part of eternity without the help
of mortar. The back of the kiln will be far back in the bank,

First lime kiln at Rockland, Maine

and the entrance will be at the top, for easy filling from the road leading up and past it.

One old lime center was at Rockland, originally known as East Thomaston, Maine. The old arches of the first kilns still remain although now become a natural part of the vine-clad landscape. There are two good-sized arches each flanked by a smaller one. In one set the "kiln wooders" threw in their "thirty cords of wood" and from the other the lime was shoveled out when finished from the burning. To have the finished product handy for shipping, the kiln was on the shore of the harbor with the cooperage near by for the making of the barrels, and although the limestone had to be drawn by oxen from some little distance, this was still the place of greatest convenience.

Eagle Rock Lime

Although there are now chimneys and stacks, the burning of lime has not changed very much from the pioneer days. There is always the stone kiln lined with brick to withstand the great heat of the furnace, the lower outlet and the upper inlet, to turn rough grey stone into whitened chunks of crushable lime. At night, Eagle Rock in the mountains of Western Virginia seems a great hulk of rock rising to forbid further passage beyond the James River, but daylight reveals at this narrow cut, vast walls punctured with caves and holes, homes of wild animals in past years and burrows of men today who seek limestone for burning in the kilns below. Close by the river stand three old kilns in a row, one fifty years old and the others coming on, with their octagonal and cylindrical brick stacks looking stunted and quaint under the great cliffs. The oldest kiln's venerable years have won it an iron support about the waist, but it still holds first place because of its "thimble."

Lime kilns at Eagle Rock, Virginia

"She's a thimble kiln," says a lime burner, "so you can push a wheelbarrow under the arch and pull the iron bars apart and let the lime fall straight into it. No shoveling like the others have to have. She used to have four eyes (furnace openings), but now she's only got two. You see she's round in the body, but the other two are square, twelve or fifteen feet across. The heat is about 1700 or 1800 degrees and at the end of every six hours when the new lime is taken out, only that nearest the eyes comes down, for the rest is so high up it hasn't melted yet so we poke it and break the wedge and she comes down. Every twenty-four hours forty per cent of gases have been burned away from the rock and twelve tons of lime manufactured."

60

THE LIME-KILN

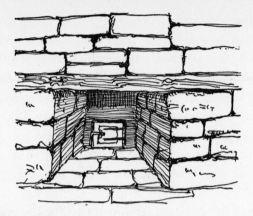

Stack stones from old canal-lock on James river

The famous old "thimble"

Of course it is a long look from the first heap of rocks built into a cone whose firebox in time burned up with the rest of the rock, to even these crude-looking kilns of today, with their flashing, door "eyes," the funnel-shaped thimble to open at the bottom and drop its horde of new lime into the waiting barrow, and the rough but massive mountain rock which makes up their sides. On the outside one might guess that a fortress stood there beneath the overhanging cliff, its lengthy porch-platform piled with a solid wall of cannon-balls ready to be fired at the enemy, the rocks which have been hauled in from the hillsides and placed handily close to the high hopper doors of the kilns. Like so many places of industry carried on in country sections, these kilns do not offend the eye, but are rather tiny man-made devices which shrink into insignificance before the beauty all about them.

Because of the constant erosion of their lands, some farmers in the South are burning their own limestone again to quicken the earth, and they are using the old method of building a stone foundation with arches left open for the fire, and then raising the structure with alternate layers of small lump coal and soft limestone. The fire burns all the way up through the kiln which is later covered with mud, and for six weeks the burning and cooling go slowly on. At the "lighting of the lime kiln" the word travels quickly through the countryside, for here is something real afoot, certain floors of the earth being called on to save others from being carried away.

V. THE BRICK YARD

The brick men burnt their brick, the spade men fell to digging, the carpenter fell to squaring out, the sawyers to sawing, and every man to somewhat.

— Virginia 1612

Brickery Requirements

A MAN who had set his heart upon having a brick house, or even a brick chimney in the New World, had to be sure of certain conditions. He must find a clay-pit, be sure of plenty of firewood for running his kiln, have plenty of water close at hand, and then he must be sure of his lime, for no matter how many bricks he might make, nor how well, he could not build them into walls without lime. Then one other item, he must have workmen "who understood the burning and the brickmaking."

One of New York City's 1416 houses in the 1730s

The first boatload of settlers to reach Jamestown included some bricklayers. The first Dutchmen to reach New Amsterdam in 1626 soon found the clay, the oyster shells for grinding into lime, and the wood for burning, but lacked the workmen. Salem, Massachusetts, had its brick kiln in 1629 and Haverhill granted "three quarters of an acre and the clay pits" to John Hoitt in 1650, while before 1674 Maine was making her own brick. Two years after Philadelphia was laid out there were "divers brickeries going on and many cellars already Stoned or Bricked and some Brick Houses going up," with "only the meanest Sort of People" building themselves houses with timber; in 1690 there were brick makers "with their Brick kills"; Germantown not only had her brick kilns but also her tile-ovens for roofing tiles; even in 1683 Penn boasted that he had a canoe "of one tree yt fetches four tunns of bricks," which must have been a sizable dugout, and gives us some idea of the amount of brick which was being turned out within a year of his arrival. Under these circumstances it is difficult to understand the claims which are made by the owners of many old houses, to having "English brick in the chimneys, brought in ships as ballast." Perhaps some bricks did come for this reason but why not stones which would have cost nothing? And why not a greater pride in having bricks which were made on our own land than those brought in from a foreign one? We had the requirements for our own "brickeries" when the permanent homestead was to be built in many sections. Maryland imported some "salmon brick" made of "sand with no grit or gravel," but, again, the Governor of North Carolina wrote in 1766: "We do not import lumber or bricks either from northern colonies or from England."

Country Brick Yards

"Old brick yard? Why, yes, there used to be one up on the road to Pecks, right in the woods it would be now, with the pasture so growed up. They made the bricks there for the only four brick houses we ever had in these parts. When they was done, somehow the old brick yard just died out."

A few humps in the ground are often the only sign to mark these old countryside clay-pits. Sometimes there was not even a kiln for burning the bricks, the sun doing just as good a job as a wood fire. Take any of the pale old yellow bricks found in the walls of old homes, lining bricks, and they speak for themselves in their durability.

James H. Beebe, of Hamilton, New York, recalled the old brick yard that used to be operated below Bonney Hill when he was a boy in the 1870s, and while this is not an early date, the methods were semi-early and give us an eye-witness's remembrance of hand-made brick. "About 1873 Deacon Paine commenced the manufacture of brick in a lot on the west side of the road that leads to Lake Moraine. Whalen was the boss of the yard. Deacon Paine started making the bricks that were used in building the Colgate Academy and many times a day two ox teams drawing two-wheeled dump carts passed down Broad Street. The load for each cart was, I think, one thousand brick. When the span of horses drew the load it was eight hundred. These bricks were all made by hand, the operator dusting the mold with sand and packing the soft clay into the compartments. The laborers than carried them to the level floor of the yard and dumped them. After drying in the sun they were stacked, arches being made into which four-foot wood was thrust."

Processes

In 1792 Noah Webster wrote to his friend Timothy Pickering to ask for a recipe for making brick, having in mind at the time the building of a State-house at Hartford, and

Early Philadelphia house at South Front and Washington streets. Lower part with broad quarter boards. Brick walk and drain

stating that Connecticut was sadly ignorant on the subject. Pickering answered, saying that Philadelphia had followed closely an old Massachusetts law regarding brick making, and that her brick was superior to any in the country. He further stated that "New York, a rapidly growing city, furnishes no clay, but is supplied from New Jersey with ordinary bricks, and good ones from Philadelphia." He then gave directions that the molds be shod with iron, that each mold should be for a single brick, and that they should be thrown into a tub of fine sifted dust, not water, to prevent bricks sticking to the sides. He says further: "One moulder, one man to work the clay, and one to wheel to the tables, and a boy who bears off a single brick at a time, constitute a set who make two thousand bricks a day. This is a regular task."

At Salem, Massachusetts, bricks were made "by mixing clay and water in a container by the laborious method of men walking around the outside pushing the crank which stirred the mixture until it flowed smoothly through a hole in the form. After settling, the clay was cut in sizes and left to dry. Then burnt in a kiln with wood fire." Here we have the molds dispensed with and the drying mass of clay treated like a pan of fudge, cut before it hardened.

Saco, Maine, had mules involved in the making of its brick. A windlass was rigged up in the brick yard and a mule traveled round and round until the clay and water had been thoroughly mixed. (Some worked their "stuff" in a pug-mill.) Now the "stuff" was poured into the five sections of a flat tray. When they were filled, the brickman took a wet stick and struck across it. This "water struck" brick was considered the best kind. The bottom of the molds fell off and the bricks slipped out into the yard where they were to dry. After this they were put into the kiln for baking. These bricks were bound for Boston to make sidewalks for its narrow streets, and so must be loaded onto sailing boats. To pick up each brick separately would have taken much time, so the man on the wharf picked up five in a row, threw them the fifteen or twenty feet down to the man at the hatchway who caught them in the same even row and threw them to the man down in the hold, where they were again caught in a row and stowed away in one. In this method the single mold had been augmented by four others.

An undated report signed "H N R" gives us these particulars:

A three part house under House Mountain, Va.,
tied together with two chimneys

In the first place a spot was made level and smooth, then two thicknesses of Boards so as to break joints and then board or planks were set up edgeways and fastened there. The bin was about fourteen to sixteen feet long and seven to eight feet wide. Then clay and sand were put in what they wanted for a batch and water what was needed. Then the grinding Proces began which was quite different from nowadays. They put in frome one yoke to two yoke of oxen yoked up and a man to drive them around till all was jamed fine enough to work for the mould. The striker had a table for his mould and then he had another table for the morta; and then taken off enough for a Brick and put it into a mould and pressed with the hand into the mould, one at a time, and so on till the moulds were filled, and with a straight edge scraped on the whole and then carried away on to the yard to dry. When dry burnt as usual, a great contrast then and now.

The brick kilns were necessarily large to accomodate a large number of bricks at one burning, and we have already seen that the arches which formed the firebox of the kiln were made of the bricks themselves. The burning took from two days to a week.

Early Types

We seem to have adopted the old standards of size used in England and Holland for our first bricks, starting with the larger sizes, then making the smaller and gradually working back to the larger sizes again. The English brick measured $8\frac{1}{2}$ by 4 by 2 and five-eights, while the Dutch brick was 8 by 4 by $2\frac{1}{2}$. At Salem, New Jersey, on the Delaware in 1683 the county law required a brick $9\frac{1}{2}$ by $4\frac{1}{2}$ by $2\frac{3}{4}$. They were also to be well and "merchantably burnt" and if they were not, they were thrown out and broken by the two persons who viewed and appraised them under the authority of the courts. A little fine also did its work in procuring fewer faulty specimens.

Because of its soils the South produced bricks of dark rich colors which were not possible farther north. Some of the Virginia bricks were glazed a deep purplish red, verging on the mulberry. In Tallahassee, a famous house called "The Columns" is made of brick of a dark red shade and legend has it that inside of each brick a nickel was molded. Another oddity of this house is that the master had the main stairway come down into his first-floor bedroom so that his heiress daughter might not elope. He probably had done so himself, hence his fears. In Maryland a natural silica in the soil gave an unusual gloss or glaze to its bricks, so that a house built of them would actually glisten in certain lights, and because some of them turned out a grayish green glaze, several color combinations were available.

Plain, sun-dried, or sun-baked brick were often very rough of surface and usually large, and generally destined to be a filler for outside walls of frame houses or for tucking in between logs to fill the chinks. Their color was an anemic orange or pale cream and they had the look of having been skimped in the stirring and not tamped down hard enough in the mold, but for all their hard treatment these step-children of the brick family did their work well, although like Cinderella, they did it in the kitchen out of sight of the passing world. The names they won were "noggin" and "puggin" and "clinkin'."

"Bench brick" was the brick which had been placed closest to the firebox in the kiln, and thus been overdone, and burned and often glazed to a color darker than that received by those farther removed from the heat. By interspersing these dark ends among the lighter bricks we shall see that all sorts of designs were achieved. A rubbing-stone gave a "rubbed dressing" to bricks which were not "axed" or straightened.

Brick Bonds

To the majority of persons a brick wall is just a brick wall, for few notice the way the bricks are laid or the "bond" which has been used. The end of a brick is called a "header" and its long side a "stretcher." It is not mere caprice which causes a bricklayer to introduce a row or course of headers among several courses of stretchers, for there is need of irregularity on the inner part of the wall where the other materials are to join the brickwork, and each bricklayer has learned a certain way of achieving this. During the first half of the 1600s much of the brickwork was done by Englishmen and the "English bond" was naturally used; this bond consisted of a course of headers laid to the weather, alternating with a

1 — Flemish bond in original chimney of early 1700s and American bond in chimney in rear addition. 11—One of the South's lonely sentinels which have burned their cabins off their backs

course of stretch. The Flemish brick-layers are said to have come about the middle of the century, although St. Luke's Church, Isle of Wight County, Virginia, built in 1632, has the Flemish bond, and in 1640 when Adam Thorowgood built his brick house at Lynnhaven, he had the front laid in Flemish bond.

In this type of bond each course had alternating headers and stretchers, but so started at the beginning of each row that a stretcher always came above a header and vice versa. This gave the opportunity for decorative design already suggested, for, especially where a header was glazed in the burning and topped a plain red stretcher, the effect was most

71

pleasing. One can see that by slipping header or stretcher forward or back every so often, a design could be procured which would be visible for some distance.

The bond which developed as the native American one was five courses of stretchers and one course of headers, but the bricklayer of today uses many bonds and sometimes very ugly ones, as when he stands the bricks in a course upon their heads.

Flemish bond house and sidewalk, Philadelphia, 1692 to 1935. Exposed floor joists. American and Ionic streets

An Old Philadelphia Home

Within the last two years Philadelphia has seen the passing of one of her pioneer bricks houses built in 1692. It had been a home, a tavern, an orphanage, a saloon, and finally a restaurant, but with all of its changes it had not lost its strong fine lines nor hidden its Flemish bond signature beneath a crust of centuries. The public wanted more parking space, and when the wreckers came to demolish it, there were few to watch its passing or care that it went. Its brick measured 8 by 4 by 2, (without a ruler) and the headers were darker than the stretchers, the inner part of the brick showing a light yellow clay. At some period the rear roof was apparently changed, while a typical cut-back corner door took the place of the large entrance door of the earlier home. Watercourse at first floor level, and string course at second floor level had each the merest overhang, but the attic floor joists protruded through the outer walls and were visible in a neat row to the passer-by. Search showed that originally the first floor timbers had also protruded through the walls, but that they had been cut back at some time and filled in with brick, obliterating their good old appearance. It was appropriate that the brick sidewalk should have been laid in Flemish bond in part, even though the usual design for these passageways was the old-fashioned herring-bone pattern.

Shallow Dutch window arch in
"William Penn house," New Castle, Delaware

Down the river at New Castle, Delaware, an older brick house stands, one which was probably of Dutch construction and which stood on one of the few streets of the town before the coming of William Penn to this, then, part of Pennsylvania. The old house now is a central part of a larger structure and can be seen only by going through the tiny alley which was a goodly street when Penn walked up it to be welcomed at the door of the two-room house. A door and one window below, and one window above, looked out to the not distant river. The alley pavements are of great stones worn deeply with the weight of many wheels, and it is probable that the little house was built about the time of the building of the first portion of the Court-house which was laid out by Petrus Stuyvesant in 1655, for the same arches which top the windows of the later are found in the former, shallow to the width of a brick laid upon its side, but still a Dutch arch. At the east wing of the Court-house built in 1675, Penn received in token of his ownership "one turf with twig upon it, a porringer with river water and soyle in part of all."

The Brick Oven

No more blessed and needed structure was ever built of brick than the old "brick oven," often wrongly called the "Dutch Oven." Some of the first ones were built quite separate from the house, either under its own rude roof or in a detached kitchen. One of the primitive ones stood in Virginia in the late 1600s — "The oven in the immediate vicinity of the house, being a brick structure in a hole in the ground." Later the oven was connected with the main house chimney, a part of its great breadth, and either used the same draughts with the fireplace or had its own. These old ovens are lovely to look upon from the outside where they have been allowed to remain, whether in the bulbous beehive-dome formation or the "stepped form" which stepped out brick by brick to the needed depth of the oven and then stepped back again to rest its base upon the sill of the house. Some Jersey ovens are stepped and also topped with a dome, but this is unusual.

A good-sized oven would hold twenty-five pies; the one in the community kitchen at Ephrata, Pennsylvania, held sixty loaves of bread. An old New Jersey oven dropped the ashes of its heating fuel through a slanting slide into the fireplace.

Stepped-up oven on outside of parsonage at Scotch Plains, New Jersey, and dome-top oven in John Bowne house, Flushing, Long Island

One tricky little use for bricks is seen often up under the peak of old Delaware and Pennsylvania houses, where a slab of cement or board bearing the date of the building is encircled by them in circular or oblong form.

OF THE EARTH EARTHY

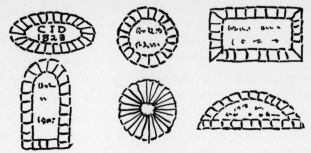

*Delaware and Pennsylvania mark their house-dates
up under the gables*

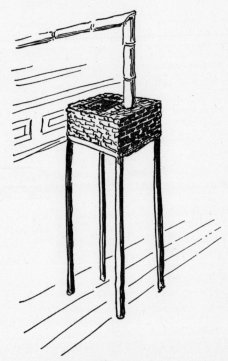

*Brick stove raised to gallery height on stilts in old
Dutch Church which stood in Schenectady,
New York in 1734*

THE BRICK YARD

Perhaps as unique a brick contrivance as one meets with was in an old Dutch church built near Schenectady, New York, in 1734. It was a small brick stove of plain rectangular form, built upon four upright posts which extended up as high as the balcony where the slaves sat. In the top was a door which opened to receive the wood. It was the duty of the slaves to keep a woodpile near by and see that the stove was stoked all through the long service. Incidentally they must have felt most of the heat, since heat rises.

VI. THE STONE-PIT

I deny that the Loadstone doth worke upon the North-pole, the pole rather works upon the stone.

"Sink stone," Ephrata, Pennsylvania, becomes a drain where it appears on the outside of house

A Curse or a Blessing

THE old stone-pit. It may have been only a hollow in the edge of the field where those who first made the clearing tossed the unwanted stones which would bother the plough; it may have been a rocky hole left where rock enough was taken out to build a tiny cabin; it may have been the beginnings of a disappointing mine soon deserted for a better one used and forgotten; whatever it was, a stone-pit often had a greater significance than appeared at first glance, for stones played a larger part in the lives of our forebears than we usually believe. When the spring frost heaved up nicely buried stones against a ploughshare or threw them down from stone-walls, the stone was a curse, and many a "spare hour" was given to toting stones across a field to dump them in the stone-pit or on the stone pile. Men wore leathern aprons for this toting, and they carried "crows" in their carts to heave rocks out of the roadway after a hard spring rain. Curses? When again it was time to leave the old log cabin and build a permanent home, or a monstrous weight was needed for the well-drum or the well-sweep, it was nothing short of a blessing to have stone a-plenty to be had for the rolling or the "hewing." If we were geologists we would call all "stones" by the more discriminating name of "rocks," and thus eliminate confusion with the fruit "stones" or pits; if we are farmers and settlers, we speak of "them stones." We would be using "stone boats" to cart them off, but never a "rock boat."

We should recognize at once that the stone family is a prolific and versatile one, with a reputation for many opposing characteristics. Here is a stone:

> A hard substance of the earth
> Mass of concreted earthy or mineral matter
> Hard shell enveloping pulp of a fruit seed
>   (Apricot, plum, cherry are drupes of such stones.)
> Calculous concretion in kidney or bladder
> A gem
> A butcher's weight of fourteen pounds
>   (Applied also to the weight of a person)
> To pelt with stone

OF THE EARTH EARTHY

The stone has long stood for the ultimate extremity:

Stone blind—perfectly sightless
Stone pitch—hardest kind of pitch
Stone deaf—without hearing
Stone "deef"—no doubt about it
Stone still—motionless

Here are some of its simple and homely uses:

Window copings
Window and door lintels
Hearth stone (and the hot stone on the hearth which
    keeps the crows out of the corn in the South)
Chimneyplace arch and whole chimney
Door rock or door stone
Stepping stones in the grass
Steps between house levels
Culverts
Corner house supports and foundations
"Heating stones" for hands and feet in a sleigh
Bed stones for warmth
Clock and gate weight
Well stones
Mortars and pestles
Dooryard and farmyard drains
Floors
Water barrel supports
Cobblestone streets and curbings
Narrow bridges
Fence posts
Paint substance
Gem pans
Milk pans
Drinking troughs
Horse blocks
Hand basins set in a wall
Sinks

THE STONE-PIT

Porch floors
Wall stiles
Guide posts
Hitching posts

*Stone through which the lightning-rods ran on the
old Henlopen Lighthouse, Lewes, Delaware*

Being stoned to death was an old ordeal, but one man,
discouraged with life and wife and strife, went out and sat
down by the brookside, and taking a great rock in each hand
clapped them against his temples and forgot it all. To one
of our religious groups the ordinary wayside stone has always
appealed as a signboard upon which warnings for life and
death should be solemnly painted. Some of these still dot the
country roadsides. And then there was the rolling stone
which gathered no moss, and the tombstone which gathered
much, and that stone which must never be left unturned.

Sermons in stones by the roadside

81

A Stone for Every Need

MILESTONES: In 1764 "The Philadelphia Contributionship for the Insurance of Houses from Loss by Fire" raised money for the first milestones of the country, by fining each member one shilling if he arrived late at a meeting of the august body, and two for not coming at all. This money went into the procuring of low curved-top stones which bore figures to show the distance between Philadelphia and New York. On May 15th, a party started forth to set the stones, the hour five in the morning, the spot, the corner of Front and Market. They traveled to within four chains of the Delaware River — the present Trenton — and set twenty-nine stones. There were two left over as a nest-egg for New Jersey's continuing the job. The Hudson River had her milestones which were a little higher than those down in Pennsylvania, and some of these still stand in the Highlands. Third Avenue, New York City, had until recently her milestone near Sixteenth Street, giving the distance to City Hall as two miles. In the Alleghanies, where slab rock abounded, they marked the old road from Lexington to White Sulphur with pointed locust posts, instead of stones, and burned the numbers of the miles with hot irons.

Mile-stone between Philadelphia and Trenton, 1764

THE STONE-PIT

MADSTONE: In 1804 was first brought to light a stone which could perform miraculous cures, such as drawing the poison from the bite of a mad dog. This stone was light and porous and greenish in color. Such stones were heard of, from time to time, in Minnesota, Iowa, Illinois — probably other Middle Western States. The mad stone grew in the heart of a deer, of a buck, and it was said that one male deer in each deer generation had a mad stone in his heart. These stones were greatly in demand, by doctors as well as laymen; but those who had the good fortune to find them rarely if ever gave them up, and their homes became places of pilgrimage for people miles around whenever any one was bitten by a mad dog.

WHETSTONE: A stone for sharpening edged tools by friction, small enough to be carried in the reaper's pocket, known also as the "scythe stone." In 1793 soft stone was found on the Monongahela River opposite Pittsburgh: "It seems good for use as whetstone and is a combination of sandy, clayey and ferruginous particles with some mica in rare instances."

GRINDSTONE: This is a flat, circular stone fixed in a permanent wooden frame and turned with a crank or pedal, and in 1753 was often called the "grin stone" as it is locally today. There were grindstone quarries, and rock known as "rockgrit" consisting of sand and small pebbles, and some as "grindstone grit." Some of the farmer's happiest moments were when he could leave the hot hayfield and sit under the apple tree at his grin'-stone, grinding his scythe. Some of the boy's sorriest were when he had to turn it.

MILLSTONE: A "run of stones" for grinding grain were set one above the other, grooved on the scarcely touching

83

inner surfaces to grind and throw off the grist or whatnot. They came from two to seven feet across and were sometimes a foot thick. There was the "nether" or bed stone, and the upper or "runner." Millstones were of quartz-shot sandstone, New England granite, buhr or "burrstones" from abroad or from Arkansas, of flint in West Virginia, and of whatever stone was hardest in the vicinity of the mill.

A "STONE": A grave marker was "a stone," and many carried very lovely carving and full epitaphs and particularly fine lettering in the old days. The sandstone of New Jersey made a popular grave marker and many of them have stood unscathed for more than two hundred years, but some of those which have scaled their faces away have, strangely enough, kept the impress of the old inscriptions. Blue slate marks the soldiers of the Revolution in New Hampshire, Vermont has fine old marble "stones," and Connecticut cherishes her field "stones." A man and his two wives lie buried in "Unity," and the stones of the wives have hands pointing to the grave of the husband and the word OURS, while his has hands pointing to either side and the word MINE.

i. Well stone
ii. Mill stone
iii. Blacksmith's ironing stone

84

THE STONE-PIT

BOUND STONES: One of these boundary stones which is of special historical as well as artistic value, is that one which in 1767 was placed between the colonies of Pennsylvania and Maryland. It is about four feet high and bears on one side the coat of arms of William Penn, on the opposite side the emblem of Lord Baltimore, and on a third, 1767. It marked the 115th mile from the eastern end. This is now in the building of the Pennsylvania Historical Society.

RUBSTONE: A stone to clean or sharpen.

WELL-STONE: These were from four to seven feet across and with a hole cut in the middle, served as a well "curb," were in fact the background of the wooden structure which bears that name with no apparent reason. They were beveled off at the edges to shed the water, and were cut in the center large or small to admit the passage of a bucket or the smaller chain or even a rope. When the early pump was introduced with its chain of cups these well-stones were often retained. One "well" is visible today only as a hole six inches long by three wide, a mere slit in the otherwise grassy dooryard, even the stones having grown out of sight. There was also the well-stone fastened to the end of the rope which passed over the drum; and the stone roped to the end of the well-sweep to make the balance for raising the bucket.

HOLY-STONE: The stone with which a ship's crew scoured the decks. Sand was thrown upon the decks and the holy-stones, with rope fastened at each end, were dragged back and forth by a pair of seamen.

IRONING STONE: To the initiated the ironing stone of the old blacksmith shop is often confused with either the mill or the well-stone. It was roughly six feet across, sometimes

85

circular, sometimes oblong, but always at least six inches thick and with a hole cut in the center to hold the hub of the wheel. When the wheelwright was ready to apply the iron tire, or "iron his wheel," he built a bonfire on the great stone and swept it off after the rock had become heated through enough to keep the iron hot while he was applying it to the felloe.

LODESTONE OR LOADSTONE: When in 1696 some one found a stone in Philadelphia which had the power to attract certain metals, it was called a loadstone. Today we know that this loadstone is a piece of magnetic iron ore posessing polarity.

THE CRACKING STONE: Some New Englanders saved their broken dishes to pound into "grits" for the hens. Any large flat stone near the house "would answer" and with a sledge hammer left handy, the task was not too unpleasant a one.

ROTTEN STONE: Siliceous limestone used for scouring wood.

PUMICE: A light porous volcanic substance for cleansing. Harder than rotten stone.

TALC: A soft magnesian mineral softer than soapstone and of a soapy feel.

SANDSTONE: This is both hard and soft. The chimney-place in the old Byrd stone cottage in Richmond, built from 1685-9, has been gently sifting to the room floor for many years, trying ever to form a sandy beach. Again, sandstone can be "as hard as a rock."

COTTON STONE: Between 1685 and 1686 the "Salamander Stone" was found near the Brandywine River in Pennsylvania. It was described as having cotton in it "which will not consume in fire though held there a long time." In Delaware, in 1724, they found the "cotton stone" with a something in it which seemed as though it might be knit into gloves and purses. This meant careful work on the spinning wheel and then there came, actually, gloves which "when foul are cleansed in the Fire, which it endures without any change." Here was our first American asbestos.

LAPSTONE: "Any old fieldstone is good enough," one old cobbler says, "to pound the leather on and make its quality." This stone rested on the knees of the old "knights of the lapstone" or shoemakers. Later it became imbedded in a piece of polished wood.

Tanner's bark crushing stone

TANNER'S STONE: This was an immensely thick stone rolled on its circumference like a cart wheel and having its edge chisled into roughness so that in passing over the tanner's bark it would crush it easily. It revolved on a great shaft and turned by a blind horse, or ox, but was taller than either.

CIDERMILL STONE: Within a circular stone trough the cider apples were dumped so that the great stone wheel might pass over and crush them. A long sweep pulled by horse or ox power turned the stone.

Freestone

"A stone composed of sand and grit and easily wrought." This definition may be all right in its place, but for our purposes the "freestone" is a very familiar and definite object, that nice smooth stone which one takes to bed with him at night, heated all day by lying on the "setting-room" chunk stove, and being slipped into its flannel cover before being carried to the northpole bedchamber. The farmers' wives of New England could hardly have lived their lives without their freestones, for these treasures traveled to the unheated Meeting-house with them safely under their feet in the sled or clutched in their otherwise cold hands, they fought off chilblains and made the children sleep at night, not to mention acting as footstools on draughty floors. Husbands could make them, large ones and small ones, because of the straight cleavage of the stone, and some had iron handles caught into whittled holes. Folks coming from the city to visit often wondered at the warm bundle which was handed to them with their candle for the trip to bed; they called them "soapstones"—which was well enough but a bit odd. The freestone or soapstone will retain heat for many hours if carefully wrapped. Stoves were made of soapstone and remained warm long after the fire was out. There were soapstone blocks fitted into the downstairs ceiling and punched with holes to carry heat above, and there were freestone squares to run the stovepipe through, with holes in a circle around it. With all the centuries of freestone warming and comfort it seems a pity to tell of one which grew overheated on the kitchen stove and exploded, knocking chunks out of the ceiling and walls. A real New Englander will not be worried by this, though, for he will be sure that that freestone harbored some alien enemy in its breast, and besides, the kitchen stove was no place for it, it should have been in the setting-room. There were "October freestones" and "January freestones," the former taking off the chill, the latter guaranteed to keep up zest under nine comforters, at thirty below.

New England's freestones for warming beds on winter nights

Freestone or soapstone neighborhoods have gone to their quarries for facings for their houses, but when the stone came from the quarry it bore the name of "ashlar"—but who ever heard of such a name for a nice warm cuddly freestone. This stone can be cut or whittled with a good jackknife, and many an old inkwell and salt cellar and pepper pot was the result of "knittin' work" by the open hearth. There were washtubs of soapstone, and sinks and footstoves, and big round griddles for griddle-cakes — words unknown before the Revolution. This soapy stone which was soft enough to turn on a lathe, was smooth enough to be ground for a lubricant.

A more careful description of this noble stone may be

welcome. This report was made in 1842 about a soapstone quarry at Grafton, Vermont:

> About two miles south from the Congregational Meeting-house is an immense quantity of excellent steatite, or soapstone, which is quarried to a great extent. Large blocks are removed from ledges by saws, wedges and bars and transported about a mile to a mill, where it is sawn by water-power. It is then manufactured into aqueducts, pumps, jambs, ovens, mouthpieces and stoves. The blocks sawn and bored for the aqueducts are two by three feet long and three or four inches square. Ready to be put down, at one dollar per rod. The potstone is of a greenish color, less frangible than the steatite.

Many of the aqueducts made of soapstone were in shorter lengths than those given above, with an opening not over the size of a thimble, and they led water from the spring to house or horsetrough after being buried underground. The quarries at Grafton were running as early as 1820, and there were others in the State at the same time, in fact, only Virginia can claim a greater production of this stone than Vermont.

The Stone Cutter

The terms "cut" and "hew" have always been applied to the work done on stone although they would seem to the layman better suited to wood. The stone "breaker" worked in the quarry and yet there were "stonecutters" who did their own quarrying. One old device for splitting rock was to lay a line of vinegar where it was to be broken, and then throw cold water over it. It would break at the mark. Some people question this old recipe and say that it must have been kerosene instead of vinegar, but vinegar apparently did the work for some folks some time. Nearly all stone would crack after heating, at the touch of cold water. The saws used in stone cutting were frequently without teeth, and the cutting made easier by pouring sand and water and steel shot into the cut just ahead of the saw.

The word of the Georgian period for stone-cutter was "lapicide" and had to do with precious stones rather than those taken from a quarry, but the next century brought the broader meaning and the man who "hewed" stone came under the same term, and one would not "hew" a gem.

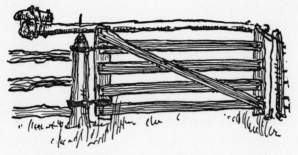

"Noddle-pin" gate with its balance stone

Stone Influence

Few of us realize that Delaware Water Gap is about the dividing line between the glacial ice movement and that more southern part of the country which was not re-formed by it. Streams north of this may have in their beds many strange bedfellows, red and purple sandstone, green, gray and brown stones, marble and granite, all mixed in together because the glacier picked up bits of rock here and there in Canada, Maine, New Hampshire, Vermont and Massachusetts and rolled them southward, sometimes a few yards, sometimes hundreds of miles. What was called native stone in some villages might have come from far north, but, where it had settled, it influenced the walls, the chimneys, the very architecture of the countryside. Some New England streams lose their bedstones to the paralleling highway during a flood, because the stones are so round that they cannot "stay put" under pressure; such stream vicinities have stone walls that topple easily under frost, while the more angular stones of the Southern districts will hang together for scores of years without a tremor. This abundance of surface rock has caused many a backache in the North and East, but stitched the land with the beloved old stone-walls which are a story in themselves. Deeply bedded and much higher than is usually believed, they stood on broad foundations and those which were to carry on through the years had each stone studied for its face and sides and base by the "stoner." Even when well "laid up" they still grew restless in the spring and threw their rocks around and had to be "mended." It took a good stone mason to lay a rod of wall a day.

Pennsylvania has a pretty way with her; wherever a greenish serpentine rock crops up through a field, there stands always a comradely cedar tree.

West Virginia has two nice stone stories:

A mountain boy was traveling home on horseback with a saddle bag, when another traveler noticed that one side of it was thumping against the animal's ribs. Questions led to the discovery that all of the grain was in one end of the double bag and a great stone in the other, to balance. The stranger showed the boy that the grain could be divided and the stone thrown away. This was done. The boy rode on a little way and began to think, "Pappy uses a stone." Another mile and he thought, "Gran' pappy used a stone." In a minute he was off of his horse. "I'll use a stone."

THE STONE-PIT

In the valley of the Kanawha River, which it follows curve for curve, and about one hundred feet from the top of Loup Creek Mountain, is an ancient wall of parts. Most of it has fallen but its stones stretch for three and a half miles. It was laid up dry of flagstone on a two-foot base which tapered upward, and was seven or eight feet high in its prime. Every so often an opening was left, like an entrance, although there is no sign of anything to enter. This wall has for many years been considered a giant game trap of the simplest technique. Directly below it on an island in the river is a famous salt lick where animals came from miles around. It is believed that in a hunt, men and dogs surprised the animals and drove them frightened up the mountain side where they came to the wall, ran along it until they came to an opening and then darted through to supposed safety. Here other hunters, hidden by the wall, caught and killed them in great numbers, for these opening were found packed with bones. When William Morris, the first settler in these parts, questioned the Indians about the wall, in 1774, he was told that when the first red men came into the valley, the wall was already out of use. Up through the fallen stones of the wall has grown an oak which is now over five hundred years old. A shorter but better built wall stood a hundred years ago above the mouth of Paint Creek, which averaged four to five feet in thickness and was in some places ten feet high.

Boston had her "Boston Stone" and her "Union Stone" which preceded the later guideposts.

To each locality and colony its own stone influence.

VII. THE QUARRY AND THE MINE

~~~~~~

"The Stone which the builders refused is become the
head stone of the corner."

~~~~~~

The Stone Pit

MOST of us know that a quarry is a place for digging stones,
an above-earth industry, but as to a mine, well, a mine is an
underground mystery, having to do with piles of rocks,
torches on miners' caps, eerie tappings along long corridors
of the earth, lines of iron tracks which slip into a black hole
carrying tiny cars which sometimes never come out again,
and if they do, are laden down with ore or minerals or metals,
all of which are but a confusion of terms to us. There are
those who know and love these mysteries, and some who
know and loathe them, but the run of us know little of the
American mines, old or new. Yet, since we are dealing with
earthy things, we certainly must not pass by the quarry —
that surface affair, nor the mine — that under-earth world,
without at least a mention of their existence, and a bit of
their history as it touched our ancestors and their development of the country.

Florida's Coquina Quarry

The very first white man's quarry in America was the one
on Anastasia Island on the Florida coast. It stands just out to
sea from St. Augustine and was therefore easily discoverable
by the Spaniards who, under Pedro Menendez Marques,
were hovering over that neck of land around 1580. Little
use was made of it until the following century when it was

94

THE QUARRY AND THE MINE

dug into so mercilessly, that soon it stretched a long distance along the island. Today the earth shows the desecration of its smooth surface, but the old "Wishing Well" is of course still there, making one wonder who first started the idea that the Spaniards dug their wells to wish by rather than to drink at. There is also the remnant of an old Spanish chimney which marks the residence here at some time of those quarrymen who dug out the soft coquina for many years and for many structures. Spanish missions standing in ruins are built of this stone from Anastasia Island, as is old Fort San Marco started in 1638 and finished, more than a hundred years later, as Fort Marion, at St. Augustine. Fort Matanza was built in 1741 of the same rock.

Perhaps the first coquina structure in the country, late 1500s. Chimney remnant of Spanish quarry-men's house on Anastasia Island, Florida

95

Coquina is a shell-rock formed eons of time ago by shell fish so tiny that the Creator must have been put to it to find a place for their hearts. This shell-rock formation is, when first dug up, still soft, but grows harder upon exposure to the air, like the heart-oak of hundreds of years ago, one defying the chisel and the other the nail.

A New Hampshire granite quarry

Vermont Marble and Granite

The first marble quarry was opened at Dorset, Vermont, in 1785, and by 1818 South Dorset was sawing its first marble blocks. Mount Ascutney Granite was being quarried not far away as early as 1793. There is a record of certain stone steps for some house, being cut at a Blue Mountain quarry, which measured forty feet in length, eight feet in width, and eight feet thick, "and cut in three pieces." It would be interesting to know just what giant walked up those eight-foot treads, but no New Englander would be surprised to learn that the full forty foot of length was cut out in one piece, for he would remember the great foundation slabs which have stood beneath farmhouses for generations, snaked to their final resting place by oxen. One stepping stone in New Hampshire which had always been partly covered by the original house, turned out to be a perfect porch floor when it was uncovered and was large enough for a dining-room for a good-sized family in front of the new building. Around this they put the real stepping stones, needing a yoke of oxen to get them into place.

The Leiper Quarries

At Avondale, Pennsylvania, Thomas Leiper did in 1785 establish himself as a quarryman. He owned a strip of land one mile wide from where Swarthmore College now stands. straight through to the Delaware River, a distance of some six miles, and in time he had achieved one of those rarely charming villages which nestle beside their own streams — in this case it was Crum Creek — in the lap of surrounding hills. Before many years he had a gristmill and a snuffmill, and a cotton mill came to join them, and all of these industries had buildings made of heavy stone from the near-by quarry. Houses for millers and quarrymen went up in little rows along stream and curving roadside, and standing back by itself on a series of terraces was the summer home of the miller. The miller himself lived in Philadelphia and rode out to Avondale each morning. His wife and the thirteen children stayed at the Avondale home because they loved it, but the miller thought " it was not healthy to sleep in the country," and would not remain over night. Today the family guesses that he thought it might be quieter in town.

The old Leiper homestead still stands on its terraces, approached by stone steps which curve into circles at the ends, one flight halfway up the walk, another at the porch, and the doorway is called the most beautiful in Delaware County.

The First Railroad

Thomas Leiper had the distinction of laying the first permanent railroad in the country. The very first one was laid in 1806 at Bunker Hill but was used only two or three months to carry gravel for a new street in Boston. Mr. Leiper held that it was easier to pull a load on rails than on the ground, and to prove this held a public test in September, 1809, in front of the old Bull Tavern which stood at the corner of Second and Poplar Streets in Philadelphia. He laid a wooden track sixty feet long with a grade of an inch and a half to the yard, with a four-foot gauge and sleepers eight feet apart. In spite of the fact that the earth was loose, making it hard going for the one horse hitched to the car, a load of 10,690 pounds was drawn to the top of the incline, something which a yoke of oxen would not have sneered at, and the hoots and derision which had been raised at the silly idea were hushed.

The railroad which was constructed at the quarry was of wood and ran to Ridley Creek three quarters of a mile away, and its cost was high. Later stone rails were substituted for the wooden ones which had become worn by the action of the metal wheel flanges. It has been claimed that the Leiper railroad was the parent of the Pennsylvania Railroad, and this claim is based upon the fact that the survey for the former was made by John Thompson, the father of Edgar Thompson, who was an early president of the "P.R.R."

In many ways Thomas Leiper was ahead of his times, for at his door is laid also, "the first practical attempt to saw stone." Here we get a typical picture of an outraged village attuned to the song of the creek and the murmurs of a wooded dell, being suddenly jolted out of their sylvan quietness by such a noise as would waken the dead. Thomas was sawing stone with a steel blade by water power. Philadelphians of that day laughed at him again but after a hundred years they were going out to Crum Creek to inquire about that "first practical method," for his design had at last been perfected. Eccentric in the 1800s, Thomas had been quite as much so in the 1700s, for in 1791 he had petitioned the Legislature for the right to build a canal as an outlet for his stone (mica schist, used in building curbs and bridges) and been refused. It was not until 1828-9 that the folks of Avondale saw a long ditch leading out to the larger world, and being built by Thomas's son, George. There were two locks in the new canal and each bore on a green stone its carved name, one was "Thomas Leiper Lock," and the other " Elizabeth Leiper Lock."

In the rear garden of the Leiper home there still stands imposingly the old office, called by the family the "fireproof building." It looks more like a Grecian temple with its pillared doorway. It is also not unlike our early forts, for the only windows in this low stone building are slits such as the Swedish Governor had made in the fort which he erected at Naaman-on-the-Delaware, in 1654. The windows in the Avondale strong-house measure five inches across the outside, but broaden to about a foot inside, giving the needed light and the maximum of protection. One of the Leipers of today says: "Thomas was an 'aye, aye, man.' He would get up and harangue at a public meeting and never give the 'nays' a chance." He got his railroad and made a fortune out of his stones and rocks.

"Doorway ay Avondale," home of Thomas Leiper, built in 1785. "Most beautiful doorway in Delaware County," Pennsylvania

THE QUARRY AND THE MINE

New Jersey Copper Mines

Many a small town in New Jersey has its copper mine, granted long ago by an English King. Few ever see these copper mines nowadays but they still do exist. At Scotch Plains, one of them can still be found if one pushes back among the underbrush up a certain ravine in the old "Blew Mountains." Somehow that old mine has always brought pre-Revolutionary days back more vividly than any other part of that ancient town, for "George the Third" was a King, and kings, having had no part in the country since then, recall the early touch. Copper mines were worked along the Passaic River "opposite the mouth of the second river" before the Revolution, and the ore there was eighty per cent pure; it was mined and sent to England "to be wrought." In 1748, near New Brunswick, lumps of virgin copper weighing from five to thirty pounds were ploughed up in the fields. In 1751 a shaft was sunk in this vicinity because a neighborhood person passing by one night saw a flame, rising from the ground, nearly as large as the body of a man. Fifteen feet down they struck a vein of blue stone two feet thick between loose walls of red sandstone, and this was covered with a sheet of pure copper somewhat thicker than gold leaf. Some of the sheets taken from between the rocks were "the thickness of two pennies," and three feet square.

Copper was not only for itself but for what it meant as bases for other metals, for it had place in brass, prince's metal, bell metal, bath metal and white copper. Zinc united most easily with copper and when properly alloyed with it, became the "prince's metal" already mentioned. Most yellow compound metals prepared in imitation of gold are but a mixture of copper with different proportions of that metal, taken either in the pure state or in its natural ore calamine. New Jersey's mines had thus a real meaning to their times.

Connecticut Silver

Connecticut was, in 1663, offering plums to "any person that will lay out himself for discovering of any mines," minerals and so forth, or "shall set themselves on work" to discover them. The memory of one of these old Connecticut mines has been perpetuated by having its name given to a near-by waterway, Silver Mine Stream, which has never failed in 249 years, as the oldest sawmill in the country which has been running continuously by its power, can testify. The mine was most active during the Revolution, but no one knows when it started operations.

Mica and Felspar at Gilsum

The largest mine in the Eastern part of the country is at Gilsum, New Hampshire, and its product is felspar. It is not so many years ago that near this spot mica, or isinglass, was being mined and the quartz and felspar tossed aside as a nuisance. Isinglass was needed for stoves which were driving the fireplaces out of business, inserted in their doors so that at least a glimpse of flame might yet be seen to cheer the heart and keep in memory the great radiance of the departed hearth blaze. Insulation and non-conductors for electricity were not yet heard of; and so felspar was only in limited demand for the making of rough crockery. One man in the neighborhood amazed the countryside by digging out some felspar, grinding it up and making his wife a toilet set.

Let it not be supposed that isinglass was not identified until the coming of stoves in the 1800s, for in 1696 the new Philadelphians had found some in their territory, and isinglass was as good for lanterns as for stoves. In 1864 mica was mined at Bath, Maine, and has been mined ever since, the Ceramic Feldspar Company there being the first to furnish our native potters with domestic spar. Felspar is also spelled "feldspar" from which comes the derivation of the word, a spar found in the fields, generally forming a stone surface easily accessible. Spar, technically, is any earthy mineral that breaks with regular surfaces, and has some degree of luster.

The Gilsum mica mine was worked in the winter only — summer being taken up with farm work — and the mica separated from the felspar so that when winter came there would be work for women and girls who gathered each day at the farmhouse of the mine owner to cut the transparent substance into squares and oblongs for commercial distribution. This work was done with ordinary household scissors, while masses of refuse clipped off and not known to be valuable, were thrown out to fill in low places in the fields, swamps, and wherever an unsightly mass would not show too plainly from the road. Now that the old "mica mine" is the "felspar mine" we learn something of that old discarded quartz and granite, despised because it made so difficult the getting of the mica. "Feldspar is used in making enamels and porcelain, china and pottery and sometimes glazes and is potassium or sodium aluminum silicate," at which our country brain reels, but steadies a bit when it finds that quartz is "just silica." Again: Large crystals of mica, felspar, and quartz are usually found where molten rock has come up through cracks in the rock and cooled very slowly, so the large crystals form. If it cools more rapidly granite is formed, and if it flows out on the surface the very fine-grained dark-colored material, like lava, forms. Slow cooling allows the individual minerals to separate like large pieces of rock candy from a sugar syrup. (Once more we are at home, for we know our maple orchards and our maple candy.) The mica in this greatest Eastern mine is of the biotite kind, clear and white.

VIII. EARTH'S COLORS — PAINT

Mocking the air with colours idly spread.
—SHAKESPEARE

Color

IT IS all very well for the scientifically minded to be content with the thought that "color is a property of light in consequence of which differences in appearance of objects are apprehended by the vision," or that the science of color is "Chromatics." If these thoughts bring joy, so be it. To the person with a reverence for science but a mind beneath it, a soul which bathes and gloats and rests in ecstasy in "Color" — regardless of its basic properties — these definitions would seem not only tragically cold but utterly inadequate. Color is as vibrant as sound, as vital as a fragrance, as disturbing as a jangle of noises, or as soothing and uplifting as the proverbial heavenly music. By many people music is interpreted best through color, and as foundation for this feeling we may turn back to that heavy word "chromatic" which means both "relation to color and a proceeding in music by the semitones of the scale." Surely color and music are kinfolks and so, equally vibrant and alive.

 Color is any hue or tint except white
 Color is pigment
 Color is paint

 Pigments are the colors for paint
 Pigments are the paint itself

 Hues are colors, tints or dyes

So say the word books, and when we have finished, we find that color, pigment, and hue are so interlocked that there is no further use in differentiating among them.

Painting is laying on colors
Painting is art of representing objects by means of colors

Painture is the art or business of painting

Limn meant to paint or draw the face
Limner was a face painter, later a picture-maker

Old-Fashioned Color Names

In talking with old people of their youthful days one often hears a word fall which is worth catching and keeping. An old New England lady tells of the wedding dress made of "mayflower silk," the faint pink of a hundred years ago; she tells of her "cherry-color sash" which she wore with her white "muslin"; to her, yellow was not yellow, but "corn color," and a rich blue was "corn-flower color." Rarely was the color called as we have it from the spectrum, but instead, our forefathers had such names as: rose-color, sage, plum, lilac, dove, wine-color, ashes of roses, ivory, punkin yaller, indigo-blue, smoke-color, sky-blue, beet-red, moss, grass-green, blood-red, and snow-white. In a dictionary printed in 1777 we find that yellow was "a glaring color," indigo "a plant for dyeing blue," gray was "white mixed with black, or hoary," yellow ochre was "a kind of earth," black was "destitute of light or very dark or gloomy," umber was "a gloomy kind of color," dun was "between brown and black," while such familiar color words as drab and orange did not exist. There is no denying the pleasantness, at least, of some of the old color nomenclature which, for musical beauty, rose far above the "vibgyor" of the spectrum and its stark violet, indigo, blue, green, yellow, orange and red.

Spiritual before Practical

It is good to find that painting's first mission was to present some vision of a man's brain, to represent a figure or object which meant something to the painter, to portray Nature, rather than being used for practical purposes. The oldest paintings thus far discovered are in the ancient caves of Les Eyzées in Southern France, where the "reindeer man" painted his familiar animals upon his cave walls in colors which are still vivid after thousands of years and surely not because he had to but because he wanted to. Later years brought painting into the field of practical usefulness, when it was found that paint was a preservative for wood, stone, brick, iron and metals of all sorts, doing its preservative work by simply "keeping the elements out."

About 1855 our first "patent paints" sold ready-mixed in cans, thrust the practical field far ahead of the spiritual and artistic one in mass production. "Ready mixed" also very largely stilled forever man's need and urge to use his ingenuity in developing his needed paint from simple sources. We speak of such a condition lightly, yet it is rather terrifying to realize that we are continually shutting doors which will remain forever shut — at least for this present civilization.

Pigments

While we find ourselves shying at the thought of analyzing color through abstruse terms, burdening a lightsome something with a heavy origin, we may still find a real delight in digging into its roots, and "digging" is used advisedly, for our paint pigments have come usually from the earthiness of the Earth. Even today we strike our foot against a lump of soft sandstone tinged with the rust color of iron ore, and are at once tempted to take it home, pound it into its original sand particles and, mixed with a sprinkling of linseed oil to hold them in suspension, find a brush and apply this new home-made paint somewhere, anywhere. The main earth pigments have been the warm colors, the reds, browns and yellows and the charred black, and these have been in the process of becoming paint for some two dozens of thousands of years: the umbers, chromes, siennas, and ochre paints, by their very names tell their beginnings. Among the metals we have had copper giving verdigris and other greens and blues, and cobalt giving us our cobalt blues, while lead, tin, zinc and more than a dozen others have entered largely into paint making. Most of our oldest red pigments are iron oxides of one kind or another, among them being rouge.

Bridal chamber in old Bidwell's Tavern, Langdon, New Hampshire. Painted c 1800 in homemade watercolors

EARTH'S COLORS — PAINT

Our first famous artist, Benjamin West, had only paint mixed from the earth by his Indian friends, for his first childish efforts.

It must not be forgotten that paint has only recently been other than a home product. That old "strong paint" of warm appealing red, put onto barns and the backs of houses — sometimes all the way around — for sweet economy's sake, is still "strong" on many an old wall after a hundred years. A homey sort of paint this was, dug from home soil perhaps, baked in the home oven and mixed with home-grown flax ground into home-made linseed oil, or skimmed milk, as the case might be.

Here is one simple recipe:

> Cheap Paint. One pound potatoes skinned and well baked. Bruise them in three or four times that weight of boiling water, pass through hair sieve. Add two pounds white chalk in powder, mixed with double its weight of water, and stir together. This mixture will form a glue to which any coloring matter may be added, even charcoal, brick dust or soot. Cheap, durable for barns and fences.

There was also the matter of dyes, and for these men and women went not so much to the earth or mineral kingdom, as to the animal and vegetable kingdoms. A few of the dyes concocted on the farms might be used to tint a basic "glue" of the above recipe, but they were generally too slight to impregnate a heavy oil base. An old lady might tint her white wool shoulder shawl with violet obtained from the root of the sweet-flag, or the purple paper which came wrapped about rock sugar cones, but her husband could not use this elusive coloring for painting the doghouse. It was the same

109

with even the heavy butternut dyes which ranged from light brown to dark as the seasons progressed, they simply could not be carried over into milk or the oils of flax or fish. Likewise the famous indigo would "color blue" whatever was put into the hearthside dye-pot, but without much expense and a different treatment offered nothing when it came to painting the house — for which we may praise heaven. Sage made a lovely line of green through a cheese, but failed in the "brustles" of a paintbrush.

The Common Colors

PRUSSIAN BLUE. Stock for this was made from cattles' hooves, their "plucks" (heart, liver, and lights) and these hooves cost $16.00 a ton. This prussian blue was known in 1868 as "stone blue" by the washerwomen who had its essence for blueing their laundered clothes.

GREEN. The greenest of all greens was verdigris, an acetate — salt or rust — of copper and the green of brass. A favorite green paint in New Hampshire a hundred years ago was so home-made that it cost not one cent. A farmer's wife who wanted to paint her unpainted best room had her husband gather a greenish clay down along the edges of the pond and mix it with oil.

YELLOW. The old "punkin yaller" was the joy of dark winter days as well as the much tramped preservative of the farmhouse kitchen floor. Powdered ochre mixed with oil made it cheap and no less strong. "Ochre looked like chunks of clay," says a man who remembers the old paint mine in Walpole, New Hampshire, which was working up until 1870. "They used to dig it out back of Paint Hill over west. They mixed it up with fish oil, or whatever kind they had on hand. I don't know why the old paint mine stopped. Whoever owned it died out, I cal'late, and then the mine just pegged out. Then, too, some one else brought in ochre that was refined better."

An old paint mine which was worked in Maine about fifty years ago is also recalled: "They had a big round vat where the ochre was put in the water, and then churned about there with a long paddle turned by a long sweep fastened to a horse that kept goin' round and round. They called it a Pug Mill. When it had been churned long enough they let it settle. Then the water was run off and the ochre run out through a spout they had ready, leading it to tanks. It was about as thick as molasses."

RED. There has been a world of wondering among the people who love our old American farm furniture, as to just what the "old red paint" or "red stain" found on so many of our old chairs and tables may be. One elderly man says that the answer is very simple, and he has seen the old red paint grow with his own eyes.

"The old red paint? Gosh, the kind they put on cheers and coffins and light stands? That was the plain yellow ochre got out of the ochre pits and roasted or burned into a soft clinker. Same as they get darker ends on the bench bricks 'cause they're laid nearest the fire, you got red instead of yellow ochre after this extry roasting. Then they ground it up. T'was awful cheap so they used it on most everything. I seem to have forgot but I reckon this was the old Venetian Red that folks bought for two cents a pound and mixed with oil or milk. Those that lived down Maine way and was handy to fish, used fish oil to stir it up with, and it kept the powder from flying off. Yes, they was uncommon generous with that old paint on all the cheers and everything round, most."

As if to substantiate this opinion, old Red Brook near

OF THE EARTH EARTHY

Kennebunkport is remembered as having received its name because it contained "ochre" which was used for "painting the outsides of buildings in early days, a tint which has been known to last seventy-five years." And buildings were painted red in droves, and not in yellow.

The old Maine gentleman was correct, for the pigment used for home-made milk or oil paints was the Venetian Red, a powder costing only about two cents a pound. Only the folks with money could go in for Vermillion.

An iron nail dropped in some of the home-made dyes would give a desired rust color. A paint authority tells the fascinating story of how the primeval Mr. Leopardskin painted his shield at the red bank, then kicked the ashes of his warming bonfire about and found a surprising silvery substance where the blaze had been hottest. These strange pellets would not yield to chewing, carving or shaping, and became useful only after they had been put back into the fire. "When the material was red hot he could hammer it into a spearhead. With a charcoal fire he had made iron from his painting clay. Later painters called Mr. Leopardskin's pigment iron ochre, mining prospectors called it hematite, miners called it iron ore, and chemists called it iron oxide." When we forget and leave our tools out in the rain, the red powder found upon it afterwards, we call rust.

Here are some old terms pertaining to ancient red:

Rubific... making red or reddening
To "redd up the hearth" was to polish the bricks with a
brick held in the hand and bring back the fresh
red surface, but later it came to mean "tidy up the
hearth" or the room or whatever.
Rubify... to make red
Rubicund... as red as a ruby
Gridelin... a color mixed of white and red

It would be inexcusable to forget to mention the busy beet in the matter of painting objects red. Beet juice was used largely both for the slenderer dyes and the sturdier paints, and gave a rosier hue than the more tawny brick. It mixed well with milk too, and made many a house gay along its "trimmin's."

CREAM COLOR. One old Massachusetts house has its early interior paint a faint cream color, and into its making went not milk or cream but eggs. This old paint was made by beating up the "yelks— preferred in the 1700s — of the eggs and mixing the froth with flour. Here we have a reversal of the usual recipe, for the pigment coloring was oftenest the heavier base, lightened with oil.

THE MADDER KILN. Although madder was used more for dyeing than in paints, the process of obtaining it seems worth our detouring. The root of the madder plant was first washed in the brook, then laid in frames to the depth of two inches in rows running west and east, their ends north and south. (This was doubtless to let the sun shine across the heavy part of the root, rather than up the stalk.) The frames were set eighteen inches from the ground at one end and six at the other. If the weather were fine for five or six days the madder would dry out enough so it could be put into the kiln for further and final drying. Here it was spread nine inches thick on frames, beneath which were six or eight small kettles or "hand furnaces," if you wanted to dignify this crude work. These kettles stood four or five feet apart and were filled with charcoal. A full day would see it so dry that it would be as brittle as a pipe stem. (Clay of course.) Now these brittle pieces were laid on the barnfloor and threshed with long hand-made flails just as grain would be.

This done, it was ground in any ordinary gristmill between its run of stones, to prevent the dampness from spoiling it.

WHITE. Since "whitewash" was a lotion for the face, wall whitener could not go under that name, but there was a wash and it was white, which was made of burned and powdered limestone, slacked with water. This was often the only "paint" which houses and outbuildings received even after paint had become the style for dwellings. White paint was white lead, and until 1809 was imported from London. At this time Samuel Wetherill of Philadelphia erected the first white lead works in the country. He had been a builder before the Revolution, but had added drugs and paints and chemicals to his building materials during the war and by 1783 was importing white lead. In building this new works he had in mind England's persistent methods of hunting out different industrial plants, getting their prices and then trying to ruin them by violent drops in their own offerings. Thus, Wetherill had his works built so that in the twinkling of an eye he could transform them into what looked like an active brewery to the snooping foreigner. White lead was actually finely ground carbonates of lead and the oxides of zinc. Since white lead became the great basic preservative as well as the common base with which colors could be mixed, it is interesting to get somewhat farther back in its history. With a hand mill, pigment, white lead and linseed oil would make a paint, but to get enough by this method to paint a house, meant weary hours, hence our "weather colored" and "black" houses scattered throughout the country for so many years. An English encyclopedia gives the beginning of white lead as it was brought about in Holland:

Pieces of sheet lead were suspended in large stone-ware pots, so as to occupy the upper part of two thirds of the vessel. A little vinegar was poured in each pot. They were covered with sheets of lead, buried in horse manure or spent tanbark, and left to corrode for a month. By that time the plates were converted into flakes of white lead, which was then knocked off, ground in water, freed from all bits of metal by elimination and the paste allowed to set and dry in small conical forms.

BLACK. Why bother trying to hunt for a black pigment *per se* when you had lamp black from the candle and forge flue, and soot from the chimney and the smut of charcoal from burned wood, and best of all the charred bones of animals — black was mostly needed for darkening other colors, anyway? But for shoes and Sunday boots there should be "blacking" and this was generally kept mixed up in an iron skillet on the cellar stairs shelf. Recipes were many:

"Bone-black and sperm-oil, with treacle and vinegar."

"Bone-black" is animal charcoal made by heating the bones of animals in a crucible, until the organic constituents are decomposed and carbonized. With gases, oils, water salts drawn off, the residue is a finely divided carbon in intimate mixture with the inorganic parts of the bones. The sperm-oil was the preservative, the treacle for obtaining a gloss from friction or elbow-grease, and the vinegar cut the resultant clogginess. Sometimes in blacking one used powdered gall-nuts, sulphate of iron, indigo, and even Russian blue. Another black substance with which one might "color black" under stress, was ink, made of lamp black, linseed oil, and boiled onions. This ink was used by Ambrose Henkel of Hagerstown, Virginia, in 1794, when he deviled for the printer. There would have been an early black lead mill at

Lynn, Massachusetts, if Dr. Child, who tried to start one, had not been undone because of his belief in religious toleration.

Paint Mills

As we have seen, many of the paint pigments were only available as paint after they had been well ground or pounded. Some of this grinding was done on the little old hand quarnes or quernes, our first American grinding mills, which were small stones less than twenty inches across, a "pair of stone" or a "run of stones" set in a stout wooden frame, table high, and turned by holding in the hand a stick which ran from a hole above to one hollowed in the upper stone, and pushed it round and round. The rough surfaces of these stones worked upon each other, the nether stone generally immovable, the upper one revolving and casting off the ground material along the radiating furrows. Often paint was ground between the large stones of an ordinary gristmill.

Stone querne for grinding pigments

EARTH'S COLORS — PAINT

There was the even more primitive way of grinding paint by the use of stones rubbed against each other. Occasionally a long slender stone will turn up either from under a barn or perhaps in a garret, and some will call it a window-weight of modern times, others a clock weight or a rolling pin or a pestle from a stone mortar. It may just as easily have been a stone for pounding color pigments. The real "mullar" or "mulling stone" was a stone paint stick somewhat more conically shaped than these other objects. Again the round stone was used in long troughs of stone.

America's first paint-mill stood in Boston about 1700. Later a guidepost

The Boston Stone

What is believed to be the first paint mill in America, is to be found in Boston as one goes out of Hanover Street into Marshal Street—old Marshall's Lane. Here, set into the rear wall of the house which stands on the corner of Blackstone and Hanover Streets, is a block of stone about four feet long, with a two-foot stone ball perched upon it, and bearing upon its face the sign "BOSTON STONE, 1737." The history of the stone includes its arrival from England in 1700 for the purpose of grinding paint; it contained a trough which had been chiseled out of one side large enough to hold, according

117

to two estimates, "seventy-five gallons of paint," and "nearly two barrels." The block stone is now but one fourth its original size, and the great stone sphere was lost for many years and finally found again under the ground. This ball was the paint "grinder" of the stone-trough mill and was rolled back and forth by man power to crush the pigments. Who the painter was who ordered this stone from across the waters, history does not make sure, but old Judge Sewall may have given us the answer when he wrote in his diary, "November 10, 1706. This morning Tom Child the Painter died." Was he the Dr. Child who had so wanted to erect a black lead mill? Thirty-seven years after its arrival the town of Boston used this old mill to copy the town of London and set up its "Boston Stone," dating it, unfortunately, just thirty-seven years too young. "London Stone" served as a direction for the shops in the neighborhood, but "Boston Stone" did not only this, but served as a focal point for surveyors, and marked the spot of our first paint mill. The sign of the miller who ran this mill was a carved reproduction of the London Painters' Guild, which is still standing by.

Oil and Other Binders

It was all very well to find the red bank by the river's side and carry its powder home for paint, but unless there were some sort of vehicle to "hold the particles in suspension" and allow them to be spread easily and evenly upon surfaces, the bank would not mean very much in the way of decorative or preservative paint. Pigment and oil would seem to tell the whole story of paint, but, as we have seen a variety in pigments, so was there a variety in the binders. We have already seen fish oil, linseed oil, and skimmed milk doing their part, but in time there came to be resins and albumins which proved to be invaluable to the industry. While alcohol entered largely into paint making in after years, it had nothing to do with the first mineral pigments paint.

When we recall that the middle of the 1800s first saw paint ready mixed in cans, it behooves us to look further into the home-made oils, the greasy, the oily, and the fatty. Maine had her pogie oil:

"Pogies was like herrings for oil, greasy, oily fish, yes, you could eat 'em, but I 'd rather have chicken. They caught 'em by the ton in a net. Would go out in boats with the nets and rowed 'til they got 'round 'em and could pull 'em in. They ground 'em up and pressed 'em. The "pogie chum" that was left was dumped on the fields for fertilizer. They used to make pogie oil in Maine and the Cape. Have to go down to Delaware Bay, they tell me, if you want to git 'em now. A pogie was about a generous foot long, sort of a herring, but Menhaden, by rights."

Linseed oil has always been the great standby where paint was concerned and was made from ground-up flax seeds; a pigment which could resist linseed oil was surely heart hardened. Oil was made out of various things in various ways; cotton seed finally — after years of waste — was rescued to the good work of oiling things up; and even the cedar tree had to yield its branches to great vats, have steam piped among them and be cooled in coils. Its job was supposed to be scaring moths away but trust an ingenious farmer to find more and more ways to use any sort of oil. We must not forget that simple binder of egg yelk, already mentioned, which gave paint its solid, heavy look, without gloss or life — known among artists as tempera — but still acted as a binder in perpetuity.

IX. THE INDIGO DYE-POT

~~~~~~

A plant for dyeing blue.

~~~~~~

The Fireside Blue

TO MOST of us the word indigo means little more than one of the colors of the rainbow whose initials spell that strange word "vibgyor," made up to help us to remember that violet, indigo, blue, yellow, orange and red are the seven colors which form the universal spectrum of light, as seen through a prism. Just why indigo, which is really a kind of blue, should have been placed in this honored position with the primal red, yellow and blue, and their intermediates, violet, green and orange, is hard for the layman to understand. Search as we may the summer rainbows for the elusive indigo between the violet and the blue, it never seems to be there.

After all it matters little to us today whether it be there or not, for the word is not a familiar one. Less than fifty years ago the word indigo was a household familiar, like "chair" or "stove," while the mother's pod of indigo — that chunk of dark earthiness — was as much a part of the household equipment as either of those pieces of furniture. Indigo was tied up with the home center, the open chimneyplace, with the weaving of homespun, and the "coloring blue" of garments for daily wear; also it belonged with the making of fine old bedquilts, and years of turning the plain and the drab into the bright and the colorful.

It is impossible too not to remember the "indigo dye-pot" which stood at one side of the open hearth, made occasionally of wood but usually of a heavy rust-colored earthen-ware, a pot which held from two gallons upward, was heavily glazed on the inside and generally left unglazed on the outer, and always, always had a firmly fitting cover to keep its odors in. The principal ingredient of indigo dye was carefully saved chamber-lye, a rather alarming one to be given a place close to the hearth where the family cooking was done, but seldom did a housewife allow her dyepot to become a nuisance, for always there was a snug bag of wood ashes floating in it to quench all odor, or the root of sweet flag. The latter, that faintest and daintiest of deodorant perfumes, persisted for years in the garments upon which it cast its slender spell. Because the dye must be kept always warm, the dyepot was kept close to the fire and thus became a favorite seat of the children on winter days. Indigo and its pot were intimate members of the family.

Localities

One of the few things which a New England farm could not produce, indigo brought the pedlar to the door twice a year, just before snow blew and just after mud time. It was not raised north of South Carolina in any quantity, so that a family to whom the pedlar could not penetrate was apt to go clothed in sombre brown and dark yellows. Says an old lady: "If the indigo pedlar didn't make out to get through to the farm some springs, Mother would have to dye the socks and mittens with butternut dye instead of dyeing blue, and blue was a sight prettier."

In a resumé of the Province of Carolina written in 1666, "indico" was mentioned, and the manufacture of this commodity as a salable article was confined largely to this section where it continued to be a profitable business until about

1796 when cotton stepped in as a more alluring livelihood. "Indico doth here grow very well," though, and in 1772 there were forty thousand pounds of it shipped to England.

During the English occupancy of Florida which began in 1763, we find Dr. Andrew Turnbull and Sir William Duncan being sent over by the English Crown to develop the new land "to sugar and indigo," but while some advance was made in the former in the Turnbull Hammocks, little seems to have been made in the latter. Still, whatever was done left its mark, for seventy years later, in spite of time and cultivation, some of the "old fields" were still sending up new growths of indigo and the pine barrens becoming less barren because of them.

While cotton was putting a detaining finger on indigo in South Carolina, sugar cane was doing the same thing to it in Louisiana.

The Indigo Plant

To many it comes as a surprise to learn that indigo seed was ever imported and raised in America in any quantity, and to many more, that while the East and West Indies, Europe and Africa are its chief stamping grounds, it was ever found natively in our own Southern States, but such was the case. The indigo plant grows on an average about three feet high and looks much like white clover, with slender small leaves and purple blossoms. It is ready for cutting just before or at the bursting of the bud into flower, and when a leaf, turned back double, breaks easily. The stem is so tough that it will not break under the hand, yet the leaves must be carefully guarded against rubbing, which necessitated the harvesting of it by hand. In spite of its toughness it is easily hurt by the sun after cutting, so that harvesting was done in the afternoons when the plant could be at once rushed to the rotting vat and there carefully laid out at once. There is "virtue" in the indigo plant, for in the mountains of Virginia the wild indigo is broken into small bunches and fastened in the bridles of beasts of burden to drive away the May-fly and prevent its sucking the blood from the animals' ears.

From letters written by Mrs. Eliza Lucas Pinckney of South Carolina in 1785 we have some close-ups on this subject of indigo growing. She had been a girl fond of the growing vegetable world and to encourage her in this fondness, her father brought to her from the West Indies a handful of seeds of the indigo plant. Her first crop was so successful that she was able to give away seeds to many of her friends who in turn planted and thus started a broad agricultural interest. It was from some French prisoners who were brought into Charleston harbor that Eliza Lucas was able to gain information regarding the care of her new crop. Two or three years later her husband became interested and carried on the work. One year later the wild indigo was discovered but soon proved itself not adapted to production in a large way although of a fine quality. In passing on to her son the story of her girlish industry Mrs. Pinckney said: "A man by the name of Cromwell was brought from the island of Monserat to make indigo for us. He made some brick vats on Wappo Creek on my father's plantation and there made the first indigo."

Simplest indigo-making equipment

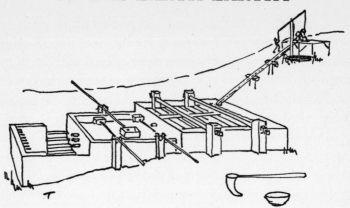

Indigo vats in South Carolina, 1700.
Steeper, beater and limer

A Recipe of 1770

In a general way the making of indigo might be simply expressed as taking a part of the leaf of the plant and by fermentation turning it into a violet-blue substance. Needed for this work was a vat for rotting the weed or plant, one for beating it, and a place for drying. A recipe which goes back to before the Revolution shows us the indigo plants a-soak for twelve or thirteen hours at which time the fermentation caused the mass to rise against the wooden bars which had been laid across the top to keep it within bounds. When the peak had been reached, the stopcock in the side of the vat was opened and the liquid allowed to flow into the next vat where it was beaten with long-handled ladles, fastened to the edges of the vat like stationary oars on an old flatboat. Fermentation in time brought the foam to the level of the vat brim and was controlled when it became too violent by the pouring on of oil. For half an hour this beating would continue until the beater could see small crystals forming. Now was the time for testing with a long-handled cowhorn dipper;

124

some of the liquid was taken out and poured into a silver cup or other silver vessel. When ready for the next step the stopcocks in the lower part of this vat were opened and the liquid drained out, whereupon the sediment appeared at the bottom ready for putting into bags which would be hung on pegs in a drying shed.

1812

By those who continued the manufacture of indigo in the next century the methods were somewhat changed. We see now the time of steeping being cut to about seven hours in the day and eleven at night, determined by the olive color and the smell of the liquor; the succeeding beating taking only forty or fifty minutes or until all of the particles were enough acidized to sink. Then the settling begins and lime water is added to slow up fermentation, while oil keeps the froth down. Only the larger part of the water is drained off through the spigots, the rest being left with the indigo to be strained through a cloth laid in a box with holes pierced through the bottom. Now we come to the indigo press into which the indigo is put for twenty-four hours. This press is a wooden frame placed on a bench, with saw-cut grooves running across it to allow any remaining water to run out. When the indigo is still wet although firm, it is taken out, ruled into squares, cut into pieces and placed in the sun to dry, no other method of drying having been found up to that time.

The "steeper vat" had to be impervious to all leakage. It was twenty feet square and three feet deep, made of two-inch planks and kept tight with wedges driven into the sleepers upon which the planks rested. When the weed was laid in it to a depth of two and a half feet, water was pumped upon it from a well or spring, and the warmer the better. Next to this a ten-by-twenty-foot vat was built as high as the steeper, where the churning and beating took place, and at its ends stood a barrel or cask for holding lime water. To be exact we must quote from an old authority:

> Liquor drawn from steeper by spigot at bottom of vat along the beater. Lengthwise this a beam resting on its upper end, and revolving on journalls, furnished with cross arms to ends of which are fixed open buckets without bottoms, containing two gallons each. Two men stand on beams with handpike fixed to long beam, alternately plunging open buckets right and left, thus churning liquid until it lightens in color and begins to show a blue fecula, or starchy looking substance drawn from the lime cask. The vat is now left to repose for four hours.

The man who wrote the above was remembering back to the first sixteen years of his life when he watched his father at the work. By 1846 he himself had made some changes in method, and he had discovered that it was best not to dry the indigo in the sun, and used "commonly the upper part of the house." He found also that the faster the work was done the lighter the indigo became, and even suggested turning steam into the vat for ten or fifteen minutes to hasten matters.

1868

At this time the rotting or steeping method is still taking nine or ten hours, and we find that the bubbles which first arise are formed like tiny pyramids which change to grey, blue, and finally to a deep purple-red. The fermentation becomes so violent that the mass seems to be boiling, while a copper-colored scum covers it, but as long as this continues the liquor is left alone and only drawn off when it becomes tranquil. It has been discovered also that by pushing fermentation too far the quality is injured, but that by cutting short and making for a better quality, the weight will be less. The liquor now is a glistening yellow, which changes to green as soon as the indigo "precipitates" or sinks to the bottom. Now it is beaten by men with oars or four-foot shovels, for about an hour and a half, or until the indigo begins to "agglomerate in flocks" and drop below, and it is not until the granulations become as small as grains of fine sand that the indigo is allowed to subside.

Indigo seems to contain, at various periods of its working, practically every color of the rainbow, for when it leaves the steeper a bright green it is on its way to become the color of Madeira wine in the next vat. At this date we see also that lime water is not always a necessity but rather a hastener, and that after the beating is done and the water drawn off, a man has entered the second vat and swept the "Precipitate" into a corner; the thinner parts are run through a bag to catch impurities, and then go into a boiler where later the froth subsides, leaving an oily film, the residue of yellow color which has been extracted to intensify the blue color and increase the weight. A night of draining produces the "drained magma" which is then squeezed inside a strong bag, cut with a brass wire into three-inch cubes, and dried on shelves of wicker-work in an airy house. Even now the indigo is not ready for the pedlar, for it has grown a whitish efflorescence on its surface which must be rubbed off. An old lady who lived all of her life in New England and remembered the coming of the pedlar with his indigo for dyeing blue, was firm in her assertion that the best indigo always showed a line of gilt in its cracks.

OF THE EARTH EARTHY

We do not know how many of our ingenious grandfathers and mothers achieved their blue coloring dyes from the simpler method obtaining in India, but judging from their other accomplishments there may have been many. It was this way: Gather any indigo leaves which one finds from time to time and when enough have been found, dry them in the sun for two days, from nine in the morning until four in the afternoon. Then thresh them by hand. Within four weeks the dry leaves will begin to change color from their green tint to a blue-grey. An even simpler way was to steep the leaves as one would steep tea, and something there was which would be left to give the homespun a touch of the sky.

The old rust-colored dyepot, the lovely blue and white quilt, the "blue'nwhite" mittens, the sturdy blue "feetin'," the long knee-length frock of the busy farmer, may all hold a different meaning for us, if we dabble a little with even a sprig of our wild indigo.

X. THE HOP-YARD

Headquarters for Hop Goods: We are prepared to furnish Hop Growers...with Hop Bagging, Burlap, Kiln Cloth Twines and Brimstone.

—*Morrisville, New York*

The father of all Madison County hop kilns, built by James Cooledge in 1815, of stone, in circular form

Wild Hops

FLOWING placidly to bring the newly arriving "land-lookers" into its valley and later to carry their families and household goods much of the journey from somewhere else, the "Old Chenang," or the Chenango River, continued its placid flowing, to water and make rich the land all about them, and, conspicuously, to create fertile fields and "yards" for taming and exploiting the native wild hops. It was to this valley in the County of Madison, New York, that James D. Cooledge came in 1808, and with his neighbor Solomon

129

Root, started the hop culture of that section. The valley is still rich with memory of James Cooledge tramping back and forth from his forest land to his newly cleared fields, carrying the precious green vines which had been dug in the former to be transplanted in the latter. For many weeks he labored at this tiring work, and soon Solomon Root was doing the same on his new land. There was the breathless waiting during the winter months to see whether the spring would do its part and call the tender little plantings up to the light of the spring sunshine, and when it did just this, a culture and industry which was to dominate the farmlands thereabouts for the best part of a century had had its beginning. There is record of Solomon Root's selling 2000 bushels of hops in 1818 for $2000. Just forty-seven years from that fall of tender planting of wild vines into "yards" of their own, this one County of Madison, in the center of the State, was producing a million pounds of hops, and three other Counties, Oneida, Otsego, and Schoharie, were also outstanding for their hop successes, making the State crop total over seven million pounds. This section has been called the finest spot for the raising of hops in the whole country, although Massachusetts had her "eminent hopgrowers."

The hop vine is a great democrat and grows in all sorts of soil, but, like a human, does best in the best soil. Planters called "good corn ground" quite perfect for hop ground, and since there was plenty of good "corn country"—as evidenced by the well-known "Johnnycake Hills"—hops began to spring up in yards measuring from one to fifty acres in this part of the State. Driving along the country roads one could see hop yards stretching away before the eye, rolling up and down hill, pole tied to pole as though great armies were dancing the polka across the land, their hands on each others' shoulders, forming miles of vine-covered vistas to entice the traveler from the sun-hot roads. Prices soared from thirty cents a pound to a dollar and hop growers lived on the fat of the land. In the winter great tents of countless poles stacked together in the fields told the story of the summer which was past and the one still to come. Then came a great slump and the hop yards were noticed because they were there at all. In 1879 the four hop Counties had thirty-eight thousand acres in hop yards, and in 1930 there were just seventeen. Today this section of the Empire State has proven that it can grow the finest English hops better than they can be grown in their native land, and hop yards are coming back.

The reason for hops in a man's life and their general usefulness may be drawn from this note made in 1839:

> The estimated number of inhabitants in the United States is fifteen millions. Allowing five individuals to a family, the quantity of hops raised in the country would give about half a pound to a family through the nation. This is evidently a small supply, for yest and small beer, to say nothing of the bakers, who are regular and free consumers of the article. However, much of it goes with a far greater quantity of barley to be consumed by the brewers of pale ale and porter. . . . In one respect hops are an exception to the farinaceous and most other kinds of agricultural crops, as neither by fementation, distillation, or any other process, can they be made to produce an intoxicating liquor. They are a strong antiseptick, and are used to preserve yest and beer of all kinds, and perhaps other materials.

Some said that hops "flavored" the beer; others that "the flower scales and fruit are used in brewing," and certainly the great brewers of New York and Philadelphia had to have their hops if they were to have their beer ready for the market:

as "yest" the bakers used it as leaven to raise their bread, and the housewives made their home-made yeast with the aid of "the pretty little green hop." One man says: "When I was a lad, Mother always saved hops to make yeast. It was a little cake, dry and mealy and tasted bitter."

A Typical Hop Kiln

Since the old stone and wooden hop kilns have been the familiar sign and symbol of hop-growing in the hop country, they should have our first attention, and fortunately that first kiln of James Cooledge built in 1815, is still standing in good condition for us to study. It is of solid cobble-stone and stands close to the road, outliving many of its near-contemporaries which stand scattered here and there in the near-by towns in sad but picturesque ruins, notably in Irish Hollow just north of Pine Woods. After some years another kiln made of wood came to snuggle up at its rear, and then a "hop house" was erected touching on one side, to be used for storage of the hops, housing the hop-press, and for "sleeping" the pickers during the four weeks of hop-picking time.

Hops kilns were of various shapes, but the Cooledge kiln was circular in form, and being "the daddy of all later hop kilns," naturally influenced their form. It, and they, stood alone, with their conical roofs and their strange turning cowls atop of their heads, silhouetting grotesquely against rolling field of skyline. Many kilns were square or of some rectangular form, with a pyramidal roof, also topped with the cowl. This cowl was a most familiar sight throughout the hop lands, for on nearly all of the farms at least one building wore its pointed headdress. Today many of these have been torn down or blown away and the old kiln has become a circular or square barn with a sharp peak at the top. Where the remnants of the old cowls remain, they look like fingers with the joints broken, sticking out wildly in all directions, for there was a strong outstuck arm to catch the wind, and the hood or cowl itself was of boards heading up to a point around a center post, generally of wood throughout. The purpose of the cowl was to catch the prevailing wind and keep the outside moisture from creeping within as well as ventilating the kiln during the drying process.

The versatile stove, doing duty this time in a country store at Hancock, New Hampshire

133

OF THE EARTH EARTHY

To enter the old Cooledge kiln is to feel that one is entering a mediaeval tower, since circular buildings are most unusual and the stones seem to speak of ancient times. In the center was a huge stove from which a long line of stove pipe started forth to travel around the circular wall about three-fourths of the way up from the ground, so that there might be an even heat for the hops which would be placed just above for drying. Unless one has had close association with the great stoves of a past day, it would be impossible to appreciate the glory of their radiating heat. Today they are still found as bulwarks of strength against the winter blasts in country stores, not quite the focal point which they used to be for marksmen in spit, but still lovingly encircled by local habitués. A New York State man says: "We use one still in the town of Lebanon, to keep our Snow Plough truck warm and ready to use." Sometimes these kiln stoves burned wood cut three or four feet long, and sometimes they were fed coal when that article was finally accepted as something less than the work of the devil. About four feet down from the top of the wall was the "drying floor," which was of wooden slats an inch and a half wide and placed one inch apart.

The Hop Yard

There was little difference between the methods of hop culture from the 1830s until the 1900s, and what a "Correspondent" wrote for the *Farmer's Monthly Visitor*, at the former date was good advice to be followed at the later one.

> The roots for planting must be taken, as is well known among all hopgrowers, from what is called the sprout roots. These are entirely different from the ground-roots. The latter, like roots of other plants, support the stock,

and having no eyes, would not, if planted, produce a blade. Whereas, the sprout-roots appear to be arms, shooting out under ground, and if unmolested, would throw up tops from every pair of eyes at every distance of about six inches. These sprouts are cut, as I have said, into lengths of about one foot for planting, allowing three pairs of eyes to a piece. Upon the tops of the ploughed in manure, near the centre of the hill we drop three cuts of hop-roots, nine to twelve inches long, and then cover the depth of corn. On rich soil I put the hills eight and a half feet apart, on poor soil seven feet.

When the frost had come out of the ground the field was cross-furrowed and then the hills had their top and side earth removed with the prong-hoes, so that the sprout, or grub, roots might be hauled up and the hill opened up as far down as possible without injuring the ground-roots. Trimming came next and with a knife. The sprout roots were cut two or three inches from the stump, care being taken not to amputate the old snout, that is, the stump of the old vine down for two sets of eyes, and perhaps more.

Hop Poles

Some one has described hops as "slender vines which climb counter-clockwise up high poles." While this is limited in explanation, it would seem to show that it was impossible to think "hops" without at the same time thinking "poles." After all, it was only the wild hop which could prosper without its pole, and the great green arbors which were the hop-yards or fields, were possible only because of the army of poles which built them up. A hop grower in Madison County says: "Poles were usually of cedar, and mostly tamarack. Sometimes when the old poles wore out I stuck willow poles in between the hardwood and the cedars. You know, those darned willows would sprout. I didn't hire out to pull trees, but I had the galdurndest time pulling willow boughs out of those hop vines."

A hundred years ago some one said: "The best species of trees for hop poles are cedar, spruce, hemlock and white pine; white birch and hard wood are sometimes used, but they are poor things, and the sooner they are converted to firewood the better. The poles should be cut in winter, drawn home and shaved all over lightly, except near the top, and sharpened ready for use." Poles were set out as soon as the frost was out of the ground and two were generally set into the same hole or hill. The "holing" had to be done first with an iron bar or something which would drive a good deep hole to hold a pole from fifteen to twenty feet tall. One old-fashioned "holer" was funnel-shaped; others had an "auger handle" or a straight handle set on at right angles to the iron bar; some recall a "round implement shod with iron, having a crutch at the top and a peg through the middle to tread upon," and this called a "poy."

Some of the earlier hop growers kept themselves busy tying their vines to the poles as they shot upwards, and continued to do so until they were nearly to the top. They found that a raveled woolen sock gave the softest and strongest "tie yarn" for this work. Later we see a regular hop twine being advertised and used for stringing the poles themselves so that the vines, when they reached high up, might be supported on them. If poles were plentiful and strong, strings were not necessary, for with two in a hill they could take care of the vine nicely. Sometimes hopfields were veritable arbors hung with drooping vines which formed a green roof over the whole yard. This was not considered good for the hops which then grew singly rather than in groups while the vines became so bushy that the picking was made difficult, not to mention the fact that the hops themselves were "soft, green, and feeble." Says a hop-man:

"When the poles began to get worn and break off some, we'd put a row of tall poles and then a row of short ones, and tie string from the top of the short ones over to the tall ones, nearly to the top. If we tied them only from east to west you got a sort of slanting effect, but if we tied them both ways to the same tall poles you got a sort of tent. When we had to string the poles we did it in May before the vines got too high. We took a pole about six feet long with a hole through the end, or a loop of wire to run the twine through, and then with that we could guide the twine and loop it over the poles."

The Pickers

A book might easily be written on the social life of the countryside during hop-picking season, of those early days when the neighborhood young folks did the picking and thought it great fun, and of later when these hop sections became the focal point for tramps from all over the country and the local pickers withdrew in their favor. Much could be told of the farmer's wife who must arise at four in the morning to do the baking for a hundred men or more who must be fed by her their three big meals a day, of the bedding down of these stranger crews in house and barn and annex, of the dancing at night in the great barns, and the visiting between the pickers on neighboring farms, and the music of mouth-organ and accordion which stole out on the air of the summer evenings and floated, weighted with human voices, far across the now dishevelled hopyards and along the dusty highroads.

New York hops were picked in the height of summer heat. Massachusetts did some of its picking as late as the middle of September. When the hops were ripe the seeds were black, the fruit (the calices) approached more or less a straw color, and when rubbed in the hand gave out a strong and fragrant odor. When they were ripe all else in the world must be set aside for their immediate picking. At once the great hop wagons with board seats running down the sides were pressed into service as well as any other large wagons which could carry the large "hop boxes" out to the fields, where they were set up some distance from each other. Sometimes they were regular board boxes, again they might be frames covered with burlap, but always they had uprights at the sides to hold a pole laid across them over which a burlap awning might be fastened as a guard against the sun. Each box had four separate apartments holding seven bushels each, and so four pickers were placed at each one, two facing the other two under the awning. What the hop pickers meant to the hop-fields after the poles had been poled down and the vines dragged from them, was a spatter of brilliant color from the sunbonnets and dresses of the girls and the broad straw hats and neckerchiefs of the men and boys. To the owner of the yard they meant groups of four busy human machines standing at their different boxes. As fast as the workers pulled the hops from the vines, leaving no stems or leaves to make "dirty hops," and filled their section of the box, men drove across the fields collecting the harvest in great seven-bushel sacks, and carrying them off to the kiln. More and more vines were supplied and so the work went on for a month or more. In some sections the name "binge" was given to this frame-covered hop-box, but apparently not in New York.

138

THE HOP-YARD

A later square hop-kiln of wood

Kiln Drying

In the kiln already partially described, were three doors, one for entrance on the ground, one large one up under the eaves and another under the eaves on another side of lesser size. A platform extended a few feet below the larger of these upper doors, upon which the bags were tossed from the wagon before it hurried back to the field. Stairs ran up the outside of some kilns to reach these platforms and the kiln workers emptied the bags from the platform through the door down onto the raised slat floor of the kiln where it stretched, burlap covered, above the great kiln stove. Thorough drying could best be accomplished if but a half pound of the hops were scattered on a square foot of floor, and the best priced hops were those which were treated carefully. One old hop grower tells us: "Brimstone and sulphur's laid around the top of the kiln edge and the fumes from it percolates up through the slats to color the hops and make them change from green to a golden color." Another one says: "Brimstone is melted sulphur and cast into sticks about an inch and a half in diameter. It's very brittle and breaks up in pieces. You put

139

this onto the stove and into skillets or pots and burned it in different parts of the kiln to evenly bleach and color the drying product. At the end of the day you took that day's pick and started the drying for it would take until the next evening to finish it generally, sometimes less time. You always had to get the last harvest out to be ready for the next one when it had all got in at the close of the day. Before they had the hop houses, they'd take the finished hops and store them in the big unfinished chamber of the farmhouse as soon as they bagged them and threw them out through the smaller upstairs window.

Into the Press

"At the old Cooledge kiln now, after they'd got the hop-house right next to the kiln, they'd shove the dried hops through a window into the upper floor of that building. There was a square hole in the floor, sort of a trapdoor about eighteen inches across, and right under this was the press, down below. A sack minus one end was tacked around the hole and hung down so that a man could keep the lower end in his hand and allow the hops to get into the press only as fast as two men could tramp them down. (Apparently careful treatment was no longer necessary, at least at this kiln.) Then when the press was full they would place a follower (press board) on top, and with a lever and ratchet, work them down to the required size. The bales varied in weight but were always well over a hundred pounds. Before another bale was made, a piece of baling cloth or heavy burlap was laid over the bottom of the press, then the press filled by heading in, then another piece of sacking was laid on under the follower. When these pieces of sacking met squarely they were sewed with strong twine and a crooked needle, then released.

Sometime after when convenient they were capped with a Pop hop-sacking about one and a half foot square on each end, to complete the baling."

Said one wise old grower, regarding clean picking: "If any one thinks that stems and leaves are of little consequence, let him pick those separately and make his own small beer and yest from that stock, and send the clear, clean, dry-picked, well-dried, ripe fruit to those who are ready to pay cash and the highest price therefor."

An unwise Sandford hopgrower nearly queered hop trade with England at an early date by dropping an occasional stone into his finished bales, but each of his ill-starred chickens came home to roost.

The very first hops raised in the Cooledge district were sold to local breweries and we shall hear more of the one at Eaton, five miles distant. Cooledge finally made himself a New York market where there was a sudden demand for "western New York hops," the central part of the State in 1816 being decidedly "western." Not far away at Waterville a man by the name of Lawrence had soon started a "Hop Extract Factory."

XI. THE MALT-HOUSE

The wheat's so growed out you could almost call it malt.

"Five Points Rum & Liquor Shop,"
New York City. From Valentine's Manuel

Malt for Good Livers

AMONG those buildings which grew up in the dooryards of "good livers" in the late 1600s and early 1700s, was the malt-house. It was neither a mill nor a shop, but just the home spot for making malt and producing "home-made strong beer." Philadelphia achieved her malt-houses, both private and public, as soon after settlement as any of the coast towns, for the first English settlers began to come in 1682 and within four years the foundations of the Francis Perot's Sons Malting Company had been laid at Thirteenth and Juniper Streets on the east side of Front Street. Today this is claimed as the oldest business concern in America and is actually older than the Bank of England. It was founded by Anthony Morris, one of Philadelphia's moving spirits — and no joke intended — and has descended from father to son through eight generations. The malt-house is now in Buffalo, but after 250 years the old office still remains in the old city.

In 1701 some Philadelphians in petitioning for a road in the north end, included the statement that "the German-town road is most traveled taking thereby much lime and meal from three mills, with much malt and a great deal of wood etc." This glimpse of what went over that road tells pretty well what would go into the building up of a real business in malt if it extended beyond its first purpose of keeping its owner in beer.

A Brewery Village

At Eaton, New York, the Morse family laid out a typical little village industry whose plant was a little village in itself. First a sawmill went up a little way back from the highroad through the valley, where trees could be sawed for the various buildings to make up the new brewery group. Close to the road rose the fine stone mansion, not facing it but siding it, giving the first exclusive touch to this almost feudal plan. A private road was cut back from the highroad, which ran past the house and almost to the mill, and then scalloped off along the brook to meet the highway again after it had served its owners well on the private domain, and was now bent on reaching the village of Eaton proper. A glance at this old layout tells the story of the industry with almost no words to describe it. Across from the house on the other side of the road at a respectful distance, stood cattle, horse and hay

*Morse Distillery, Eaton, New York, as it stood with
its sawmill, gristmill, malt house, cooper shop and
other buildings*

barns. Across from the house over the new lane stood a compact stone office, a fine little building to take care of the business side of the concern. Near it stood firehouse and storehouse, edging the lane. Now in a long wavering row, on the lane which would grow to be "Mill Street," and outlining the brook, came, first, the gristmill where the grain was ground for the malt-house; this done the grain traveled over to the malt-house where the maltman or maltster added the hops and steeped all in water and dried it in a kiln or on the malt floor; from the malt-house the result was carried to the distillery where the spirits were extracted; while just over a little bridge across the brook stood the cooper shop where the barrels were made on the home grounds to hold the distilled liquor. A man driving in at the mansion-office corner would proceed past all of the steps in the establishment and drive out at the other end without leaving his buggy seat, and if he wished, proceed to the door of the Eaton tavern to sample the product as finished. Says a neighbor who remembers the old malt-house: "I've seen several pounds of hops used in a ten-gallon keg of home-made beer and it sure had a kick in it."

Malt-House, Brew House and Still

Throughout the making of the various old drinks the malting, brewing and distilling and all other processes were closely interwoven, often being carried on under the same roof. In the 1660s John Whipple of Ipswich had "a malt house with a license to still strong water for a year." While the rest of the Philadelphia gentlemen were erecting their private "malt houses," William Penn's order was for "a brew house." In the 1660s, Oloff Stevenson Van Cortlandt, one of the important New Amsterdamites, had his residence on Browers Stratt (Brewer) to the northeast of the Fort, and his whole brewery plant attached at the rear and running around the rest of the block. One plan was the combination brewery and bakery, such as Robert Turner had in Philadelphia in 1685, with a bricked underground passage leading clandestinely to the river.

In 1764 there were upwards of thirty "distel houses" in Rhode Island, making rum from molasses. New Jersey advertised "a good distil house for making apple whiskey. It is convenient for distillers as there is a dam already made on the brook, with a gentle descent so as to fill his cisterns without a pump."

MALT
a   Name given to grain in which germination has been caused to proceed to a certain stage and has then been arrested by removal of the water and the application of heat. Made soluble.
b   Barley or other grain steeped in water and dried in a kiln.
c   Hops gave the bitter taste necessary to good malt liquors.

William Penn's brew jug, 1680s

BREW
a   Preparation from malt or other materials, by steeping, boiling, fermentation.

b   Preparation of liquors from malt and hops.

c   A "brewage" is malt liquor.

d   Fermentation. The changing of organic substances by which their starch, sugar, gluton, etc. are decomposed and their elements recombined in new compounds.

DISTILL

a   To extract the spirit from a substance.

b   To fall in drops.

For the work of steeping, a fire and pot were necessary. For the work of brewing, a stone jar would serve well. For the work of distillation there must be some sort of "still" with its under fire, boiling vessel, coils and spouts, to extract the "sperrits."

The Grog Shop

Back in 1729 the New Jersey Courts in Salem County were controlling the prices of drinks, and from their rulings we have a list of West Jersey beverages:

Each public house keeper within the county shall take for their several measures of liquors hereafter named as follows:

Each nib of punch made with double refined sugar & ½ gill of rum	9p
Each nib made with single refined sugar & 1½ gills of rum	8p
Each nib of Muscovado sugar & 1½ gill of rum	7p
Each quart of tiff made with ½ pint of rum	9p
Each pint of wine	1sh
Each quart strong beer	4p

147

*From Valentine's Manuel, Five Points Brewery,
and old Reynolds Beer House, Thames and
Temple streets, New York City*

What with malting and brewing and distilling, some
great combinations were concocted to be poured down the
"gullet" or "meat pipes" of men. Here are some of them:

148

THE MALT-HOUSE

Tiff—any drink of liquor

Lees—dregs of wine or beer

Yeast—the flower of malt liquor when working

Spirits—liquid produced by distillation

Grog—spirits and water, generally unsweetened

Gin—spirit distilled from rye and barley flavored with juniper shrub. The "Spirit of Juniper" was called "Geneva"—the derivation of "Gin."

Ale—liquor made by infusing malt and hops in boiling water and fermenting

Rum, or Rhum—spirit distilled from molasses or sugar. East India molasses and an East India word

Beer—fermented liquor from any malted grain and farinaceous plants. Also malt and hops

Rotgut—bad small beer

Wort—new beer unfermented. Also unfermented infusion of malt that when fermented becomes beer

Persimmon beer—North Carolina

"Strong" Beer—New Jersey brew

Apple Whiskey—New Jersey distillation

Whiskey—Spirit distilled from barley, wheat, maize, or **rye**

Whiskey handy in the taproom

Bock Beer—Linked with the coming of spring and used in spring festivals by the ancients. "It gushed from the newly tapped vats, and because it came from the bottom of the vats, owned a rich darkness and potency." Always thought of with a goat, symbolic of manly vigor at this season of the year.

Wine—the expressed and usually fermented juice of grapes and other fruits

Peachy—peach drink

Perry—made from pears

Cider—made from apples

Apple Jack—New Jersey whiskey

Brandy—distilled from wine

Syllabub—brandy in heavy whipped cream

Eggnog—whiskey with egg, milk, and sugar—Southern Christmas drink

Black Strap—New Hampshire—forgotten

Mead—Fermented honey and water, yeast or malt

Metheglin—Same as above

Flip—Beer, brandy, and sugar

Hum—ingredients forgotten

Corn Whiskey, or "Cawn"—corn, yeast, sugar, water

Moonshine—Illicit liquors originally of the Southern sections

Bootleg—   "   "   "   "   "

Persimmon beer—Layer of corn pone and layer of mashed fruit

One Large Still

At one time West Virginia had probably one of the largest, if not the largest, stills in the world. A man who visited it says: "One day a friend and I went into a cave and penetrated quite a distance to where the stream divided. Soon two young fellows came in and began to build a fire. We got to talking to them and one of them said that his grandpap and pappy had made whiskey here for years. By going beyond the dividing of the streams you could not be seen by the casual searcher, and the mash of ground malt and warm water could be made so close to the stream that all signs of it could be washed away by the flow of water. The smoke, that usual give-away to Government agents, had just one vent and that was on the other side of the mountain, a mile and a half away, where the cave had its exit.''

Barroom, old Central House, Stoddard,
New Hampshire, showing grained and gilded door

That still was in the district where even the most careful agent could find little to report and nothing to smash. One day one arrived at the store which centered up that part of the mountains and confidentially threw himself upon the mercies of the storekeeper. "I'm here to clean out the boot-leggers and moonshiners. Of course I don't know the ways through these mountains, and I'd make it worth your while if you could get me a competent guide."

"Sure, that can be done easy, mister. There comes old Hickory Jones now. He knows these mountains like a book. Hey, Hick. This here gentleman wants some one to help him run down the stills through the mountains. Like the job at good pay?"

At the end of three weeks, after the guide had faithfully led the agent through pass after pass and up "branch" and down "run," he said: "Say, I reckon the boys has all stopped makin' shine these days. I done the best I can but I don't seem to be givin' you anything for your money. I reckon we better be startin' home." Like a great hushed room those mountains had remained during this visit of the "furriner," stills and jugs and coils and mash hidden far out of sight, for after all, Old Hick might have to cross their trail now and then, in spite of himself.

Moonshining taught these mountaineers to be mighty clever and original in their methods of work. One way to fool a possible inspector was to go to town and buy a new cook-stove and on the way home lose one of the legs. This necessitated building up a little brick support to take its place . . . and through this brickwork a secret pipe could be run with no one the wiser. Some of them had the pigsty close to the still so that all pipes and coils could be run through it, and the stiller benefit both from the shelter of the dungheaps and the misleading of their odors.

The mash was generally of corn, yeast, sugar, water, and sometimes potatoes since they fermented quickly. This was left to ferment and came out beer or wine. The poor whiskey had an overdose of sugar to form the alcohol. The juice was taken out and put into a still and heated almost to the boiling point, for alcohol boils just before the water does. Then this liquor passed out of the top through coils or copper worms,

THE MALT-HOUSE

and as these ran through cold water the spirits were distilled, the result being about half water and half alcohol. To make it really good raw whiskey the process was often repeated. Many of the moonshiners who resented interference of the Government in the making of their bootleg for their own and the neighbors' use, quit their illicit distilling when Prohibition came in, stating very emphatically that they were not outlaws or lawbreakers, and if the law of the land was against everybody's making it, they would keep that law. What they had resented before was the disproportion between the license tax which they were supposed to pay and that which was paid by the great money-making distilleries in the cities. "Cawn" was a part of their regular diet and no man should be taxed for eating his home-grown food, said they.

Bartender's folding bed in above barroom, closed during the day with a triple folding door decorated with yellow, brown and gilt design

XII. SILK AND MULBERRY TREES

Yet may I not this Wondrous Worm pass by,
Of fly turned Worm, and of a Worm a Fly.
Two Births, two Deaths, here Nature hath assigned her,
Leaving a Posthume, dead,—live Seed behind her.
                                        —DU BARTAS, 1655

An American Product

SILK seems an exotic thing to have been grown in this land, a something smacking too much of the Orient to have had a place in our ordinary living, and yet America has produced some of her own silk and done it almost as simply as she has turned out hen's eggs. Sometimes it was the handiwork of the daughters of the family, and sometimes it was undertaken in a large way. We cannot claim to have been a great silk-producing country, and yet from time to time the culture of silk has been undertaken and accomplished from New Hampshire to the Carolinas.

Early Colony and State Efforts

The French are responsible for our having received the first "silk-wormes seed" or eggs, for in 1620 some Frenchmen settled at Buckroe, Virginia, where they had been sent by their Government to plant mulberry trees and grapevines. In 1622 eighty ounces of seed were sent here from England. In 1623 the Assembly of the Colony, made up of Englishmen, ordered the Colonists to busy themselves planting at least ten mulberry trees to each hundred acres which they owned, the failure to accomplish this to cost them ten pounds of their beloved tobacco. The claim is made by some that the very first silk culture in the country was on the Digges plantation, at Yorktown, remembered as the famous "Belle-field."

In 1682 William Penn was starting his new city of Philadelphia, and it was not long before he was encouraging the planting of mulberry trees for feeding silkworms. Like the French he planted grapevines as well, some two thousand for the production of wine.

The Carolinas were finding about the same time, that their soil was as the smile of God to mulberry trees, and they said: "There is in Carolina great plenty of Mulberry Trees, such as are by experience found to feed the Silkworm very well, yea, as well as the white Mulberry, but there is of that sort also, which are propagated with a great deal of ease, stick a new cut and thrust into the ground seldom failing to grow." It was however in the 1730s that this Colony got well into its silk culture.

Georgia, established as a Colony in 1733-4, lost no time in setting about silk production. What is now known as Wormslow Gardens, near Savannah, was at this early date an eight-hundred-acre silk plantation, and today some of the old mulberry trees upon which the silkworms fed, are still standing. Was the plantation name significant? In 1741 it was said ". . . you shall see numbers of silk balls sticking to the boughs of trees even in the woods." The height of the industry in this colony was about 1759.

Six years later, New Jersey, Delaware, and Pennsylvania had to offer substantial bounties to get the work of silk culture under way, and then but little success attended it. "The silk was badly reeled on hand looms and roughly spun on the large wool wheel. It was too fine and uneven to compete with Italian silk and badly colored."

Parts of New Hampshire were undertaking silk development around 1800 but in a small way. One girl raised her own silkworms and spun the silk, then wove it into a wedding veil of lovely sheerness about a yard long. The wedding veil of that rural section was not worn as a bridal veil at the wedding but was a part of the wedding outfit to be affixed to the huge "Meeting" poke bonnet with its huge crown and huger brim, the veil being shirred and fastened about the root of the crown, to be thrown back when not wanted over the face. Sadly enough the little silk raiser never became a bride, her lover dying too soon. She dyed the veil black for mourning and wore it until she died as an old lady. Such was the quality of silk raised and spun and woven on a New Hampshire farm.

Over in Vermont, quite a bit of silk was raised in the southern part along the Connecticut River, in "a flurry of interest between 1835 and 1845." Mulberry trees measuring from two to twenty feet in height were set out and later their leaves plucked and fed to the worms. Buildings much like the tobacco barns which now stand on the opposite side of the river for curing tobacco — with their sides made of hinged boards to raise and lower — were built for the work. At the end of this busy decade the trees had all been frozen, and Italy had one less competitor.

At Mansfield, Connecticut, the first silk factory in that section was erected and from 1810 until 1839, several hundred pounds of silk were turned out annually. But there was something which Italy had, which America lacked, and although so many of the Colonies and States, including Maryland, made their attempt at silk culture, our product could never be brought up to the Italian quality.

SILK AND MULBERRY TREES

The Silk of Joseph Clarke

It is always a boon to find some one who knows definite and intimate facts about work done by our forebears, and the following, recalled by Miss Anne L. Clarke, is invaluable to the subject:

> My father, Mr. Joseph Clarke of Northampton, commenced raising silkworms soon after the close of the Revolutionary War, as early as '89 or '90, and continued it more than thirty years. At first he was altogether unacquainted with the business, except through some European publications, and the little oral information obtained occasionally from the Mansfield people.
>
> "Every year, however, added to his stock of knowledge and consequently he was enabled to produce raw silk (reeled upon the true Italian reel) equal to any imported from India to England. He had cloths and handkerchiefs wove; they resembled in texture the foreign. Cloth for my mother, a cloak, was woven at Long Meadow by an Englishman and is still worn by an old lady at Northampton. Mr. John L. Sullivan took some raw silk to England and it was returned to my father in very beautiful stockings. The manufacturer pronounced it as good as any imported from India.

It would seem from this that Joseph Clarke had that something which had seemed lacking to so many other American silk producers.

The Mulberry Trees

We have already found that the South abounded in the mulberry tree. There were, however, different kinds of mulberries, that kind upon which the silkworm would feed and the other which it would not touch. From the Carolina reports we know that the "right" kind was found there natively;

from early Virginia reports we find that no mulberry tree might be cut in the making of a clearing, because of its usefulness in silk culture, but that the crop was also augmented by importations. The "right" kind of mulberry tree was either the black or the white, and some of these coming to our shores came via England and China. At old Williamsburg there are some ancient mulberry trees of the "paper" variety, and it is said that these were brought into Virginia before or about 1735, long after silk production had been abandoned.

Virginia's Leaves and Worms

It is to Virginia that we must look for the details of this interesting old industry, even although all of the silk made there was made under bonus urge and protest, due to the settlers' eyes being fastened upon the beloved tobacco plant. By 1650 her warm climate and many mulberry trees made her seem to Englishmen as the ideal spot for silk culture, where much of the work could be done indoors by the women and children. It was done "at that time of the year in May, that it hinders not any other work of planting, sowing. . . ." It is to E. W. Gent, writing "At the Signe of the Sun below Ludgate, London," in that same year, that we go for the following story of silk culture in Virginia:

"A man and a boy if their hands be not sleeping in their pockets, will feede as many Wormes as come of sixe or eight ounces of seed till they be past their foure first sicknesses, and within some fourteen days of spinning: Indeed the last fourteen days require a more extraordinary diligence and attendance, a more frequent and carefull feeding, because in that time they conceive, gather and store up the disposing matter from whence the Silke comes, which by an inconceivable mystery of Nature, they after as it were, vomit out of their mouths, and spinne out of their bowells. At this more particular season, there is a necessity of adding the labor of three or foure helpers more . . . their labor which is nothing but to feede them within doores, cleanse, dry and perfume their lodgings, with some strengthening, but not overstrong odour. . . .

"When they spinne their Silke, that creature be then very obnoxious to be stifled with too much heate. . . . Again, to temper a season inclining to a preternaturall coolnesse with an artificiall heat. Mulberry leaves must be dried in a moist season after their gathering before they be administered for food to the Silke-worme. In drought season let the leave lye and shade a little for cooling — or water the roots of the Mulberry tree.

"Set up a house in the middle of a grove of Mulberries where the Silkewormes in a dry cabinet of Boards, may be kept set up with stones in it, in case the season require it eyther to correct the ill sents, or to give the ayre a temper and qualification, which if not prevented may destroy your work by killing the Silkeworme. The Silkeworme house should be long like a Bowling-Alley. To erect these slight silken lodgings, cleave and saw out small quarters, rafters, planks, poles and boards. The Country afford woods which will run out, slit and cleave into long lengths and breadths, which by the directnesse of the Ground will rive in a manner, as if they had been sawne for the work. All which must be so close layd, joyned, and nayled together, the one still lapped over the other, that no Winde or Raine may penetrate there-in to offend that laborious Creature . . . stop such chinkes . . . with Lome Clay and Lime . . . with what speed may such a house be clapped up together with a few nailes one lopping over another. . . ."

OF THE EARTH EARTHY

"The Reformed Virginia Silk Worm"

It is now 1655 and hopes are still running high for Virginia silk. "Mulberry Seeds. Ground well dunged in the sun. Dig two feet deep, divide into several small beds not over five feet in breadth. Lay Mulberry seeds in water for twenty-two hours, dry again half dry. Cast upon the beds, not as thickly as garden seed, cover with fine earth (past through a Sive), about one half inch. In dry weather water every other day. Transplant twice. When leaves of Mulberry buds forth a little, lay eggs of Silk Worm in a say (woolen cloth) in a little safe box, carry them in some warm place about you by day, at night in your bed or between two warm pillows. When worms come forth punch holes in a paper and lay it over them in the box. Lay Mulberry leaves thereon. After second sickness remove worms to two foot shelves eighteen inches one above another. Let each worm hatch by itself for two days to understand their several sicknesses or sleepings, which are four in the time of their feeding. First generally twelve days after hatching, then every eight days for three days. Whole time of feeding is about nine weeks. Give a few leaves twice every day and increase the food, and after fourth sickness as much as they want. Keep boxes clean. Keep warm first five weeks. In cold weather set a pan of coals with Juniper or Benjamin in it yielding sweet smells. Store the room with herbs and flowers."

This use of the "Benjamin," or the "Purple Benjamin flower" for yielding a sweet smell, gives us pause. The "Purple Benjamin" smells to heaven, in the words of some, but since it is the dark branch of the family of trillium, the lovely sweet flower of our spring woods, we may guess that "Benjamin" was the family name at that early date. To continue:

160

"Separate worms more as they grow. When bodies are clear amber colored they are ready to give their silk. Make arches between aforesaid shelves, with clean heath, or branches of Rosemary; stalks of lavender, and so forth." (Still the Old Country terminology) "Upon these the worms will fasten and make their bottoms, which in fourteen days can be taken away. The best must be presently wound or the worms within them killed by laying bottoms in the sun for two or three days or in some oven after bread is taken out. Other bottoms for seed lay aside until the worms come forth. Sixteen or twenty days from the beginning of their work, when they do put them upon some piece of old Say, Grogran, backside of old Velvet, made fast against the wall or hangings. There they will ingender, and the male having spent himself falleth down and soon dies, likewise the female when the eggs are laid. These will be grey on the Grogran. Take them off gently with a Knife and put them into a piece of Say, keep in covered box among woolen clothes until next year. A wheel for winding. 'Sickness' casting out of their skins Worms either placed on bowers or booths and leaves taken to them or put upon the trees themselves."

Once More, Vermont

Somewhat simpler is the story of silk culture as carried on in the Green Mountains, as referred to above. We know of the large buildings with opening board sides, and here were the tables and shelves upon which the leaves were spread, and upon which the worms were placed for feeding. In about thirty-one days from the date of hatching of the insects, during which time they fed upon the leaves, they formed their cocoons which took three days. A day or two later they were carefully picked and the moths killed by boiling or steaming. The cocoons were then unwound and the threads prepared for use. In this vicinity the winding or spinning was done by the old flax wheels which were abundant. As we have seen, this climate was not made for mulberry trees, for one bad season made a clean sweep of them and ended the silk culture of that section.

Between tobacco in the South and cold weather in the North, the silk business came to a bad end in America.

> Wee all are creeping Worms of th' earth,
> Some are Silk-Worms great by birth,
> Glow-Worms some that shine by night,
> Slow-Worms others, apt to bite,
> Some are Muck-Worms, slaves to wealth,
> Maw-Worms some that wrong the health,
> Some to the publique no good willers,
> Canker-Worms and Cater-pillers,
> Found about the earth wee'r crawling,
> For a sorry life we'r sprawling,
> Putrid stuff we suck, it fills us,
> Death then sets his foot and kills us.
>
> —SAMUEL HARTLIB 1655

Shipped by the Grace of God in good order and well conditioned by mee, Robert Bauldry, in and upon the good ship called the Thomas and Edward . . . now riding at anchor in Yorke River and by God's grace bound for London — to say, Tenn hodds of sweet scented tobaccoe. . . .

Five Points Segar Store, New York City

Coin of the Colony

EVEN a bill of lading can be musical and artistic when written in the simple words of the English tongue, and tinted with appeal to an approachable Providence. Robert Bauldry lived and shipped his sweet scented Virginia tobaccoe during the 1600s, and gave a picture of its setting forth upon the high seas to reach the money markets of a foreign land. While beaver skins were the coin of the northern parts of the new world, "tobaccoe" was the coin of Virginia and those other Southern Colonies which raised it, and taxes

163

were met with it, bills settled in it and fines paid with it for many years.

The casks or "hodds" for shipping the tobacco at this early period, were made of staves which had been seasoned for three long months, and they measured a third of an inch in thickness and forty inches in length. This made a high cask which was "thirty inches in the drain of the head," and had the initials of its cooper stamped upon it, and those of its owner and shipper, not stamped, but "inscribed thereon." Naturally all of the plantations could not be situated upon the shore front and so there was the matter of getting these great casks to the ships after they were packed. This was done by having the slaves roll them along by main strength, with the sailors sometimes having to lend a hand, not only in storing their cargoes in the hold, but in getting it to the wharves. It was a job fit only for a heavy beast of burden, and sweat and agony followed in its trail.

Later the "tumbling barrel" appeared and became a familiar sight on the old "rolling" or "tobacco roads" of the South. The tumbling barrel was the great tobacco cask turned on its side, with a hole bored in each end through which a stave was passed for an axle to the conveyance and to which the traces were fastened so that an animal might draw the load. The rolling roads were the shortest routes between the tobacco fields and the harbor where the English ships rode at anchor, and went over hill and dale, through woods and across everything which they met except a stream which must be avoided at all costs. Drawn by oxen or bulls or mules, or a team made up of an ox and a mule, these tumbling barrels, or "clod crushers" wore broad cartways through the country, cartways which later became highroads through the land, their vast size — eight long by six feet broad — doing the work of many roadmen.

Tobacco Raising in 1680

As soon as the tobacco plants were ripe they were cut, but only on a day which was dry and clear so that the leaf might shrink and fall before being put under a roof. The plants were then carried to the barns and received by men who drove a wooden peg into each one and hung it up to dry. These pegs were apparently "knittin' work" for the workers during off seasons, and yet sometimes they were neglected until October when there was a great to-do to get them done in sufficient numbers for the incoming plants. The barns measured anywhere from thirty to sixty feet in length and although they were cased and weatherboarded were still built so that air could circulate freely through them, for drying fires were not resorted to at that time. Sometimes there were smudges to smoke out the "horn wormes" and other insects. "Sitting at the tobacco house making pegs, his master told him they had hung the tobac and now there must be a smuther made." Over-sweating and fire of all sorts must be guarded against, else the leaf deteriorate. When the tobacco was taken down it had to be done on a day when there was enough moisture in the atmosphere to penetrate the leaves so that they would go limp and thus show no bruises from handling. The leaves were stripped from the stems, or were not, and the sorting accomplished. Even back in 1686 the lowest grades were called the "lugs." As early as 1611 there was a tobacco trading post near the site of Richmond.

OF THE EARTH EARTHY

Tobac in the Carolinas

"Flue curing" or curing the plants with heat, became popular and today along the winding roads of the Carolinas, for instance, quaint hewn-log buildings appear, their chinks made air-tight with smearings of red clay, their brick furnaces

Tobacco Dry Houses, near Troublesome Creek, North Carolina, with different arrangements of furnace and flue

166

showing along their bases in all sorts of shapes and ways, their great pipes or flues to carry off the smoke of the burning pine, protruding at all angles. These strange little log buildings are sometimes shaded by a gnarled tree, sometimes they wear a shed roof of vines held up by high poles, sometimes their protecting bushes show that they have stood there for many a year, but always shade has been provided against the hot suns, and a woodpile stands handy. Inside, the tobacco plant hangs upon the "tobacco sticks," slender but strong and fixed side by side in rows.

The children draw the tobacco plants in from the fields, sliding it along between the rows in long slender sledges with wooden runners. The processes of its curing are much the same as those used years ago. The furnaces are filled and lighted and the days of careful waiting and watching begin, for if a single leaf should flutter down and catch fire on the hot furnace bricks, the work of a whole year might be lost in a few minutes. In the old days a man sensed when the temperature was just right for the curing, but today the thermometer does the careful work and the man has lost his technique to that extent. To the flue-curers the thermometer therefor is king during these anxious days, and the planter delegates the task of watching it to no subordinates. Once a planter was called away for a few hours and carefully impressed upon his colored helper, the importance of not letting the thermometer go higher than a certain point. The helper was a dependable old negro and did his work well, and the master coming home praised him when he found that all was well and the thermometer where it should be.

"Yessir," the negro answered with all seriousness, "some six or eight times he went up, but each time I fotched him out and cooled him off and put him back again."

OF THE EARTH EARTHY

Today in the Southern newspapers the tobacco news is as regular as the weather prophecies, and the terms used therein often quite as pleasant as were those in the Robert Bauldry bill of ladings from this same land nearly two hundred and fifty years ago.

BRIGHT TOBACCO MARKETS
Much of the tobacco is damaged due to continuous moisture...
Much of the leaf sold today remained on the floors over the weekend (a term unknown in the past) which was detrimental to its quality.
Sufficient leaf is on hand...
Very little of the better quality leaf appears to remain in the hands of the farmers...

Still other ways of connecting flue and furnace in the Carolina tobacco sections

DARK MARKET
Sales on the Blackstone dark-fired market were blocked today...
Sales of dark leaf tobacco on the Farmville market today...
Tobacco appeared high in order because of the continuous rains...
The Georgia growers of flue-cured tobacco report...

TOBACCO BARNS

Whether sun cured or flue cured, the words are all nice ones.

Along the Connecticut
Northern tobacco fields have their long barns where the tobacco hangs in rows, curing by the air which passes through the river valley and in and out of the movable slats which are hinged for easy moving. Through the season the fields change from yellow ploughed land, to dark green nobs in slender rows, to the great spreading verdue of the full green plant in its perfection for cutting and hauling to barn.

> Sublime tobacco! which from east to west
> Cheers the tar's labour or the Turkman's rest.

Double flues for curing the leaf

XIV. THE ASHERY

~~~~~~

If the trees be very great, the ashes will be good and
melt to hard lumps, but if they be small, it will be but
powder, and not so good as the other for sope.
                                CAPTAIN JOHN SMITH, 1606

~~~~~~

Why Ashes

AN ASHERY is a place for keeping ashes, and that seems as
it should be, but just why ashes should ever have been kept
at all is the question. Several interesting answers pop up,
among which such humble things as soap and hulled corn
and potash and pearlash are mentioned. Surely such things
should be beneath the notice of the historian and yet, they
are recorded as filling a large place in the life of the early
comers. Today soap appears ready-made on shop counters
and we know not whence it cometh although we do know
whither it goeth, but years ago each member of the family
helped in saving "soap fat" from the cooking or the killings
and saw the needed ingredients go through the leaching and
boiling, and knew that no matter how much grease they
saved, it could never know the glory of soap without the help
of ashes. As with soap, so it was with potash, and its gentler
sister, pearlash, and other leached products, they all needed
the alkali of common wood ashes for their make-up.

Old asheries were numerous in both town and countryside, for until the middle of the 1800s America was making
all of her own potash, which was reason enough for establish-
ing these dusty old repositories. The old ash-house shown in
the illustration stands in New Hampshire, not far from an
old sawmill. It was built well up on a great boulder so that

THE ASHERY

there should be no danger from red sparks still left alive, for the woods were close by. The daughter of the old miller says:

Where "Old Morse" collected ashes to carry to Keene, New Hampshire, for the making of yellow soap

"When the water power gave out in late summer, Father had to use steam to run the mill. Hardwood ashes made the best potash but all of the ashes were taken from the engine and put here in the ash-house, and those from the house too. He'd climb up on the big rock, open the sliding door in the roof, and pour the hot ashes in where they could lie safe against the stones. The bottom door was only opened when Old Morse came from Keene several times a year, to cart the ashes away. The folks would trade with him for yellow soap to wash the dishes with, and some soft soap too. He'd made them of lye and potash. I'm afraid the old ash-house won't stay up much longer."

*Oven-door and opening for warm ashes, in the
Brown-Bryant house at East Alstead,
New Hampshire, c 1782*

Some of the later built brick-ovens in homes had an open space beneath them for holding the ashes after they were brushed out of the oven, the wood fire for heating having burned down and gone out. This lower opening had its own iron door hinged on, or some sort of makeshift door. We laugh sometimes today when we find these doors, which protected the house from hot ashes, made of *wood,* and many of them are badly charred; but in comparison with the "green-wood" lugpoles of a century before which held the great iron pots and their contents before iron cranes came in, they seem almost asbestos-like in their make-up.

Wood Ashes

Ashes are, technically, the earthy or mineral particles of wood which remain after combustion in fire. If there was one thing in which the settlers were rich it was in their supply of trees and wood and if there was one thing which they wanted to make way with, it was these same limitless forests which everywhere met their eyes. Trees as they stood in phalanxes forbade cultivation of the soil, they shaded whatever land may have already been cleared, from the warmth of the sun, and snuffed out all hope of pasturage for the would-be grazing stock. Down then with the trees, acres and acres of them, but after they were down they still cluttered the earth unless they were burned in great windrows or mighty piles, and burn they did for days before the last spark of life had been withered within them. Then were left great masses of grey ashes to be scattered to the wind and mingled with the earth again, or carried to the ashery for making into potash. There was England though, crying aloud for ashes, and "potashes" began traveling the great way to Europe as soon as the Pilgrims landed, and crediting their senders with thirty-five shillings a ton.

We can see then that trees were worth more in their ash form than they were either standing or cut into planks, and continued to be so wherever there was an ashery in the neighborhood. In 1717 it was said that one man could in a year's time, cut, clear and burn the wood from four acres of land and that this would yield eight tons of potash; while a gang of three men, cutting, burning, boiling and managing the ashes on twelve acres could produce twenty-four tons of potash which would be worth forty to sixty pounds a ton. Already the forests were showing their clearings.

The Public Potash

Then came the time when the forests had been pretty well destroyed and farmers no longer needed to mow them down by the acre. In the first half of the 1800s many country newspapers carried alluring bids for ashes, the two given here being typical. The one from New York reads:

> SAVE YOUR ASHES. The subscriber will pay one shilling and sixpence in goods at the lowest cash price per bushel, for good house ashes, delivered at his ashery in Hamilton. 1823.

Another from Vermont read:

> The subscriber will purchase good house ASHES, delivered at his Potash in Windsor or at the Potash opposite Campbell's Tavern in Hartland, at 10 d per bushel, payable in goods at a cheap rate. All orders drawn for Ashes by Joseph Grow, will be paid as above stated.

Here we come across the different names given to the old workplace of ashes, for they were "the ashery," the "potashery," and "the potash," and perhaps other things in our countrysides.

There was probably no less attractive work center than the old asheries. They are remembered as being ramshackle affairs, buildings which, to be sure, would keep out the dampness from the collected ashes, but roughly constructed and spreading in their shedlike form along a country road or even in a village yet shouldering with buildings of real respectability. Although they looked temporary and shambling they were still dignified by the name "works," sometimes the "potash works," and again the "pearlash works." Their equipment consisted principally of huge leaches and great cauldrons or kettles, and the processes undergone there were of the simplest.

Gum, or leach tub, on leaching stone

Leaching

An easy and favorable leaching vessel, leach tub or ash gum or lye tub, was a section of a hollow tree, a sycamore or gum being the favorite. This would be raised a few inches from the ground on stones or stumps and the inside bottom formed of a thick network of branches and straw. Below this bottom some sort of trough would be fixed to catch the liquor which came trickling through from the top, and send it on to a vessel. Other leaching vessels were barrels set up in the same fashion but resting on a "leach stone" or "lie stone," a large flat stone which had a little furrow chiseled in a circle around

Southern ash leach-tub

its edge, a little larger than the circle of the barrel bottom, so
that the liquor falling through the straw would leak down
and out to the little trough and then follow a straight cut in
the stone leading to a waiting trough or bucket. Some con-
traptions for leaching were the roughest collection of boards
of all lengths whacked together inside of a supporting frame
of heavy posts and timbers, with their feet in a great trough
leading off to a bucket. The whole reason for such a contrap-
tion was the simple holding of a quantity of ashes through
which water could seep slowly and pass out at the bottom,
dragging along with it the alkali from the burned wood, to
form a lye, or as some of our grandfathers said, the "lie."
"Leaching" was not in the dictionary before the Revolution
and may have been a word which grew at about that time,
but the process was going on under some name and the
vehicle, so it fulfilled requirements, did not need to be ele-
gant. Between the leaching barrels for the making of potash

and soap there was no difference, the irregularities coming only with the locality.

An old ashery at St. Johnsbury, Vermont, is remembered as set up against a bank so that the gathered ashes could be dumped from a cart from the road above directly through a window built under the ridgepole. Once inside the building, the ashes were shoveled into large casks, mixed with quicklime, covered with water and left to settle. After a day or two the clear liquor, which was now the salts of lye, was drawn off. The building against a hill was the usual device for avoiding much handling of the ashes, for ashes are like feathers and love a sudden foray into the far blue. Caleb and Joseph Wilder are remembered in that Vermont section as having advanced the methods of leaching ashes.

Potash Kettles

With the ashes drained of their alkali and a good strong lye now ready for doing business, the next necessity was a good sound iron kettle for boiling. From the questionable vantage point of today, one sees the fine old potash kettles left here and there on prosperous old farms, and wonders how farmers would ever have kept farm without these antique symbols of a past industry, so necessary do they seem to present-day farming in any of several capacities. Some of these old potash kettles, a good inch thick in the wall, have been standing for decades along country roads as public watertroughs, some do home duty along the same line, some grow morning-glories about their sturdy ears, and some become the cauldrons over roaring fires when the December killing comes, or the steaming pots for boiling maple sap when March rolls around. Kettles of this sort have generally come down from the days of home-made potash, but others have been rescued from the

ruins of an old public ashery; and they were used for boiling
clothes and cooking swill as well as good family eatables, at
different times, for after all, to own one potash kettle was
something to boast of, let alone having one for each kind of
work.

*A well sooted potash kettle now standing on a
millstone as a wayside watering trough, in the
foothills of the White Mountains*

Since the potash kettle did its work hanging up, it was
quite differently shaped from the more familiar cauldron
kettle which stood firmly upon a stone support and was
used for scalding newly killed hogs to loosen their hair, or
for boiling syrup. It was larger than the latter, a good three
or four feet across the top opening, and running quickly
under to a much smaller base. Three-inch iron ears stood out
on two sides quite close to the top, slanting down just enough
to prevent the chains which held it from slipping. In 1753
potash kettles used in New Hampshire were cast from "Salisbury iron ore": in 1790 in New Jersey, one air-furnace was
chiefly employed in casting "Kettles to make Pot ash"; while
Vermont was turning these same kettles out at Sheldon in
1798. Today many of these old servants of the past stand

slightly browbeaten and the worse for their cracks, but their active life is said to have covered, as a rule, the making of about thirty tons of potash, so that they deserve consideration for that even if no thought be given to their really lovely form.

Potash

Such a simple name — "pot ash" and telling the story of its growth too. After the wood ashes had been leached and a strong lye resulted, this lye was put into the potash kettle, or big iron pot, and set to boiling. Two centuries ago they said that potash was the ashes of vegetables, but the vegetable kingdom is a large one and includes along with carrots and turnips the trees of the forest. Weeden, old historian, called potash the "fixed and vegetable salt of ashes from the onset of the pioneer's ax and the purification of the settler's torch." An ax and a flame, and that was all there was to it — given the wood. Above the flame the lye was boiled down until there was nothing left in the pot but a dark, thickish mass of residue, which for want of a better name was called the "pot ash." In 1770 potash was bringing thirty-four shillings a hundredweight, and in a review of the New York stock market in June, 1824, potash was bringing $120.00 a ton, and pearlash, $122.50.

Pearlash

Pearlash has already been spoken of as the gentler sister of potash, and was in reality a further reduced and purified ingredient. Pearlash was another of our "after the Revolution" products. It was the more refined baking powder and yet had its own short-cut to existence in some homes. It was found that ordinary corn cobs which had been burned on the hearth, or "cob coals," had natural pearlash at their heart. After they had been put to soak for a while, the water was drawn off and put into bottles ready for use. Another way to get pearlash was to dissolve the pure potash again by filtering or leaching it through straw, then evaporating the result. This would leave lumpy bits of pearl white color which contained about fifty per cent of pure potassa, or potash. This pearlash was for many years used as money for barter between the farmers and their tradesmen.

Here again we have the name of the building, the same as the product made therein. At the "pearlash" where the new baking soda was made in some quantity, were large ovens into which the potash was put for baking. After a large mass of the refined substance had been baked into a somewhat solid form, it was stirred about and broken up into small lumps for convenient size in baking. In many an old ashery the leaching, boiling for potash, and baking for pearlash, were done one after the other; in fact this seems to have been the usual procedure until pearlash became so popular in the second quarter of the 1800s. Our next lead is that "pearlash was used in the making of soap by women."

Leaching for Soap

And when t'would eat a piece of rope,
We knew t'was time to make the soap."
—DANIEL CADY:
Rhymes of Vermont Rural Life

As soon as one begins to dabble with the old-fashioned making of soap one is immediately pitched headlong into the mysteries of the heavenly bodies, for there were times when soap should and should not be made, depending upon the "dark" and the "light" of the moon, just as there are moon rules to govern all planting, and cutting of brush and hair, and the butchering of hogs.

> Sow peasen and beans in the wane of the moon;
> Who soweth them sooner, he soweth too soon.

Said an old New England woman: "I cal'late as how I ought to know. You let the menfolks butcher their beef and pork on the increase of the moon and the meat'll shrink in the cooking. And then if you don't make soap on the increase it'll go thin on you."

The first mention of potash being applied in the making of soap seems to have been about 1767. While every farm may not have had its own potash until after the Revolution, every farm made its own soap, and had its own leach barrel or tub into which the ashes were put until leaching day. The trickle of water which came through the branches at the bottom of the tub and flowed out, was the same as that which had been sought for the making of potash, but from here on the process was different although nearly as simple. It was however very necessary that the lye be exactly strong enough, and the Cady lines give us one of the tried and accepted ways. Different homes had different tests, but floating an egg on it was the usual one, and when the shell showed the size of a threepenny piece — some thought a sixpence — the strength was believed just right.

The boiling of soap was done in a copper or brass pot, for this was generally the woman's work though often done in the open. The small settling pit in the bottom of the kettle was called the "hat." When the accumulated fats had been put into the pot the lye was poured in in a slow stream, while

the stirring was kept up evenly all of the time that the boiling continued, and then the dark-colored mass must be
poured into a tub for keeping in the cellar. It must be remembered that soap came in spoonfuls more often than in cakes
in those days, but there were "hard soaps" for the luxurious
and the spare chamber, and one of these could be made of
cream which was too sour for butter, mixed with lye and
becoming soap without any cooking. Sometimes tomato
juice was called upon for a sweet pink coloring for this dressy
soap.

Lucky indeed were the settlers in Ohio who found the
caves where the Indians' ashes still remained from their camp
fires, for there were ashes still to be dug out and carted away
after a hundred years of digging and carting.

> "I remember the old road to the ashery, it had on the
> average sixteen heavy loaded teams going to and from."

XV. SALTPETRE BEDS

Salt peeter, that fiereth at the first, and yet proueth but
a flash.   —1590

Genealogy

FOR a simple substance with a questionable family tree,
saltpetre caused a most remarkable furore in the country
throughout the entire period of the Revolutionary War, and
a good bit of excitement during the wars of 1812 and the
1860s. This was due to its ability to hide itself away from
the eyes of man when those eyes were combing the country
far and wide for any fragment which might be found. Surely
nothing ever had a better chance to hide than saltpetre, for
by its very nature it formed only in those out-of-the-way
places where man might not see, such as in deep caves and
dark lairs, in overhanging ledges of rock, or in the top layers
of the earth itself. Saltpetre was to gunpowder what yeast
is to bread, and since no more powder could be bought from
England during our rebellion, it was now worth its weight in
gold to the fighting yearling which had never before put
its brains to work on so subtle a mining proposition. There
were times when it looked as though the Colonies might have
to give up the fight because of the lack of saltpetre.

Just What Is It

There are several definitions of saltpetre, both polite and im-
polite, the former found of course in the more courteous days
of the past, the latter in the modern days of forthrightness
and scientific exactness. Here are some of the former: "Nitre

183

— mineral salt — rock salt because it exudes from rocks or walls — nitrate of potassium." Here are others: "Deposits of bat manure collecting for ages in ancient caves — dove cot scrapings — wild pigeon droppings, also crystallization of the earth beneath stables and barns for farm animals." One old New Hampshirite of over eighty says: "The white dirt that is found under the barn floor where the horses drive in and stand while the men unload the hay from the fields, always that has saltpetre in it. We use it for fertilizer for corn, but not too much."

New Jersey's Effort

In 1775 a man in Princeton, New Jersey, wrote to the *Pennsylvania Packet* as follows:

> I remember about fifteen years ago, a miller in this neighborhood began to exhibit the singular phenomenon of setting his millpond on fire. The fact is that in stagnated waters where great quantities of weeds, brush, leaves of trees and other rubbish have fallen together to the bottom and there putrified, if you stir up this mass of filth in the heat of summer when the waters are low, great numbers of bubbles will rise to the top. To these apply a lighted candle and they will for some yards around, or as far as the bubbles extend, emit a sudden flash, not unlike the explosion of gunpowder. From this incident I have been led to conjecture that this trash may possibly contain large quantities of saltpetre."

He then tells of having read that in ancient Macedonia large quantities of nitre were afforded during the dogdays from some of its lakes and other waters; and that the New Jersey masses of fermenting trash were not widely different from the pits of rubbish from which Germany had formerly produced saltpetre.

184

*Typical home in saltpetre sections of the
Alleghany Mountains*

The Caves of Maryland and Virginia

Maryland's and Virginia's donation to the problem of saltpetre in wartime was considerable and we have the following
communication sent to its Convention by Dr. C. Weisenthall
of Baltimore-Town in 1776. The doctor had been ordered to

185

examine the saltpetre works on the south bank of the
Potomack on Patterson's Creek, about twelve to fourteen
miles from the South Branch:

> If stones are broken off or lifted up, there is some-
> times a good quantity of real saltpetre in its white colour
> found, which can be scraped off of the interstices where
> it collects. As for its formation, there is a similarity with
> old cellars which are known to contain often (according
> to their age) great quantities, with this difference only,
> that the collection of nitre in these caverns may be form-
> ed thousands of years, which accounts for their richness.
> It is evident that our mountains contain everywhere
> such caverns full of saltpetre as to furnish the colonies
> with that desirable article to the fullest extent, at reason-
> able rates. The people on the spot now make saltpetre for

Saltpetre cave near Natural Bridge, Virginia,
used before the War of 1812

186

gunpowder and salting meat, that being a scarce article there, and no doubt squander away great quantities, not being sufficiently skilled to make it to advantage.

On Lost River, a few hundred yards from Natural Bridge, Virginia, is Saltpetre Cave where during the war of 1812 and that of the 1860s, saltpetre was scraped from the crevices in the rock wall, and finally removed with a diamond point steel drill worked by hand. Today the overhanging rock surface, wherever the whitish streaks of saltpetre once lodged and stained the rock, looks lank and ossified. Fissures leading back into the mountain have been traced and scraped to their uttermost limit for those droppings which the ages have turned into saltpetre.

Tobacco Houses

There was still another way in which these two cavernous States were able to help in producing saltpetre, and that was through their tobacco houses. In August, 1775, orders went forth from the Virginian Convention that the inspectors of the Colony should preserve the "trash Tobacco" on their inspections for the purpose of making saltpetre, while in October the planters had to cut down and preserve all their tobacco suckers, trash and stalks, and save sweepings of their tobacco houses. That month the watchful London ran this news story: "The people in Maryland and Virginia have begun to dig up their tobacco houses, and lixivate the earth for nitre; and what would seem incredible . . . two ounces of saltpetre have been obtained from two quarts of loom. This success has excited a perfect enthusiasm throughout the country, and manufacture of nitre will be everywhere dominant." In reality that period was a continuous cry for more and more saltpetre which was produced much too slowly to meet the demands.

Manufacturing Methods
Although it was the Revolutionary War which drove the colonists into this precipitate race for saltpetre, and it is to that period that we are driven for clues as to its rustic manufacture, the following quotation leads us to believe that vigorous attempts were made a good hundred and thirty years before this time for this vital catalyst among the ingredients of gunpowder. About 1640 the Commonwealth of Massachusetts took a unique step toward procuring this commodity "out of the domestic economy."

> To make saltpetre each plantation shall erect a house about 30 by 20. Military companies are to carry earth. Careful and conscionable members of this commonwealth are to carry urine and manure, and all is to be mixed.

It is not surprising that this order was soon countermanded, but still each family was enjoined under a penalty to make the needed saltpetre, for gunpowder was a necessity of pioneer living. Boston built a house for making saltpetre in the prison-yard, while Concord "tried the breeding of it" and hunted for the nitre in their henhouses.

Those who discovered the value of the "white dirt" beneath their stables and barns, if they desired to use it for more than fertilizer, took the simplest of means to extract the saltpetre from it, means as simple and ingenious as those used for all of their living in those days of many handicaps. They would remove the earth gently and lay it in a cask into which they poured water. The resultant lye was then strained in a leach of ashes from which the strength had been taken, and it was then boiled until it had cleared to a desired consistency. After cooling, the saltpetre formed immediately and was ready for use. From one bushel of earth about three-fourths of a pound of saltpetre could be made.

The great wooden sweeps, widely familiar for drawing water from deep wells, but known in the 1600s and 1700s as the power of a "pounding mill," "plumping," "beating," or "hammer mill," were pressed into service in Greenbriar County in the western part of Virginia near the saltpetre caves, where gunpowder was made. The sweep was about thirty feet long and braced from beneath the house or some stump, and at about one third of its length supported on a couple of crotched sticks which made it slant up and out. Mortised into the upper end was a fifteen-foot sapling (sometimes a sugar tree) which could swing easily up and down as the sweep was raised and lowered. The end of the sapling was hewn into pestle form and came down into a hollowed gum, or gouged tree base, which was formed narrowly at the bottom and broader at the top; this shaped receptacle would cause the saltpetre and powder to fly up the sides at each stroke of the pestle, and then come swooping down again into the exact center of the bowl where it was ready for more pounding. A bar of wood was inserted through the sapling above the pestle so that two men might work at the mill at the same time, their strength bringing the pestle down, and the natural inclination of the sweep doing the hard work of lifting it.

A Recipe of 1775

At Windsor, Connecticut, Messrs. Blakerlige and Wilson made saltpetre after this manner:

Erected house 30 by 20 feet square. Three vats containing about 45 bushels each. Also 2 potash kettles, conveniently set in brick for boiling. From one boiling would result 27 pounds of fine saltpetre crystals. He found that there was some saltpetre in almost any earth, even the uncovered, but that the best was under old buildings standing on pretty high land, of a light, sandy or loamy nature, that loose dirt on top contained the largest proportion of nitre, but when he got below this, the lower he dug, the better it yielded, and went on down about three feet. With this he filled the vat, leaving it hollow on the top, and sprinkling it with lie drawn from common ashes, in the proportion of 1 pint to a bushel of earth, which should be about milk warm. Took about the same quantity of water as earth and kept repouring it into the vat until it came out perfectly pure. Saved the lie for boiling as soon as it came through clear, but as soon as it appeared yellow or brownish, he put it into the next vat of earth. Began boiling as soon as he had enough lie to fill two kettles, and kept refilling the one which was boiling off, from the other, and filling the latter with the cold liquor from the vats, skimming his scum to put into his next vat. Boiled until liquor was two or three times the quantity desired for crystallization and poured it into a tub. After standing, drained off liquor to leave in bottom of tub. A gentle boiling now with about two spoonfuls of alum thrown in, if one expected fifteen pounds of nitre—which brought the impurities to the top. If crystallization was now formed in a test spoon after cooling, the substance was returned to the cleaned settling kettle and drawn off before cool enough to crystallize. This process was repeated twice after first crystallization. The remaining liquor went into the next vat of earth as an added nestegg. Fifteen pounds of saltpetre a day were turned out.

To the statement of these Connecticut workers that saltpetre might in some quantity be found in almost any sort of earth, may be added the discovery by one of our forebears, that "we seldom find saltpetre in the earth but that is sea-salt mixed with it, which must be separated."

After perusing the subject of saltpetre and its strange and interesting origins, one is filled again with wonder at the cleverness of those early settlers who, often with no previous experience to warrant their findings, did yet seek and find what they needed for their hardy living, even though the finding lay among the droppings of their fowls and the manure in their "mixin' " or dungheaps. After all, this resourcefulness and ingenuity were only the outcroppings of a divine heritage from that Parent Power which had been ingenious and wise enough to create a universe whose slogan surely must have been NO WASTE HERE.

Put your trust in God, my boys, and keep your powder dry.
—Colonel Blacker

Necessity is a Mother

WHEN a settlement is made in a new land, it is necessity which guides its development far more than chance or whim, or even heartfelt longing for the ways of the old life. It was necessity which drove our forebears in the early Colonies to become, in time, makers of gunpowder. Part of this necessity was of course due to their own misunderstanding of the natives among whom they had come, and the rest to the overwhelming greed of the countries back home which wanted land and more land, and finally bought off the redmen to assist in the colossal grab of their own lands. It was as early as 1666 that the first attempt was made here to manufacture gunpowder and thus become independent of supply from the Old World. Failure at this time did not deter the insistent ones from making another attempt in 1672, but it was not until 1675 that, under expert advice from an imported Englishman, William Everden, or Everenden, the experimenters at Dorchester, Massachusetts, were successful in making what was claimed by outsiders to be as strong and good gunpowder as the best which England was producing. A gunpowder miller was granted land in 1639, but success apparently did not dog his footsteps either.

If, as some one has said, "powdermills spring from the atmosphere of the time," it is easy to understand why when the Revolutionary War started, an impetus was given to the making of powder throughout the thirteen Colonies, and mushrooms had nothing on these little upstart powder mills of the time in the matter of growth. Such notes as the following show the powder activities of 1775 and 1776:

The Committee of Walkill, Ulster County, New York, certified to Representatives of New York State, that between March 1 and June 9, 1776, Henry Wisner, Jr. had made 918 pounds of gunpowder and that Henry Wisner, Jr. and Morris Phillips "had erected a Powder Mill in this precinct and had her complete at work by the 20th of May last," and that there was manufactured at said mill 1459 pounds of good merchantable powder in seven days successively. From Dutchess County came the report that John R. Livingston's powder mill was completed before May 20th and that it had produced 1000 pounds of good merchantable powder in one week of seven days. In 1775 powder mills sprang into existence at Stoughton, Andover and Bradford, Massachusetts. One of the old mills which was standing before the Revolution and busy at this time has left to us its great stone foundation built into the side of a steep hill at Feltville, New Jersey. Its virtue is greater today than when it was active, for it no longer helps in the murder of mankind, but presents to the passer-by a most splendid example of how to make stones stand one upon another without the help of mortar and keep on doing it for nearly a couple of hundred years.

Gunpowder Recipes

Having heard already of the speed and skill of Henry Wisner it will be interesting to know his recipe for his special brand of powder. Here it is as it was set down by his own hand:

OF THE EARTH EARTHY

Gunpowder is composed of nothing more than the four plain simple articles, saltpetre, brimstone, charcoal and water. The first three of which are to be made as fine as possible so as to be sifted through a gauze sieve, or fine bolt, as fine as for common flour.

He detours here to tell of the difficulty found in making saltpetre fine enough and of how all that would not go through the sieve had to be dissolved in "soft warm water." Then he continues:

Then let the sulphur saltpetre and charcoal be each separately weighed. Take one cwt of saltpetre, 15 pounds of sulphur, 18 pounds charcoal. Mix together in large vessel such as potash kettle, when mixed, moisten with aforesaid nitrous water till it is as moist as dough for baking bread. Put equal quantity in each mortar and pound for 20 hours, if mill runs slowly then 24. The paste will dry, therefore keep it moist with said water, and when finished put in tub.

Graining of it: Take box 5 feet square, sides 18 inches deep, bottom tight, top entirely open, fix across the box two rods, or laths, near the middle, about 4 inches below top, ten inches apart, then have 6 sieves made of wooden splits same manner as a wheat riddle, but much finer, the coarsest as fine as a cockle sieve, and each sieve growing finer, and each be made of wire. Then take a quart of paste, put it into the coarsest sieve, set sieve on rods, work with circular motion, then through finer and finer sieves.

To break up large balls of paste which gather, place board in sieve to shake among them, in circumference as a common pewter plate, about one inch thick on the center declining to the edge, of some hard wood turned in a lathe, and made as smooth as possible. When the powder is well grained it must be rolled in a barrel, inside of which must be smooth, with a small door in one side capable of being shut tight, and the barrel to be so fixed as to turn with the shaft of the mill. Put in a few pounds at a time, the rolling mill will make the powder smooth, then sift in finest sieve till the fine parts that work off in the barrel pass through the sieve, which is to be returned again into the mortars. The powder must then be put in flat trays or dishes, and set by to dry either in a small room where it will be kept warm with a large stove, or if the weather be dry, in the shining of the sun.

In reading the above it is hard to realize that we are having to do with implements and materials of war, much easier would it be to believe that we were reading some simple kitchen recipe for making soup or the bolting of flour, or the concocting of some farm tool, for most definitely are de· scribed the temz, or temse, as it passes over the bread trough, the tumbling barrel in which hayrake teeth were smoothed, the mortar and pestle of the country doctor's herb grinding, the riddle sieve for bouncing the dust out of the wheat, while surely the mention of dishes and pewter plates are more akin to cookery than to a death-dealing substance. And yet it was with these simple implements of the farmhouse and the barn that the powder was made which won the Revolutionary War, and, we must not forget, "the shining of the sun."

If one will glance through the old Committee records of the different counties, as kept through that war, one will find constant mention of the need for powder to carry on the various campaigns, and the inducements offered for its manufacture by the ruling group in Philadelphia, and will get some idea of what it meant to the cause of freedom to be without this material which was yet made of "nothing more than four plain articles." We shall see in a later chapter the desperate straits to which need of one of these simple and plain articles, saltpetre, drove the scampering patriots. It was bad enough to need it and see plenty of it in the hands of the enemy, but when it was plentiful for the use of the Indians, who had been paid to fight against them, matters had come to a pretty pass.

During 1777 the Indians attacked Fort Henry on Wheeling Creek, using a field piece which was the work of their own heads and hands. Having been supplied with plenty of powder they hollowed out a maple tree, plugged one end with a block of wood, and bound it round and round and up and down with iron chains, then charged it heavily with powder and filled it to the muzzle with bits of stone and slugs of iron. The torch being applied, it straightway burst into a thousand pieces, killing several of the Indians and sending the rest of them off with fiendish yells of disappointment, surprise, and fear.

A "short horn" carrying only six ounces of powder

Carriers

Among personal conveniences which were contrived and have come down to us in countless forms, are the carriers of powder which were buckled or hung or strapped upon the person who carried firearms. Because powder must be kept dry, and because, being powder, it was so finely powdered, it needed some sort of receptacle without loophole of escape and impervious to dampness and hard rain. There probably is no older type of powder flask than the horn of an animal, severed or dropped, blocked at the large end with a chunk of wood, and fitted at the tip with a tiny wooden or bone stopper. An early definition of the word flask is, a narrow-necked vessel for fluids, and another is, "powder horn," but these do not quarrel, for powder is extremely fluid when running away. There were horns of great size and immense swirl, and horns of small size holding but three or six ounces and with but little curve in their stumpy shapes, and there was the very lovely middle-size horn upon which various designs were cut for adornment. The owner's name had a place among curls and flowing lines, sometimes a picture of the owner's house was engraved or carved thereon, sometimes the mountain range seen from the kitchen window, as was done on one horn still cherished in New Hampshire and bearing the date 1700. One old horn had a border of flowering vines around the heavy end, cut with the most meticulous care with the point of some old jackknife. One bore, with much elaboration, the old threat:

> Steal not this horn for fear of shame
> For here ye see the owner's name.

The name, alas, is gone, whittled and scraped off by some later owner probably — perhaps by some one who did steal it after all.

George Washington's powder horn, which he carried during the Indian wars, had come from the head of a buffalo and is of a deep, dappled ivory. It is large and gracefully curved and bears at the broad end a mirror set in for field service.

*George Washington's powder horn carried in the
Indian wars with a mirror in the larger end*

An old New Englander says: "Powder horns have not been used since we stopped using the muzzle-loading guns. You shook the powder out of the horn into your hand, holding your finger over to moderate the amount, then you put the horn aside and poured the powder into the muzzle of the gun. Then you shook it down good, striking the gun down toward the lock to shake the powder into the tube. Then you put in the wadding, mostly old paper and wadded up, put it in and pushed it down with the ramrod. Sometimes you could use tow, but that was worth something and the old paper wasn't. Then you poured the shot in, usually from the leather bag — it poured out and in through the same opening — and a wad put on that. Then put the cap on the tube and you're ready to fire." In his district during the Revolution the authorities arranged for the distribution of ammunition thus: "One pound of powder, four flints and a sufficient portion of lead to every man who owned a gun."

While the white man carried his powder and shot about with him and his flints for striking fire, he did not achieve the carrying of fire itself, as did the Florida Indians. They cut the growing reeds — whose edges were incidentally sharper than a steel blade and good for scalping and beheading men — kindled a fire with them which they kept burning in moss wrapped about with skins, and carried in their belts.

Metal cannisters, generally flattened to carry in a pocket without too much bulge, were made at home out of pieces of saved-up tin, or other metal, and had many rough and home-made seams, which yet served well. More elaborate ones were turned out in shops, and always they had the large and the small end, growing in intricacy as the years advanced, and becoming quite tricky in their stoppers and ways of checking the powder's flow when enough had passed.

Common metal powder flask toward the end of powder-carrying days

Powder Magazines

Where to harbor quantities of powder so that it would remain safe and dry was a problem presented to local communities. New England was apt to hide it away in the garret of the

Meeting-house, knowing that there the roof would not leak
and no enemy could come without being seen. Several old
powder houses remain which were built for the purpose, and
one of these is at Eastport, Maine. It was finished as a fort
in 1818, and called Fort Sullivan. It is of stone and brick

*Powder house at Eastport, Maine, finished in 1818
as Fort Sullivan*

and now so well covered with growth of bush and vine that
one would almost pass it by without giving it more attention
than to think it an old receiving vault in a wellnigh obliter-
ated burying ground.

The old stone powder magazine at Charleston, South
Carolina, was built in 1703 and is among the oldest buildings left in that old and lovely city.

Virginia has her old powder repository which was built
as an arsenal in 1714. It stands in Williamsburg and is an
octagonal building with walls measuring twenty-two inches
through and laid in Flemish bond. The roof flows into a
slender peak from the eight sides, and the building was

originally surrounded by a ten-foot wall standing twenty-one feet from the magazine. Because of its contents and its pointed shape the building soon won for itself the name of

"Old Powder Horn" 1714, at Williamsburg, Virginia

the "Powder Horn" which it has always retained. Naturally it stands rather apart from other buildings and has seen many changes both without and within, during the 222 years of its existence. Time brought a protective coat of earth and vines, both of which have come and gone in spots, giving the old bricks a chance to peep out on old Duke of Gloucester Street hard by. Within the building things far stranger have taken place. Used as an arsenal from 1714 until 1783, it became the tinder box for Virginia's entry into the Revolution, when, on the very day after the battle of Lexington, the English removed the powder which had been stored there and carried it off to one of their ships six miles away at Burwell's Ferry. After the war the Powder Horn became a much needed markethouse within its conveniently placed wall; and then it became a church. Unfortunately the worshippers tore down its outer wall to get brick for the foundation of a new church building, and having thus skinned the property, allowed it to pass to others for a dancing school. The need of an arsenal in 1861 brought the old building back once more as a "powder horn," but the coming of peace turned it into a livery stable. Then fortune smiled upon it once more, for in 1890 it was rescued by the Association for the Preservation of Virginia's Antiquities, and turned into a museum. In this care it will probably achieve a right venerable old age.

"Mad Ann" Bailey

Farther west, near Covington, there stood a plain little stone house measuring about eight by fifteen feet and standing not over seven feet high. In this unadorned, flat little abode of gunpowder there was kept a large quantity of ammunition, which had to be relayed still farther west to the settlers around Lewisburg. No men could be found to undertake the perilous errand and the dangerous trip through the mountains and Indians, but Mad Ann Bailey — mad at the Indians for killing her husband, but correct as to brains — offered her services, and was accepted on her reputation as scout and Indian fighter.

She was a Welsh woman of low stature but strongly built and with a most engaging countenance and smile. Her task was to load the powder upon a packhorse wearing a bell, which would follow her over rock and mountain gorge. She "steered" by the trace of Lewis's army and the help of a pocket compass, forded some of the streams, made rafts for others, and swam the rest. Once when she was deep in the mountains she suddenly became conscious that something was wrong with the ringing of the bell. She turned just in time to get in a deadly shot at the Indian who was leading the horse off into the underbrush. Her pay for these dangerous trips to transport powder was the acknowledgment of the General that she was a "brave woman," and the gift of the coveted "dram." Once when an Indian was going to kill her he was stopped by his companion who said: "God damn, too good a soger," and thus saved her life. Her dialect was much appreciated in the countryside, where she lived in a cabin in a clearing close to lovely Falling Spring; she "halways carried a hax and a Hauger," and once told some one about the "howl upon the helm on the bank of the Helk." The little old powder house was torn down some years ago with no thought for its history.

XVII. GUNS

"Ay me! what perils do environ
The man that meddles with cold iron."

Gunsmiths

MANY a man who loved his gun was his own gunsmith, straightening a crooked barrel by holding it in a hollow of a stump and pounding with a wooden mallet, making his saw from some odd bit of steel and deepening the furrows when the rifling had worn down, even detecting the smallest bend in a barrel without the aid of the usual bowstring.

Only as carriers of powder and shot dug from the various floors of earth, do guns come into our picture, for after all, guns are hardly of the earth, earthy, in themselves.

Perhaps the first gunsmith in this country who hung out his shingle as a public smith at arms, was he of the unknown name who was busy at his trade in the Bay Colony in 1636. What is known as the "Audrey House" at Williamsburg, Virginia, was built about 1717 by John Brush. Brush was a gunsmith and the armorer to Governor Spotswoods, the first keeper of the arms and munitions in the public magazine which we have already learned to know as the "Powder Horn." In the same town we find that Neel House is identified with James Geddy and his son, both silversmiths and gunsmiths — a usual combination — from 1737 to 1774. Philadelphia had John Drinker making guns in 1751, and one Krider in his gunshop at Second and Walnut Streets. This combination of silversmith and gunsmith, which to the uninitiated in gunmaking seems a strange bringing together of the lovely and the dangerous, was found throughout the Colonies, for although not all jewelers were gunsmiths, it was only such skill as the gold and silver-makers possessed which could do the careful work on a gun.

From about 1725 to 1735 there seems to have been an influx of gunsmiths from the southern part of Germany, and from Switzerland came others later. Lancaster County, Pennsylvania, became the center for gun manufacture and here guns were made entire, and in part, for because guns are more or less personal implements, they had to be made to fit the men who were to carry and use them. Thus, throughout the country could be found American gunsmiths who depended for certain parts of their guns upon the workers in Lancaster, but put them together according to local order, with a certain length barrel, such and such bore, so much fall to the stock, and so forth. "I got a long arm, you'll have to drop the stock some and make it longer than common," or "I want a rifle to handle a bullet running a hundred to the pound," or "Better cut the cheek-piece a hair higher than usual."

Gun Development

"I use' t'bring down pa'tridge on the wing at fifteen rod, and kill 'em too," said an old New Englander, fondling his old shotgun. "She carried the shot thick and good." Thus did the old gun toters love and praise their fowling pieces. Old gun names are intriguing and while some of them will mean nothing to many of us, they are worth recording within their period of supremacy, or those overlapping years to which inheritance carried them.

1600s   Flintlock, early part.
The old-fashioned lock for firearms in which the cock held a piece of flint, and came glancing down upon the steel cap of the pan containing the priming. From this came the expression: "Only a flash in the pan."

1676   A few matchlocks.

1738   Stocklock.
Muskets with rests. (High standards were carried along within whose top prongs the great gun barrels were rested while the shot was taken. Of little use for Indian fighting.)

1750   Firelocks.
Fowling pieces.

1775   Last of matchlocks
to   Flintlock, or "Queen's Arm."
1783   Firelock
Brass Blunderbuss
Riffle
Rifle gun
Bell Muzzle (shooting slugs and stones.)

1811   Breechloading guns, which followed the muzzle loading. These were poor affairs and the old muzzleloading gun kept first place for many years more, before the former were perfected. Our soldiers went into the Civil War with "muzzleloading guns," but many came out with "breech loading," the Spencer rifle of '64 making this change possible.

The change from the old smooth-bore musket to the rifle with its spiral "lands" was of American origin and meant the difference between inexactness and exactness in hitting the bull's-eye. A long bullet coming out of the old smooth-bore would sometimes follow a zigzag track and "like as not" turn over in the air and hit the mark with the blunt end instead of the point, a little stunt which was known as "keyholing." When the six slender grooves or "lands" were cut on the inside of the barrel in a spiral path the bullet would attain a terrific speed of several thousand feet a second before it left the rifle and, spinning, go straight as a die to the mark, and when an object spins at great speed it cannot wobble.

Unfinished, home-whittled gunstock, found in a New Hampshire barn

In the general progression of guns the farmer on the land had his part too. There was much of a gun which he could make in his own shop. A partly whittled stock came to light in an old barn one day, the form made from cherry wood entirely complete, but the smoothing and polishing for some reason never accomplished. Light-colored stocks were not desirable and if one were made of fine curly maple it must be made to grow dark under a stain of soot and oil well rubbed in. Even though a ramrod must be straight and no question, and smooth, and no question about that either, since the bore of a gun must be kept perfect and "clean" and without imperfection if the bullet is to travel straight, the farmer could make his jackknife turn out a pretty one with a little patience and elbow grease. One thing there was which the novice could not hope to do, and that was to make the "patch box." This was an exquisite little brass frame inlaid in one side of the stock, with its own little brass door fitting to perfection. Out of the stock wood a little hole was hollowed beneath this brass frame for the holding of patches of linen cloth which were wrapped about the bullets, or laid over the muzzle before the bullet was inserted. Here it is in a nutshell: "A brass trap in the side of the stock held a greased linen cloth cut in a circle a little less than the size of a half dollar. This was pressed into the barrel by the ball which it cleaned, and protected it from ramming or becoming misshapen and stripping. It also kept the powder from slipping by the ball, and hushed all noise." Since a gun's work is generally done on the sly, some sort of anti-noise campaign was quite necessary, and the hickory ramrod proved to be much better than a metal one for this reason.

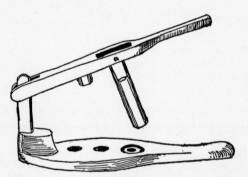

Homemade cartridge filler, New Hampshire

The coming of the cartridge was an event, doing away with the tedious and slow earlier loading which poured in so many drams of powder, then the wad, then the shot, then another wad, all of which had to be tromped down together. When the brass shell came for loading at home, things were speeded up, and these shells would last a long time and could be refilled in quantity and kept on hand for the quick coming of a hawk to the henhouse, or the end of a red nose telling of the red tail which was pluming out behind it.

For the Military

Taken by and large a man with lead, powder, and flint was equipped for defending his family and pulling down enough food to keep them alive, but the soldier of the Revolution was supposed to have:

    Musket, Blunderbuss or Flintlock
    Powder Horn
    Bullet Flask
    Buckshot Pouch
    Bullet Molds
    Melting Pot
    Balls
    Cartridges
    Hunting shirt
    Wooden Canteen
    Welded Bayonet
    Gray Cartridge Paper

Different periods of the war provoked different needs and the militia which was kept up afterward had its own requirements, to wit:

> You are hereby warned to appear at Milton Meeting house the 2 Day of May next at twelve o'Clock, with a good Musket, with an Iron Rod, Bayonet and Belt, priming Wire and Brush, Cartridge Box, a Pouch, twenty fore Cartridges, suitable for the Bore of your Musket. Hereof fail not, as you would avoid the Penalty of the Law, per Order of the Captain, Benjamin Canady, Clerk. April 14 1797.

OF THE EARTH EARTHY

In the military huts used during the Revolution and later unearthed behind the old Dyckman House in New York City, squarish pieces of tinder, slightly thicker on one side than the other, were found, and the steel striker which was used against them to fire the tinder in the gun. With such arduous practices to be gone through before a shot could be fired, the wonder is that any one was ever killed or even hit.

The following notice shows how precious an old firearm could be even when it was little more than a wreck:

> Williamsburg, Nov 1775
> Stolen out of my company a few days past, a small rifle gun with a yellow stock somewhat defaced, without a box, and broken just below the lock; the breech is mended with three iron pins. Whoever will produce the said gun to the commanding officer at this place shall have 20s reward and on conviction of the thief 40s.

Not long ago a Civil War bugle was carried into Ava, Missouri, for repairs. It measured five feet and three inches long. Those were days of size.

Pouch and Belt

For powder it was the horn or the flask which proved to be the best carriers; for shot it was the "bag," the "buckshot pouch," the "conister" or "cannister" with now and then a "bullet flask." A fighter of the 1750s carried his powder horn under his right arm and his home-made bag for home-made bullets at his waist. With the horn under his right arm, it was necessary only to tip it up, guide the powder with the forefinger, recork and reach for the waist bag of shot. Some of the shot bags were the simplest affairs, crudely sewed around the edges with thongs or beeswaxed homespun

Shot Pouch, worn over left shoulder and under right arm; carries powder and shot with "measuring caps" at ends. 20 by 3 inches

thread, and one which was found was sewed up around an old spool which served as a natural outlet for the shot. There was also the cartouch, a box which held the balls or a charge for a firearm. Then there was the great belt, killing many birds with one stone. It had long pockets under the right arm which made loading very easy. It was about three inches wide, a flat piece of leather at the front and left side, widening or swelling out to include the necessary compartments for both powder and shot. In some of these home-made belts the hunter simply squeezed the stopper which immediately slipped out bringing the powder with it, while from the tip of the other ridge there was a device for releasing the shot. Similar belts of many designs were produced.

Before the Revolution in "western Pennsylvania" the young blades wore a costume closely resembling that of the Indians, even to the exposing of their thighs part way down to the knees, their coarse linen hunting shirts — loose frocks — hanging behind and before but missing at the sides. The bosom of these great frocks served as a sort of wallet in which, along with food, was carried a little mass of tow with which the gun barrel was kept wiped clean. The shot pouch was suspended from the belt with a strap which had been woven on the home loom; to this strap was also fastened a buck-skin-handle moccasin-awl made from the backspring of a caseknife, and a roll of buckskin for mending the footwear with buckskin thongs or whangs, untanned but oiled.

Life on the Range

Of all the sports which were a part of the life of the early American men and boys, none seems to have equalled that of shooting at the bull's-eye. A study of early outdoor sports shows that there was scarcely one which did not have some ulterior motive behind it, and that motive was oftenest, protection. Hardly a village in the Colonies which did not have its "range" and its Saturday afternoon meets for "shoot-in' at a mark." and when a man could hit an appleseed at some amazing distance, he was cock of the walk among his neighbors. It was these ranges and years of practice which made our men such marksmen. Only ten years ago there was still a shooting group of old men who continued their "gun matches" in an Ohio town, and they used the old

muzzle-loading guns and would not let a "breech loader"
onto the range.

The Kentucky Squirrel Rifle

One day the Reverend Charles F. Magee was having dinner
with the Abbot family of Spruce Run, West Virginia. He
says: "After dinner I picked up the gun I saw standing in
the corner, took out the plug and looked down the barrel.
'That's the first clean gun I've seen in a farmhouse,' I said.
'You like guns?' Abbot asked, and then told me that he
could stand on his back porch and break a fruit jar on the
paling fence fifty yards away with that gun. You see they
do their canning out in the yard always, and they turn their
empty jars upside down on the palings of the fence and leave
them there for months to keep sterile, or until they need
them the next season. So there was a row of them out there.
'I can do it with a gun I've got in my grip,' I told him. It
was a pocket rifle with a detachable stock that went on with
a thumb screw, and as luck was with me, I did hit my jar.
The man was surprised and grabbed the gun out of my hands,
broke it open and looked down the barrel. 'How long you
had this?' he asked. 'About six years.' Then he said, 'When
I die I'm going to give you that gun of mine—give it somebody that'll appreciate it.' Six years later the archdeacon
who was circuit riding through my part of the State brought
me the gun. 'The old lady heard I was coming this way and
wanted me to bring you the gun now that her brother is
dead, and I'm glad to get rid of it.' He'd ridden horseback
with it for a good many miles and it weighed over twelve
pounds.

"It's one of the old Kentucky squirrel rifles and made
about 1840 by a local gunsmith near Buckhannon, West

Virginia. The 'set trigger' and the hammer, the brass trigger guard and the brass on the end of the stock, and the barrel were made by G. Goulcher of Lancaster: he was one of the fine goldsmiths of the country and a good many local men sent to him for the finely finished parts of the guns they put together. You understand, the barrel came as a smooth bore and was rifled by the local man, and a nice job he did too, making about two turns in the length, and it's a forty-inch barrel. Gun itself is about five feet or a little over. The ramrod's of hickory, the stock of curly maple, and a fine piece too, and do you notice how it's finished at the end where it joins the barrel? He's cut those designs out in the maple and then run in hot lead or babbit to make it hold more firmly.

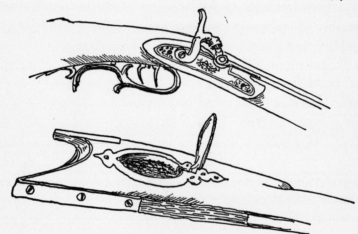

Old Kentucky Squirrel Rifle of West Virginia, with
"set trigger," and patchbox set in end of stock

"Why did they make the guns so long? Why, they thought the longer the barrel and the distance between sights the better the aim would be. This one has the blade sight at the front and the open sight back. My little detachable rifle had the peep sight, a pinhole through a small piece of metal that came close up to the eye on the stock, with a pin sticking up in a little tube down at the end. The hole and the pin had to come together. I want you to notice this cheek-piece, how he's whittled it out from the left side of the stock to fit against your cheek when you're firing. You see it was things like that made a man want his own gun made to order. As it happens, old Abbot's gun fits me perfectly. I want you to notice this little piece of copper the gunsmith put on under where the hammer strikes to keep the fire from hitting the wooden stock. You can see that the barrel itself around that part has been roughed by the flame. He's made a nice little brass plate here to carry the screw that holds the lock, and this patch-box he's made himself, I think, for you see how roughly it's cast on the under side of the cover, and how he's had to gouge out the stock to make the hollow.

"This gun carried very little powder, and this little bullet mold he made himself on his forge to make just the right size shot to go in it. Rather nice, having the mold go along with the gun. The hammer here goes down over the tube and explodes the cap of fulminate of mercury. There isn't much fancy work on this old gun except the nice engraving Goulcher did on the hammer and plate—and that's mostly gone after nearly a hundred years—and there are no insets of silver in fancy designs as many of the old guns had, but this old gun can shoot and hit the bull's-eye every time."

The shootin'est woman in Scotland County—"Down South"—just aimed to snig the top of her man's head but killed him instead.

The souldier is sooner killed with a little Bullet then a large Sworde. 1579

*New York's first shot tower near 53rd street on
East River, built by George Youle, 1823*

The Height's the Thing

NEITHER a mill, shop, nor any sort of a yard was that place in which lead shot was made round and true enough to be shot from a gun, but, rather, a tower reaching to the heights and proportions of the lighthouses along the coast, something indeed to lift the eyes. From one hundred to two hundred and fifty feet they might rise in either brick or stone, but it was not until 1782 that the idea of dropping softened lead from a great height to give it a perfect rotundity, began to percolate through the world at large. The story goes that a roofer working on a church steeple in England accidentally dropped his pot of molten lead, and going down to recover it, found shot scattered all about the ground. At once the suggestion was acted upon with good results, but it was not until the early part of the next century that America erected her first shot tower, which is still standing in Philadelphia, at Front and Carpenter Streets. This was owned by Thomas W. Sparks for many years, and continued to turn out dropped shot until 1904.

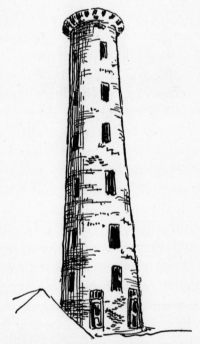

America's first shot tower which was built at Front and Carpenter streets, Philadelphia before 1821, by Thomas W. Sparks. Still standing

OF THE EARTH EARTHY

Shortly after Philadelphia had made a beginning, New York City followed suit, with George Youle buying property at Belvidere on the East River just north of the present Fifty-third Street, to erect his shot tower. It started building in 1821 and stood between the "New Alms House" and Kensington House, but when it had reached the height of one hundred and ten feet it lost from sixteen to twenty feet because of near-by blasting. In 1823 Mr. Youle had erected a new tower on the same site and begun the manufacture of shot even though the tower had not reached its designed height. Within ten years Mr. Youle had died and by 1833 "Mr. Hilton" was in possession of the "delightful situation at the Shot Tower (mansion of the late George Youle)." After this the property belonged to Commodore Vanderbilt, and in 1849 was sold again to Thomas Otis Le Roy & Company. Its record was three tons of shot a day, and although the coming of higher buildings made the old tower seem to shrink in size and more modern methods dissolved the business there, the building stood until 1917. Another shot tower was built on Centre Street in 1854 and demolished in 1908. Still another was erected in the rear of 82 Beekman Street in 1858-59 which lasted until 1907, and was known as the "Wind Shot Tower." Not one of these old towers remains in New York City. Baltimore, on the other hand, has preserved her shot tower built in the late 1820s. Other towers arose in the more western cities, St. Louis raising the largest one in the country. A few only of the old towers remain, although some modern shot is still being made in shot towers.

The ingenuity of man was shown by the use of a mine, in Dubuque, Iowa, for dropping shot, rather than building a tower above the earth. Again, some fifty miles south of St.

THE SHOT-TOWER

Louis and near some lead mines, shot was dropped from a river bluff into the river. These are spoken of today, by shot-makers, with high scorn and called "crude affairs" but to the lover of resourcefulness and originality they exude interest of a thrilling sort.

Jackson's Ferry shot tower on New River, Virginia.
230 feet high from water level

One of the most artistic of the old shot towers, perhaps the most artistic in the country, was built of stone in 1808 and still stands in Wythe County, Virginia. Lead mines were discovered along the New River by Colonel Chiswell, a British officer, about 1750. In 1756 the Colonel established Fort Chiswell a few miles away for their protection. In the meantime, however, Chiswell had journeyed to Richmond to attend a King's Council. Proud to be able to announce the discovery of the lead mines, the Colonel was amazed to have his word doubted in the matter. A gentlemanly fight ensued in which Colonel Chiswell slew his doubting colleague with his sword. Others must have believed the story or the fort would not have been established.

Fort Chiswell on Wilderness Road from Draper's Meadows to Cumberland Gap, 1756. Burned

Showering and Dropping

To drop it in a spherical form, the lead required an admixture of what is termed 'temper,' which was made by cooking arsenic with lead, and portions of this temper, were added to the large kettle of molten lead at the top of the towers, which was then percolated through sieves into a well of water at the base of the tower, then elevated, dried and screened into various sizes. In the earlier days, the taller towers were supposed to produce the best shot, and this was true especially with the larger sizes. But the, so-called Wind Towers were also used in the early days. These had difficulty in making the large sizes. A blast of air was sent up the well of the tower to counteract the fall of the shot. Hence you see why there were high and low towers.... Certain refinements also occurred in the process by which, for instance, one could produce as much as eighty-five per cent of the actual size wanted, by 'dropping' instead of what was known as 'showering,' which produced all sizes in the dropping, many of which, because of their limited demand, had to be remelted. . . . Buck shot is not dropped . . . but the shot business as it was known for over three-quarters of a century, is no more."

This valuable description has been given by Mr. John R. Wettstein of Mount Vernon, New York, who has for many years been one of the outstanding leaders in the lead business of the country, and is apparently among the very few who remember the workings of the old towers.

In terms even more simplified we find that lead was carried to the top of the tower and after being melted was poured through the holes of a colander and allowed to make its great fall of a hundred or two feet down into a vessel of water set to catch it. To make the lead more easily drawn out, a proportion of arsenic was mixed with it. Then to prevent the lead from passing through the holes of the colander too quickly— for, except for gold, lead is the heaviest of the metals—and to perfect its roundness, the bottom of the colander was coated with a spongy, creamy crust of oxide which clung to the surface of the lead. The colanders were of sheet iron pierced with varying sizes of holes through which the lead passed in fine threads which collected in globules the size of the shot, on the under surface of the colander. Strangely enough the shot was always larger than the holes through which the lead had passed. As the lead left its great height and fell, the air acted upon all of its surfaces with exactly the same strength so that the shot became perfect in form, the complete sphere, cooling as it dropped, and although still soft when it reached the water below, not being flattened by impact with it. Of course there was always some good and some bad shot, and the next step was to separate those which could be used in firearms from those which could not. Here the good old incline plane came to the fore, several of them, their job being to test the perfectness of each piece of lead and see which would leave the gun straight and true and reach its mark. The pieces of shot started down the planes and those which were perfect rolled nicely into the boxes placed at the bottom to catch them, while those which were not true went zigzagging back and forth in a crazy line, finally sliding off side to oblivion—and another melting.

To the shotmaker good shot looked a dead silvery white and his next move was to see that it received a perfect burnish, for the more polished it became the better it would travel on its one journey into the world. For this polishing the usual tumbling barrel of early days was used. The shot was placed in the barrel through the small door at one side, with it went a small quantity of ground plumbago, or black lead. The barrel or drum was attached by its shaft to some sort of water power which kept it revolving at a furious rate, during which time the shot rubbed against each other and with the help of the plumbago took on its fine steely polish and smoothness.

Sorting for Sizes

Much as the miller used his bolting mill for separating the husks from his wheat, did the shotmaker sort for different-sized shot and throw them into their own compartments. For this he used a revolving copper cylinder, with small holes at the top, larger ones in the middle and the largest of all at the bottom, and the shot that was small enough to go through the small holes naturally did so at once, while the rest kept slipping farther and farther along until they had found their places of escape and dropped into their own special compartment down below. The usual box of shot weighed twenty-five pounds, and when each was filled, the shotmaker knew that no further sorting was necessary, for each size would have found its own haven. Until about 1890 shot was sold in bags for individual needs and more than half of it was used in the South, but when breech-loading shotguns and the loaded shells were introduced and cartridge-loading companies came into existence they rang the knell of parting day for the old, individually owned and operated, shot towers.

Bullet mold, marked "200."
Iron dipper for melting bullets

A Way Back

There was that little matter of a couple of hundred years before America had shot towers and "dropped shot," when

Transportable lead-melting pot with long handle

each individual bullet or shot which was fired for food or protection, had to be made by hand with a crude iron mold.
Here and there among old farm tools and junk these old
molds sometimes come to light. The old mold is a small affair working like a pair of scissors. When the lead had been
melted in an iron dipper—wrought for the purpose—the
bullet mold was closed at the head and the hot lead poured
into a little round hole at one side. This hole led to a perfectly
round cavity formed by bringing together the two hollows in
each side of the head. The mold could then be plunged into
cold water to cool the lead, and when it was hardened the
mold was opened and the new lead shot, or bullet, rolled out.
There was still, though, the rough point which had been
left where the lead was poured through the outer hole, and
this was cut off by the sharpened cutter between the handles
of the mold. On the upper part of the handle was a number,

perhaps "170," to show how many shot could be cast in it from a pound of lead. Occasionally an old iron dipper for melting lead is found, and in such a vessel many an old pewter button, spoon, brooch, piece of lead window sashing or window weight may have lost its personality in the cause of some skirmish or war.

Chain shot and Expanding Bar shot

"Shot is any projectile thrown from firearms." This gives us a large leeway for variety and covered all kinds of "shot" from grape to bird to buck and on to cannon ball, chain-shot and bar-shot, and all of these were made by hand, if not in a mold, at the forge of the blacksmith. The chain-shot was a completely handwrought instrument of destruction made of two hemispheres of solid iron measuring three or more inches, and a joining chain of eight or ten inches whose each link had been forged on the anvil by hand: it was made to fire against masts and rigging, to cut them down as the heavy ends twisted about the solid wood. There was also the expanding bar-shot, with two heavy half balls, each fastened to bars which slid upon each other and were so interlocked that as soon as the shot was fired from the ordnance, they doubled the distance between them, whirling as they went and ruining anything which happened to be in their way. Fortunately the shot tower was innocent of such terrors.

XIX. THE SALT YARD

He's the salt of the earth.

Early Needs

EVEN before the first settlers came there was need for salt
in America by the white man. When in the 1500s foreign
fishermen haunted the waters of the New England which
was to be, they needed salt to preserve their summer's catch
until it could be slowly sailed back to the Old World. Only
a person who has gone to the uplands of a farm on a summer
Sunday morning "to salt the stock" and seen the horses,
colts, cows and calves, sheep and lambs out at pasture, come
whinneying, mooing and baa-ing rapturously around the
farm wagon for their weekly treat of salt, can quite realize
what life must be without it. Unless, perhaps, one has trod-
den those ancient trails beaten by centuries of buffalos and
all of the other wild beasts of the forests who knew, best of
all their trails, those which led to the "licks" or salt springs.
These trails were laid out by the greatest engineers of the
world, animals which made as "bee" a line for their goal as
was possible in a rough country. Scanning the early Colonies
rapidly we find that although thirty of them had their salt
licks, only two, New York and Virginia, were to produce
salt in any quantity. When in 1864 West Virginia separated herself from Virginia, she carried most of the salt licks
with her, and thus made a new salt State; while Ohio was to
do her share later.

THE SALT YARD

"There is good means for making salt, the water is salt enough and there is no want of heat in summer." So wrote the Reverend Doctor Jonas Michaelius of New Amsterdam in 1626, and one can picture the Dutch letter writer striding down to the shore in his squat costume and broad black hat, and where our Battery is today, sticking his fingers into the lapping water at his feet and then gingerly touching it to the end of his tongue. Would it be salty or would it taste flat? Would his venison saddles and wild turkey meat come in for their proper seasoning or must he forego the pleasures of the palate along with many other things now becoming obvious? In the same year his neighbor Issack de Rasiere wrote to the West India Company: "As to the making of salt. I fear this will not be successful because it sometimes rains here in summer, but with God's help we shall try it at the proper season and see whether it is feasible." We of later generations know that it does sometimes rain in New York City in the summertime, but marvel that this should have in any way interfered with the making of salt.

Back in the third century some sailors at sea found a way to separate salt from sea water. "They boil the sea water and suspend large sponges from the mouth of the brazen vessel to imbibe what is evaporated and in drawing this off from the sponge they find it to be sweet water." The American settlers' problem was reversed, for they had plenty of "sweet water" but no salt. If the summer sun were to be utilized as an evaporating agent the salt water must be left open to its blandishments, but this open exposure to the heavens meant an equally hospitable welcome to the downfalling rain. There was the simple method of boiling the water to hasten evaporation, but neither of these methods seems to have put New Amsterdam on the map as a salt-producing center.

An "Up State" Memory

"I can remember very well when I was a boy seeing the men cutting down trees and piling the logs in great piles for burning. After days of burning the women joined them and assisted in carrying the ashes from these great fires on long rough wooden trays hewn out of the lengths of tree sections which had been split in two, and with handles cut in their ends. They took them to a cucumber tree—really a hollowed trough of the catalpa tree, I think—and poured them into it and then poured on water for leaching. In the bottom of the troughs were holes bored through which the liquor drained into another cucumber tree just beneath. Then this lye was taken and boiled in a big kettle hung out of doors, until it crystallized into what we called 'black salts' as big as the tip of your finger. These were later sold to be ground into saleratus." A man not yet old saw all of this done.

Here then we are right back in the ashery chapter again, making "baking powder" or saleratus from leached ashes, and yet this New York State product was "black salts" and belonging to the salt family. Right in here should fit the following simple Salt-Making recipe:

> Set your ashes in a tub, as when soap is made; draw your lye, let it stand three or four days, then strain it, and boil over a gentle fire till the salt makes, which will settle at the bottom, then take it out with a skimming dish and lay it on a woolen cloth in the shade, and it will dry and become good salt.

The salt makers must have had to whisper to the ashes whether it was baking-powder or salt which they were after, just as we have to whisper to a "cure-all" today which ailment it is supposed to remedy, so that it can function properly.

Salt fields, Syracuse, New York

Salina

The city of Syracuse grew from a little village called Salina, which came into existence simply because of a wealth of "brine springs" near the shores of Onondaga Lake. Father Simon le Moyne, a Jesuit priest, was the first person to record these springs of salt and in his diary wrote: "The Indians dare not drink there saying there is a demon within which renders it fetid." With the coming of the 1700s the spot was called the "salt pan" and became so popular that in 1797 the State authorities laid a heavy hand upon any future operations there, demanding a tax on its output. Before the State took this step, two partners, Danforth and Tyler, came to old Salt Point. The former carried upon his head a kettle while Tyler carried the other tools upon his shoulders. They made their center of operations the lick which was later behind the "old pump house" and there planted two crotched sticks for the hanging of their kettle. A fire was built and tended for twelve hours and behold, thirteen bushels of salt. A pile of stones later held up the kettle and more heat was conserved. A rude roof soon appeared, and then a solid "arch" of stones was made into which the kettle could be permanently fixed, and have its own chamber for a fire burning beneath it. Brine was now found in the bottom of a near-

229

by creek and salt wells were sunk in the drift deposits of the underlying valley, so that soon the one kettle was increased to many and in time five salt "boiling blocks" held from twenty to over a hundred kettles. A year after the State tax was imposed, the salt "at the springs" sold for one dollar a bushel.

This "salt pan" at Salina was the only known source of salt back from the seacoast during the 1700s and early 1800s, and so naturally was worked steadily. By 1862 the entire eastern end of Onondaga Lake was surrounded by salt sheds which dotted what is now the northern end of the present Syracuse. The amount had jumped from the original thirteen bushels to over nine million barrels a year and a city had grown up all about. Strangely enough the last thirty years of Salina's activities were devoted to what is delightfully called the "solar system," or making "solar salt" through the work of the sun.

A sad spot was the old Salina when work fell off, for, since salt has a mania for rust, all of the buildings and equipment had been made of unrustable wood. There lay the countless pine vats with their connecting wooden pipes made of slender hollowed tree trunks, not rusted to be sure, but badly eaten and softened by the touch of the insatiable salt. Row upon row the old grey boarding stretched away, partly fallen into the vat holes, curled and lifeless, covering hundreds of acres of land. It had been the Gale salt works for more than half a century when it closed down and the last batch of salt in the old warehouse stood twenty-four feet high, a glistening white mound of purity. Mighty Syracuse is proud of her little mother, and her famous "Salina street" and "Salt Springs Road" are but two of the many reminders of the days when she was the Salt City.

230

THE SALT YARD

Inner view of Salt House, old Salina

Salina's Processes

The salt workers are remembered as a crowd of wild and wooly specimens, with jagged beards and ragged clothes, carrying terror to the heart of a stranger, but they knew their salt. In the boiling days the springs in the low marshlands were sunken two and three hundred feet and their water pumped into reservoirs which in turn supplied the vats in the evaporation blocks. This brine was 17 to 20 per cent salt, and was left in the reservoirs until its impurities had settled with the aid of some alum. The boiling kettles held one hundred gallons of brine and were set in eleven rows in brick blocks, which ran the length of the works or yard. To boil forty-five bushels of salt required a cord of wood and later a ton of coal. When the solar system was used, for coarse salt, and only an eighth of the output was made by that method, the far stretching wooden vats were only six inches deep and eighteen by sixteen feet on the ground with narrow salt-saturated, wood-rimmed walks running between them. Each of these vats yielded about fifty bushels a year, and a "tierce" of salt was a medium of exchange in the earlier years. By way of comparison between the two methods of salt making, a bushel of evaporated salt weighed seventy pounds while the same amount of boiled salt weighed less than fifty-five pounds.

To the passer by, the scene presented where the finer salt was being boiled, was long blocks of covered buildings stretching low along the earth hiding within themselves great rows of kettles measuring four feet across the opening; for the rougher salt for "corning" meats, one saw the low wooden troughs built out in the open with only movable wooden covers for their heads in case of rain.

New England's Salted Fish

Fish seem to have needed salt as much after the settlers came as when the Europeans were catching them in earlier years, and the New Englanders lost little time in filling this need as soon as was possible. Salem had her own "salt pond" in active operation by 1630, four years after her settlement. By 1637 "Goodman Fitt-tailor" was allowed to set up a salt-pen, "if he can live upon it and upon his trade." One would think that a tailor who could really "fit" would need no other source of income. Now comes John Winthrop the younger, who by 1635 was already returning from England with a collection of "philosophical instruments" consisting chiefly of chemical apparatus. John had been educated at Trinity College, Dublin, and was therefore well equipped to set up the first American chemical laboratory and begin the manufacture of chemicals. The prime essentials in the New World were his goal, and among these he counted lead, gunpowder, and salt. In 1638 he was getting his "salt house on Rialside" at Beverly.

It was to Samuel Winslow, though, in 1641 that the real monopoly fell when a patent, called the first in the country, was granted him by the Massachusetts Colony, for inventing a method of manufacturing salt:

> Whereas Samu: Winslow hath made a proposition to this Courth to furnish the countrey with salt at more esay rates than otherwise can bee had, & to make it by means, & way, wch hitherto hath not bene discovred. It is therefore ordered, that if the said Samu: shall within the space of one yeare, set upon the said worke, hee shall enjoy the same, to him & his assosiats, for the space of 10 yeares, so as it shall not bee lawful to any other pson to make salt after the same way during the said yeares; provided, nevrthelesse, that it shall bee lawful for any pson to bring in any salt, or to make salt after any other way dureing the said tearne.

On Nantucket and Cape Cod salt was procured through the use of windmills which pumped the sea water into vessels where the evaporation could take place through the solar system. In the first of the 1700s Nantucket had a little fleet of windmills standing in a row, all busy at this work.

Wooden pack-saddle for transporting salt

The Salt of the Virginias

After the starvation period at Jamestown, the wise in the Colony made plans against its recurrence. About 1614 Lieutenant Craddock took twenty men and went down the

James River and across Chesapeake Bay until he reached the sea-surrounded Smith's Island and there set about trying for salt with which to preserve fish against a famine. In 1616 seventeen men were established for the same purpose at Dale's Gift at Cape Charles. The failure of Argoll as a governor brought about the failure of the salt venturing and the unsalted meats being eaten in the Colony brought about severe distempers and great suffering. Finally a Miles Pirket, a skilled saltmaker, was sent to Virginia to straighten the matter out, and a John Pory tried on the Eastern Shore, but failure followed failure. Sun and salt water seemed unwilling to coöperate. In 1660 Colonel Edmund Scarburgh appears to have started the first salt-making on any real basis in the Colony and the authorities soon had salt for export, the two shillings revenue on each barrel going to Scarburgh as an "inducement."

Fate had decreed that the Virginias should find their salt in their inland springs rather than along the seashore. West Virginia's separation from Virginia in 1864 took the salt springs out of the latter and made the new State a large salt producer. From salt licks and springs she progressed to salt wells and in time to "salterns" those places where salt was made, and the saltern just east of Charleston became an important one. Deep animal traces leading to the old buffalo licks, ancient walls with intriguing gateways for trapping the animals who came to the springs, show that the Kanawha Valley has for many hundreds of years, and perhaps longer, been the home of men and beasts depending upon these salt licks for their very lives.

It was in the 1790s that the salt springs of Virginia were first vigorously attacked for their treasure by the white settlers. The Indians had been even coming from the West to make salt here and carry it back home with them, a band of them carrying off Mrs. Mary Ingalls, stopping long enough on their backward trip to make the needed salt. John Dickinson had one of the first land locations in the valley and on it was a salt lick. In 1795 Joseph Ruffner bought Dickinson out and as soon as he had leased the spring to Elisha Brooks, died. Brooks it was then who erected the first salt furnace in Kanawha, or in the western country, and this was his equipment — twenty-four small kettles set in a double row, with a flue beneath, a chimney at one end and a firebed at the other.

Old wooden stirrup in salt region, West Virginia

To obtain a supply of salt he sank two or three gums (gum tree sections hollowed out) some eight or ten feet each in length, into the mire and quicksand of the salt lick, and dipped the brine with a bucket and swape, as it oozed and seeped in through the sands below. In this crude way Brooks got about 150 pounds of salt a day which he sold "at the kettles" at eight to ten cents a pound. There was no effort made to purify the salt before it was boiled down and its color was therefore reddish, due to the oxidization of the carbonate of iron in the earth. It soon made a reputation for a strong pungent taste and its value in curing meats and butter, and was called the "strong red salt from Kanawha Licks." It was transported in saddlebags.

A swape at a salt lick

Finally the lease expired and the Ruffner sons started in to make a better salt product. Opposite this "Great Buffalo Lick" Daniel Boone made himself a shelter, for here the animals had always come in droves. The clever ways in which the Ruffner brothers finally got their salt from great depths, and invented ways to meet an unprecedented situation, is a real story of Western achievement. Always it was the "gum" through which they worked as they strove to get below the mire and ooze with the simple swape for a pump, and down to a steady clear supply of salt. The tree they cut for a gum was a sycamore four feet across in the inside, large enough for a man to work inside it with a pick and shovel. The larger end was inserted and braced on four sides with props. About the top a platform was built and a swape erected, having its fulcrum in a forked post set in the ground close by. A large bucket made from half a whiskey barrel hung from the swape at one end, and a rope for pulling at the other. Down thirteen feet they pushed that great gum, striking sand, gravel and iron, only to have clear fresh water flow in and have to abandon it all.

Then they made a twenty-foot wooden tube by boring with a long pod-auger, shod it with iron and drove it down like a spile. Through the tube they let down a glass vial on a string to test the water, only to draw up another failure. Then back again to the old stamping ground to go three or four feet further and there find the rock from which the salt came. A long iron drill capped with a $2\frac{1}{2}$ inch chisel bit of steel was set to boring, with the upper end attached to a springpole with a rope. In 1808 they were forty feet in the rock and fifty-eight from the top of the gum with a strong flow of brine for a furnace. Then came the problem of how to get the salt brine up through the layers of fresh water and weaker brines. There was no precedent for such a task, no metal tubes, nor sheet metal, only a blacksmith and he could not bore a half inch hole in a wooden tube forty feet long. But there was a way — they furrowed out one side each of two long strips of wood, fitted the furrowed sides together and then bound them the whole length with small twine. A bag of wrapping near the lower end made all water-tight. This was pressed down the $2\frac{1}{2}$ inch hole-and-worked. A bottom made water-tight was now put in the gum and held the brine raised with the swape and bucket. A tin-cup maker happened along a little later and made a tin tube for the well, soldering each piece on as the lower part disappeared down the hole. Thus was bored, tubed, rigged and worked the first rock-bored salt well west of the Alleghanies, if not in the United States, and all done in eighteen months. The first "lifting" of salt was done on February 8, 1808, during the "kettle era."

One of the most interesting things about the production of salt in this locality was its being the means of the discovery of petroleum oil in this section and gas, which in time, after many surprising explosions, proved able to keep the furnaces a-boil with no cost for fuel. In time the gas became more important than the salt through which it had been discovered. George Washington knew this section well, owned land there, and recorded finding a "burning spring." Springs in the neighborhood are still "burning," where once "particles of salt were continually exuding from the surface of the soil."

Simple Devices

Swape — bucket, rope and man-power were the first method of raising salt through the gums.

Then came the pump, with lever crank, shaft, and blind horse or mule, revolving in an orbit around shaft. The horsemill.

Next the steam engine in 1818.

An ingenious trick for shutting off the weaker waters from the joints deserves mention:

Buckskin or soft calfskin was sewed up like the sleeve of a coat, 12 to 15 inches long, and slipped over the tube and knotted against slipping. Six or eight inches of the bag were filled with flaxseed, alone, or mixed with powdered gum tragacanth (the concrete juice of several plants). The other end was then wrapped. Put down hundreds of feet perhaps, the seed and gum soon swell from the water till the joint becomes water-tight.

A less simple device was Ebenezer Oakes' who chopped

eleven cords of wood in one day for the fueling in salt making in this section in the 1790s.

The first salt shipped from the Kanawha Salines went in hollowed poplar "piroques" between sixty and eighty feet long. Later the "bitterhead," like a common flatboat was used for this purpose.

Other Wheres

Michigan became one of the leading salt States but did not share in the early days of the industry which is our especial interest. Kentucky and Tennessee "trapped the salt springs" catching their waters in iron kettles as it burst from the rocky crevices or bubbled from the ground. A trench of four-foot depth was dug, long enough to hold ten or twelve sunken brass pots, containing in all two hundred pints. At one end of the trench a fire was kindled, one which ate up the wood in large mouthfuls, and the boiling was carried on in successive stages with the different pots. These brass pots gave West Liberty, Pennsylvania, one of its livelihoods, in the making.

Recently a duck hunter wallowing through a western North Dakota slough to retrieve a dead bird, discovered large sodium sulphate beds, so that millions of tons of salt may be opening up to that State. "If the salt have lost his savour wherewith shall it be seasoned?" although a biblical question, is not one which need worry our country for some years to come. From the earliest days of settlement we have been fed salt from the seashore, through the accidental finding of salt pans, along lick ways of centuries, and now through a hunter with a good aim.

XX. THE FISH FACTORY

~~~~~~

There's just as good fish in the sea as ever was caught.

~~~~~~

"Fish factory," Eastport, Maine

Of the Earth, Watery

A LITTLE like poaching in the preserve of Providence is this use of the name "factory" for a fish house, but "factory" it was called, that little low house on the edge of the sea where fish were brought in nets and made ready for consumption. One of these old factories, still standing guard by the sea although no longer at its old trade, happens to be the most easterly house in America. Located at Eastport, Maine, the most easterly town in the country, it is the last house out on Todd's Head, the most easterly part of that town. A Cape Cod type of low house with the wing nearly as high as the main part and quite as important, it neighbors with the sea which is only as far off as you can swing a bull by the tail.

What went on at sea where the fish were being caught is not for these pages, but the little houses and dwellings which

240

THE FISH FACTORY

awaited the return of the fishermen and their catch, are certainly straws to be fitted into our structure of old workaday industries. North America's first large commercial output was fish, for long before white men had come to settle here, fishermen had been dropping in from Europe to spend the summer in New England waters so that in the fall they could carry back great cargoes of fishy foods. Some of them even remained through a winter to be early at the fishing banks when spring came round again. In fact, there were fifty fishing boats belonging to the Portuguese, the French and the Spanish on our coast in 1517. A hundred years before the Pilgrims came in the *Mayflower* or there were mills to grind corn or saw trees, or workers in the soil, or lumbermen to clear the fields, there were fish "stages" set up to hold many hundreds of pounds of salted and drying fish, on our Eastern shores.

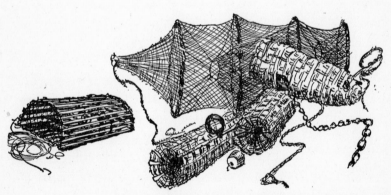

Trap for all sorts of fish, made of withes and string; basket eel-traps, at Gilpin's Point, on Choptank river, Maryland. Also lobster pot or trap

OF THE EARTH EARTHY

In 1623 David Thompson and his fellow-settlers established a fishery at Portsmouth, New Hampshire. Off the Massachusetts shores one of the islands won the name of "Stage Island" because of the curing stages which were erected there. In Virginia, Berkeley at a very early date had the oldest fishing shore on the James River, and as many as 22,931 shad and 200,000 herring were landed there in one season; the seine used there was 500 yards long, and drawn in by fifteen men, while the haul included "from roe shad to baby puch." When the haul was landed the fish were sorted into baskets and then taken to the fish house, where it was finally ready to lie on the cool bricks of the floor until the time came for its shipping abroad.

New England Fisheries

The early catches were vast quantities of haddock, cod, hake and pollock, and the fishing was done by groups of men in a shallop, a small vessel with two masts. There was the master or steersman, the midshipman, the "shore man" who washed the fish of its salt and dried it upon breast-high hurdles pitched upon stakes; and there was one man to attend to the very necessary cooking. Many hundred quintals—one hundred pounds—would be caught on one voyage so that the share for each man might be eight or nine barrels. The waters along our coasts were still practically in their virgin bloom for fishing, since the Indians had had no sails and thus kept their fishing close to shore, and so until the 1800s the catches of fish were vast ones. One of the early fishing boats was the "pinque," over whose rails the lines were managed. Following this came a square-sterned vessel.

Boats arriving from the Old World carried two distinct sets of workers, the fishermen and the shoremen, the former going off in the shallops and the latter getting ready for the first big catch which would be brought back to them for washing, splitting, drying and packing for taking home in the fall. The first simple step for this work was the erection of the stage, the platform on which the curing was done, and the frames or "drying flakes" upon which the fish were laid out to dry in the sun and air after the various cleaning processes. The stages were strongly made of stout poles, were floored with branches and brushwood, and often stood through a hard winter ready to be used again on the arrival of the spring boats. It is a pretty picture for the imagination, this spring race in such very slow boats across the great Atlantic, in order to hit shore first and win the right to use the best of the standing stages. Also there were rough shelters which had been built for dwelling places, free to the first comers.

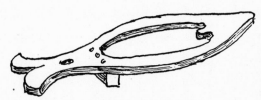

A Gloucester bootjack in fish form

A big haul finally accomplished, the shallops were turned landward and two men carried the catch to shore on two long poles. The first washing was done in deep baskets set in the water and then the fish were cleaned or dressed, slit and thrown into great troughs to await the salting. When cod had been part of the catch, there was the careful pressing of its liver to extract the precious cod-liver oil, the separating of it from the blood, each going into its own cask. Drying was done by laying the opened fish on the drying-flakes or table-

like standards, and waiting for sun and air to make it sterile
and hard for its long sea voyage.

Gloucester

From two people who remember back to their childhood in
Gloucester, the greatest of our fishing towns, come some
intimate touches of the old fishing days there, those things
which no book records would show, and few people think
worth recording.

"A 'salt trip' was one on which the fishermen brought
back the mackerel already salted at sea, and packed in barrels
carried out with them for the purpose. On a 'fresh trip' they
brought the fish home and salted them on land.

" 'Making them.' That was what they said when they
laid the fish out to dry. 'I have so many fish in the butts and
I'll be *making* them next week." From this may come the
name "factory."

"There were slender racks built up above the flakes to
hold white cotton cloth. The cloth was raised against the sun
the first thing in the morning on hot days, to keep the fish
from *burning*. Sometimes they dried the fish up on the roofs.

"A *quintal* of fish was a big bundle of them tied together,
and weighing one hundred pounds. It was a regular weight
measure, and was always called in Gloucester, a 'kentle.'

"*Fish flakes* were shelves for drying codfish after they had
been salted. They washed them first in a dory on the wharf,
then wheeled it to the butts of salt. Then they laid it in a
basket with the salt—a layer of fish and a shovelful of salt—
and let it drip through. Then it was laid in a butt of salt water
for three weeks. It was then put into a wheelbarrow and
taken to the flakes.

"A *jigger* was a long cart running close to the ground,

only a few inches up. It had a single board bottom with no sides and was hung on axles swung below, a bent-down axle. Sometimes sides were put on for carrying wet fish or salted fish. A jigger could carry twenty barrels; with one horse, ten barrels. The front was cut out so that the front wheels could cut under in turning, and the wheels behind were high ones. It was made so low so that the barrels could be easily 'cut up' or overhanded on to it.

Woolen nippers knitted by the women but worn by the men

"Do you know what *nippers* were? They were knitted of white wool round and round like a stocking leg, and about five inches across, so as to fit loosely on a man's hand. They were used for saving the cutting of the hand when they hauled the cod line in. This would be frozen and salty and cut like a knife, so the nipper was a protection. It was about two and a half inches thick when it was finished. When the band of white wool was about six inches long, it was rolled back on both edges over a padding made of thick woolen pieces which had been carefully rolled first. When the edges had been rolled back to meet each other they were sewed strongly together down between the rolls, making a sunken valley down the center, through which the cod line ran without hurting them. The salt water seemed to strengthen the wool against the heavy wear. Why, yes, there were nipper societies in every church in Gloucester.

245

"The *Sticking Tommy* was an iron candle holder, with two very sharp points, one running out from one side and the other from the bottom, so that the candlestick could be stuck into the floor or the side wall with equal ease and quickness. They could be used between decks or in the fore-castle when it was dark. Each point was five or six inches long and it was all forged in one piece."

Fresh Water Fishing Through the Ice

Fishing in streams and inland ponds necessitated no hut or factory or fish-house, for the fish which were caught in these waters were for more or less immediate home consumption. Some of the ingenious methods of catching fish by the land-lubber are worth recording here and some of the fishing tackle and implements deserve preservation.

Fishing through the ice, which in New England has always been the winter treat and fun for the farmer and his real chance to supply the home with some good fish dinners —not having to wait for the occasional rainy day which is the only excuse for this pastime in the busy summer months — is sadly enough becoming a thing of the past in many sections. Many a fish law now keeps the farmer from his old sport because in winter-fishing the larger fish were often caught, which meant that the "summer crowd" or the "city folks" would have fewer of them to catch when they came for their vacations. It is not many years ago though that the farmers had their days of utter delight hauling fish through the holes they had cut, with the temperature down below zero, and if not quite there at least cold enough to freeze out the summer visitor.

It was a sight much like a distant battle field from which most of the soldiers have retreated. What had just a few days before been a smooth glazed acreage had suddenly become a place of bivouac, with scattered white tents still left standing. The holes could not be cut nearer than ten feet apart — to avoid entangling of lines down in the water — but at that distance they had been whacked open with an ax, whose shrill voice had echoed far across the woodlots and fields. Not a large hole but one over which a "jack" could be set and a good-sized fish pulled through with ease. By each hole therefore the pile of ice chunks looking like miniature tents scattered about in broad groups of ten each. Days as cold as those which New England can boast and a good gale blowing made the need for fires, and their tiny flames licked out here and there and their smoke puffed first this way and that at the word of the gale, while the burned-out circles of yesterday's fires loomed up black and forbidding in abandoned tent villages. Hay stacked in low mounds for the blanketed horses gave the finishing note to this army-camp picture. "Fishin' through the ice" is a meditative occupation, for there may be whole half hours of waiting to see the signal red flag fly up from one of ten jacks, and although much visiting goes on, each fisherman must keep his eye out for the sudden red flash. So there is plenty of time to "jes' think" or enjoy the holiday while the farmer-fisher stamps his feet to keep them warm and hugs himself against the cold. An apparently lonely day of fishing through the ice, may however be a day of vivid excitement to a farmer tied to his barns and stock through the rest of the year. Earcaps and five pairs of socks inside his moccasins and inch-thick home-knitted mittens have not been donned for nothing.

The old-fashioned fishing-jacks were often home-made affairs, slender pieces of whittled wood with a slice cut off part way down one side and fastened back again with a brad so that

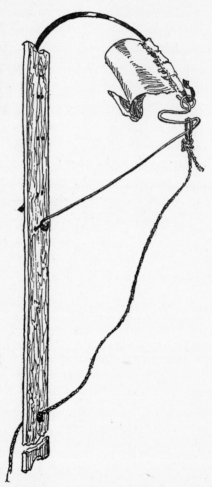

"Jack" for ice fishing. When the fish bites, the jack "trips" and sends the bit of red flannel shirt up into the air

it could swing around and come bottom to top with lightning swiftness. The fish line ran from this up through a slender ring on one end and the slightest nibble from the water below would start it trembling, while a real bite would yank the slender wooden shaft up and over. Now at the free end will be blowing a tiny red flag, some old piece of woolen underwear. Out across the far-stretched sombreness of the pond's whiteness, this bit of red would catch the eye of the most meditative fisherman and send him trudging — not running — to the designated hole to haul up his catch. Sometimes there was no time for meditation, for often flag after flag would spring into the air about the same time and keep the moccasined feet a-trot, and the mittened hands a-jump.

On one New Hampshire pond, and many just like it, the early settlers had an abundance of trout, so many that they did not bother with hook and line in summer, but made themselves fish traps, two long slender baskets of ash or willow, the smaller placed within the larger. The outer basket was complete, but the inner had an opening in its peak end, where the sharp strands stood out in a small pointed circle, through which the fish might pass out into the larger basket but could not pass in again to reach the open water. These baskets are gone from New England today but are still found newly woven in the open curb markets of Columbia, South Carolina, made from strong peeled willow.

By Hook and by Spear

All the way up and down the Atlantic States men have been catching fish since the 1500s, different kinds of fish in different kinds of water, and the means for catching them have been different and yet much the same. Hook and line, net and trap and spear, have all done their deadly work, but all of these contrivances have had to be made before they were used, and many of them were made in the home or at the forge of the user. Fishlines were spun and twisted by the women-folks upon their spinning wheels and reels; hooks have been beaten out on the anvil, traps have been made and bound with the pounded wood and bark of trees, and great spears many feet long have been fashioned at the forge and by whittling, and some by both methods. These old implements of warfare against swimming, darting fish have been clever and are worth remembering. Back in the beginning of all this fishing fun John Smith was talking about "spining thread for fishing engines." If only we knew what they were.

New Hampshire sucker spear, and eel spear

There are almost as many kinds of spears as there are men who made them. One old "sucker spear" still measures off more than seven feet where it lies up under the porch roof of an old New England farmhouse. At first glance it looks more like a seven-branch candlestick than a vicious weapon of death. It was made many years ago by a village blacksmith who fashioned it with exquisite care. Six feet go into the slender but strong wooden handle, while thirteen inches go into the iron end, the spear part of which measures five inches both ways. The center rod is of one piece so carefully fashioned that its four edges have even been lightly chamfered for beautification; the lower section of this shaft has been left open so that the curving spear points might gain strength by passing through it. Three of these curves of wrought iron make a set of six points, and each is flattened at the ends, while the point of the central rod which is in line with them is sharpened to a point for quick piercing of the fishy scales, and all seven parts are toothed or jagged backward from the tips to keep the fish from slipping off. The iron rod is fastened into the wooden handle with an iron ring.

Another spear of the same general vicinity has the same seven points but the three on each side of the center are made into long sharp hooks with the center part broadened flat.

Virginia had her wooden "gig." This has varied in make-up but was generally a spear of but three prongs, each with an arrow-like point at the end. They measured scarcely two inches across so that they could be cast into the smallest kind of a crevice between the rocks. A man who knows the deep tangled places of the Virginia mountains where the bears still roam, tells of a fishing excursion he made with some old mountaineers one night about forty years ago.

Virginia's Gigging Parties

"One night I was riding home through the mountains with

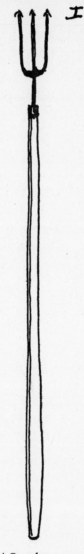

A Southern gig

a man and as we came along one place we heard chopping
and I said I thought it must be Isaiah Smith up to something,
so we stopped. You know a mountain man will never come
out if you holla to him. He'll peek through the underbrush
and if he knows you he'll call to you to come, but if he don't
he'll go back into the woods and wait for you to go, Well,
he knew me so he called us to come in from the road. He
was getting ready to do some gigging. You know what a gig
is? It has a wooden handle about five feet long with an iron
piece on one end, less than two inches across, with three
prongs not larger than wheat straw and very sharp. Well,
the fish stay right still when they see a light at night, and
you sight them and aim the gig at them and pull out a trout.
Didn't always hit them, but as one old fellow said: 'I didn't
git him, but damn him, he'll die.' Well, Isaiah called to us:
'Git out of that buggy and come on in, we're goin' to have a
big time.' He didn't even have a real iron gig but he'd made
his own. It was something like a boat oar trimmed out of
wood, and he aimed to hit the fish on the head and knock
him out — seemed like he never failed, too. A dead fish
always floats so he would reach down and pick 'em up just
as fast.

"He was splitting up some lightwood—pine splinters—
and now he tied them up with a piece of hickory bark. They
were about two feet long. Then he made a sort of surcingle
of hickory bark and hung that round his neck, letting it hang
down some so that he could slide one end of the bundle into
it against his chest so it would slant upward and out from his
face and yet not drop. Then he lighted the far end. That was
the light he worked by, flaring out there in front of him. He
stepped down into the stream and began to creep up through
it, watching the water all the time, until he'd see a trout and

out would flash his wooden gig, catch the fellar on the head and bring it floating into his hand, and then he'd slip it into the crocus sack hanging on his left hip, watching the water all the time. When we got through with gigging, me and my friend found it was about two in the morning, and decided we'd better go on home, but Isaiah was set on our staying a while longer for the big fish-fry he was going to have. So they built up the fire and brought out the worst looking pones of flour bread I ever saw. They'd made them themselves in the ashes, with bear's grease. Poor as he was Isaiah had coffee pots hid all over that mountain so he could have one handy wherever he camped for the night, and they made coffee and drank it boiling hot out of tin cups. We ate the fish, but I didn't tackle that bread. And the moon came up over the mountain, I remember."

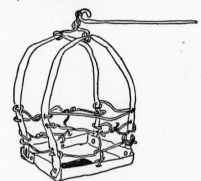

A New Hampshire pickerel jack to carry fire for night fishing

The Pickerel Jack

One New Hampshire farmer invented his own light-bearer when he wanted to go after pickerel at night. This "pickerel jack" was made about a century ago. It is really an iron-strap basket, with a sheet-iron bottom turned up like a shallow box cover with an oblong hole cut in it to make a draught. This base had two thin iron straps which arched up from it at the corners and down on the other side, and were riveted in. Three holes were cut into these straps and in and out of them ran strands of heavy wire which formed the sides of the jack part way up. The straps were fastened together across the top and from them extended a heavy iron hook with a shank a foot long coming out of it, and this shank went through a hole in the bow of the flatboat and held the basket sticking out ahead. A fire of twigs in the jack was fed from the boat, and the slow motion kept it burning steadily.

Fishing pier, Atlantic Beach, Florida

Time Marches On

From Maine to Florida the fishing times and ways are changing. Great fishing wharfs extend into the Southern waters for rich and poor, child and grown-up to try their luck in the fishy deeps. It would seem as though the simple old methods were still producing results though, when a man in Florida can catch a nine-pound bass on a bent pin. Down East in Maine where the fishing customs have changed little from year to year, old fishermen are sitting idly on many a smelly wharf, sighing for the good old days of the past before politics ruined their livelihood. "It was haddock in the old days, and we've owned our own homes and boats and trawls, and now these men in Washington with their codes have made it so we've had to stop all that and go mackerlin'. I don't know how we're goin' to live nor what we're all comin' to."

The hated "drudge" or modern dredge, is causing havoc along many shores. The following letter of a few weeks ago gives us a peep into the life of the old trotline crabbers along Chesapeake Bay, where with their ordinary dipnets they could make a good living for themselves and families right at their own shore edge:

> ...Twenty years ago I married a young riverman and we started shedding crabs and selling the peelers to fishermen who came from every part of Virginia and lots of them from other states. My man would crab with a trotline and all the buck's wives and others that had the sign and buy whatever he could. In ten years he injured his lungs by crashing over the stem of his bateau running his line, and got an ailment that took him away from me. I didn't know what else to do so I kept on selling peelers. I had to buy crabs to shade, except the ones I could pick up myself near my little house on the river shore.
>
> The crabs kept getting scarcer, and I finally lost my home, so my four little girls and I moved into an old shack near the waters of a little creek that runs into the York River. In the river is what we call a crab lump, where the crabs bed down in the winter. When spring comes they would come in this creek to spawn. Last Thursday, Friday and Saturday a bunch of dredge-

boats came up the York from the bay and they dredged this lump thoroughly. They left one little crab and he climbed a broken-off net stake and a big seagull caught him. So my prospect of a chance to make a cent this summer is gone.

Mrs——

The old trotline crabbers along this shore say:

> The drudges kill more than they catch, and the crabs are caught—or killed—when they are numb with cold. It began to slack up in '29 when they brought out a new dredge, heavier, with stronger teeth. I remember when we could dip up as high as eight barrels a day—and it was a living. There soon won't be any crabs to fish with.

Fishing for buttons with a trot line

One of perhaps our least known old industries in the fishing line was that of fishing for clams, the shells of which were made into buttons. This was carried on until a few years ago in the St. Croix River near Minneapolis, and one of these fishermen was a woman who poled out into the stream with her trotline resting on wooden uprights and its double row of hooks hanging down into the water, baited them and hauled them in when the catch was caught. Sometimes she added a pearl to her harvest, and at the age of seventy-six Mrs.

Mary Houdek in her sunbonnet and apron was still fishing for buttons.

A string of whiting in Florida

Gone too is the old picket-fence trap which used to stand across Campbell's Creek in West Virginia. The fence had a gate in it and when the river rose this was opened to let the fish through, and when the river sank the gate was quickly closed, leaving a wagonload of fish for the lazy fisherman.

XXI. THE SEINE LOFT AND FIELD

The seine is a net, of about fortie fathome in length,
with which they encompasse a part of the sea and drawe
the same on land by two ropes fastened at his ends, together with such fish as lighteth within his precinct."

1602

The Massachusetts Seine

NOT in a shop, but in a loft, were the Down East seines
made for the wholesale catching of fish. Close to the water,
generally in a loft above some other active work, these long
nets were made that they might be handy to the sea, their
destined scene of labor. The seine is a net netted by hand,
and by the hand of man rather than of woman, and used for
the catching of mackerel and herring. We have read of seines
since the days of Bible happenings, but the purse seine which
came to our waters during the latter half of the last century
was something a bit different. So ominous indeed was it that
those of the generation which saw its advent here, shook their
heads, prophesying: "These seines will spoil the fishing,"
so great were the draughts which they brought in after one
casting. Surely the sea must run short of fish with such a
greedy octopus at work upon its waters. Hundreds of barrels
of fish came home from fishing expeditions when a purse
seine was used, as against the smaller number caught at the
weirs, where single nets stretched from pole to pole to catch
fish in the old way.

One of the more intimate names for the seine or net was
the "twine." Made of twine they came in time to carry that
name. Up in the seine loft several men would be at work upon

their individual nets, for by the very nature of its make-up, the net could be worked upon by only one person at a time. Seines might measure several hundred feet in length and, in width or "depth," about ten feet. From this word "depth" we get a suggestion of how a seine was used when out for its prey. Sighting a school of mackerel, two boats would put out from the schooner, the smaller one, or dory, would drop its anchor and take a permanent stand, while the larger "seine boat" would begin to row away to encircle the school. Carefully folded back and forth in the seine boat was the hand-made seine, so laid as to keep it from snarling as the men began to pay it out and drop its width or depth down into the water, while they held tightly to the rope which ran around the top. Finally the circle would be completed, and, if the school of mackerel had not suddenly grown wise and dropped to the bottom of the ocean to elude these tricky humans, the men would draw together the bottom rope, or "purse the seine at the bottom" and make a bag of it in which the catch was securely fastened.

Knowing then the use of the seine, it is easier to understand why hundreds of feet of net must be woven in one lengthy strip, and also what a task the seine-maker had. The making of the seine was similar to the making of the gill-net, which was fastened on uprights driven into the bottom of the bay and caught the fish by the gills as they came head-on against it. It seems to have been largely a difference of the size of the mesh, if any existed between the trap nets at the weirs, or the gill-net, and the long seines. A Gloucester woman remembers her father's weaving his fish nets and what she tells of the treatment of the smaller net will tell us also of the seine.

New England netting needle

Weaving the Net

"The netting needle was of thin wood about eight inches long and perhaps an inch wide, with a blunt hollow end with a point of wood running up into it, and at the bottom it would be open with a point at each side, and he would make that little needle fly, I tell you. Why, the nets grew so fast with that little thing going in and under and out again. I remember Father would take his twine and cast a loop over a hook he had in a shelf. Then with his netting needle he'd make two loops in that one. Then in the next row there'd be one more loop and so he kept adding until he'd made a row which was just the right width for the net. When he'd finished the net he coiled it round and round inside a great tub, oh, it must have been a hogshead sawed off. That kept it from snarling. Then the whole thing was carried off to a shed, I remember, where the net was to be tarred.

The Tarring Shed

"Old Mr. Maker had that little tarring shed with a great big tank in it. On the edge of the tank there was a roller about eight inches in diameter and five feet long. Inside, the tar was set boiling by pipes which ran from a water boiler at one side. The tar was always ready when Father got there. Then they had to get the net out without snarling, and the last end in would be the first end out, of course, and Father would pay it out over the roller which let it fall down easily into the tar, and lie there in folds which ran back and forth.

261

I remember that the seine was always light twine color when it went into the tank or vat, but black when it came out. This tar of course strengthened it. Those men that worked there in the tarring shed, I remember how their hair turned green after a while, and they got sort of greenish looking all over."

Tarring a Gloucester seine

Here a neighbor man volunteered: "When the seine was well tarred, the ropes which had been holding it back over the roller, were pulled and the net came back and with the men guiding it, was folded back and forth in a two-horse wagon with a roller on it, and sides that made it look like a hayrick. We had a field on our farm which was always called the 'seine field' and there the seines were laid out to dry for days. The men would drive the wagon into the field and then drive round and round carefully paying out the tarred seine and spreading it out on the grass as they went, until the field would be well covered with its great length.

"After the seine was well dried it was gathered up in the same careful manner and taken back to the seine loft where the corks were added, the corks which kept the top of the net afloat. Years ago they used glass balls to hold the nets up, and at the bottom there was an anchor at each end to keep it down. Oh, yes, and the seines had to be well salted after they were tarred, and every once in a while after they were on the boats at sea."

Still another neighbor had something to tell, and she said it with a light of youth in her eye: "Father had a little dory and would sometimes take me out in it. He would row around and then set the net where the fish would likely come. The little 'boys'—buoys—would hold the net up. Next day, or perhaps in the evening, he would row out again and pull the net, and so many, many fish he would have. When the nets were broken he had lots of work mending them all up again."

The Weirs

There is no finer trip in all the world than a trip to some far-out weirs, at three o'clock in the morning when the moon is over Cape Cod. There will be a mess of squids to throw their ink wildly about, but there will be also many pounds of great fish for eating, to roll from the nets into the hold of the boat. There will be also the early twinkling lights of the houses on the circle of the shore—where the laggards are arising at five in the morning—on the trip back home, and the shine and beauty of many colored scales and satiny sides curled against each other. In 1633 a charter for a fish weir was granted to one Israel Stoughton along the Atlantic coast so that he might sell alewives to the men of the plantation at five shillings per thousand. This was back in the days when blown glass balls of almost any color were caught into the upper edges of the nets, to keep them afloat, balls which had been blown and shirred off from the ponsil or blow-stick,

and left roughly projecting. These balls are sometimes confused with the Witch Balls which hung in some chimney-
places to keep the witches from coming into the house via
the open chimney. These latter were blown and left open
where the ponsil was broken off, so that a twig might be
inserted and pass across the hole, by which to hang the ball.

We laugh today when people speak of the "wear" where
the fish are caught, but that was the original way to spell
the word, "weir" being a later spelling.

*Fishermen's rope reel for hauling in nets on Gwyn's
Island near Norfolk. 1700s*

An Evening Fantasy

Fortunately there are still many sections where old working
habits are still in vogue and others where the shadows of old
ways are only just faded away. A young mother relates a
scene of her childhood which might well be told of two
hundred years ago. "I remember how as a girl I used to love
to go to the beach at night and see the fishermen pull in their
nets, great long ones, I don't know how long. It was near

Norfolk and on the beach was built a great wooden reel like a turning table. It had three cross pieces on a turning post and these of course made six ends, and at each of these ends a donkey was hooked on and each donkey led by a negro. When the ropes of the net had been fastened to the post the negroes started the donkeys, and drove them round and round in a great beaten circle of a path until the net had been drawn close to the water's edge. Then the negroes waded in up to their waists and got hold of the two sides of the net to keep the fish from rolling out and then drew it up on shore. There were big pine chunks burning all around so they could see, and their flames flooded the whole scene so that it looked more like a stage scene than everyday fishing."

XXII. SPONGE BEDS

~~~~~~

Every man is but a spunge and but a spunge filled with
teares.   1622

~~~~~~

Greek Cross Day

EACH year when January the sixth comes around, the
Southern papers carry a story of what has happened that day
at Tarpon Springs, Florida, of the arrival of the Archbishop
of the Greek Church in this country accompanied by other
church dignitaries, to observe the Feast of the Epiphany in
that community of many Grecians. They tell of how visitors
come by the thousands to watch the high priest of the
Hellenic Eastern Orthodox Greek Church march to the
waterfront followed by singing ecclesiastics, see him hurl a
golden cross into Spring Bayou (an arm of the Gulf of
Mexico), to rescue which a dozen young men dive into the
crystal-clear water. When the winner has found and returned
the golden cross to the high priest, and received his praise, a
white dove symbolic of the Holy Spirit is released over the
waters. Once more the symbolic ritual of the baptism of
Jesus has been celebrated. But why a strong Hellenic Church
in Tarpon Springs? The answer is that Tarpon Springs is the
largest sponge market in the world, and the Grecians the
greatest sponge fishermen. So in this town on the west coast
of Florida, just a little north of Tampa Bay on the Gulf of
Mexico, where the Greeks make up a greater proportion of
the population than in any other town in America, the great
Archbishop himself appears each January to celebrate his
church's great day.

SPONGE BEDS

Adventurous young travelers in 1894-5 made a trip in a twenty-eight-foot sailboat from Tampa to Miami, making stops along the southern coast of Florida and visiting many of its southernmost keys. Stormbound for a week on Bamboo Key they had their first introduction to the sponge industry and it came by way of their olfactory sense, for "the smell of dying sponges and their final kick in the crawls" could not be easily ignored. The sponge station was on Sugar Loaf Key, a little to the northeast of Key West, farther to the west was Crawl Key, named from the industry, for after the sponges had been brought to shore they were laid out on "crawls" so that the tides could wash out the animal impurities.

At this time the only sponge fishing in the country was being done on these lowest Florida keys near Key West, and although the industry was hardly noticed by the world, it had been carried on since 1849. The first sponge fishers were native Americans who used long poles with a three-pronged hook bent at right angles on the end of them, and they never ventured beyond the depth of twenty feet, or the reach of their poles.

A sponge is really only a skeleton of an animal which has adhered to the bottom of the sea, to the top of, or in the crevices of, a rock, or fastened itself to a coral reef. The Greeks had their name for this too and called it "zo-ofiton" which means half plant and half animal. It is one of the oldest and lowest forms of marine life and is, in its native state, covered with a tenacious black skin, with its cells filled with a gelatinous grey matter called "gurry." After these living animal elements have been removed, the skeleton which remains is our well-known sponge.

OF THE EARTH EARTHY

To the early Key West sponge-getter, the twenty-foot pole seemed the best possible means of wrenching the clinging creatures from their lowly beds, and wrench them they did, tearing them ruthlessly but drawing them to the surface with the greatest of skill. It seems not to have entered these fishermen's heads that sponges might be dived for, or perhaps they knew what had been happening to naked Greek divers back home, who went below and cut the sponges with knives, only to be cut in two themselves sometimes, by curious and unfriendly sharks. The only trouble with fishing with a long pole was that the water must be clear and untroubled so that the "hooker" might peer down through it to locate his destined prey. It was not until 1905 that some one concocted what became the grandsire of our glass-bottom boats, and thus overcame this bad-weather difficulty. Somewhere in this inventor's mind must have been a memory of men's going down into deep wells if they wanted to see the stars by day, for he rigged up a bucket with a piece of heavy glass for its bottom, and found that by pressing this down against the roughened water, he could see the bottom plainly, sometimes to a depth of sixty feet. This "water glass" proved to be a great boost to the sponge industry.

Quite early an attempt had been made to market these American sponges and some had been shipped to the New York market, only to be met with the rebuff which greeted many domestic products at that time. They were priced at ten cents a pound. Still the sponge fishing continued along the keys until "hooker boats" had been sent out in some numbers. In the meantime John K. Cheyney, an early settler at Tarpon Springs, had determined to put sponge fishing upon a real commercial basis, and in 1890 sent out his first hooker boats to be followed soon by other Tarpon Springers.

SPONGE BEDS

During the Spanish-American war, the fear of Spanish war-ships along the keys caused the Key West sponge fleet to run their cargoes of sponges into Tarpon Springs for market-ing. It was this safety act which made the beginnings of the great sponge market at the latter place.

Greek Sponge Divers

The first Greek to come to Tarpon Springs was John Corcoris who worked in the Cheyney storehouses, and it was he who finally persuaded John Cheyney and his associates to import trained Greek divers to build up the baby industry on this side of the Atlantic. The first group which arrived in 1905 came from Greece and was equipped with divers' paraphernalia and all the fishing comforts of the Mediterranean. What they have accomplished in modern sponge fishing is hardly in place here, but it is interesting to know that although Tarpon Springs has a great sponge fleet and has left Key West far behind in the business of sponging, there are still the old-fashioned "hookers" at the Springs. At Key West hooking is still the preferred method, and carried on by native fishermen. There is even a law there which prohibits the use of diving suits in the harvesting of sponges.

Cleaning the Skeletons

The "crawls" have already been mentioned, where, on the beach, the harvested sponges were left over night to allow the cell substances and outer coating to disintegrate. Naturally the aroma arising from this decaying matter did not add to the gayety of that part of the seashore, but the tide was the great cleanser and remover. During this period of purification workmen assisted Nature by beating the sponges occasionally until they were "clean and strong." Beating in the sun was also a cleansing method; while burying in the warm sand seems to have acted upon the sponge's unpleasant-nesses much as common earth does upon clothes buried after an encounter with a woodpussy. The black outer membrane died in one night and was quickly scraped away, so that in a short time the sponge was ready to be threaded upon strings and called a finished product. There is no open season, or rather no closed season, for sponges in Florida and so the hookers, from the keys to far northern Apalachicola, and the deep-sea fishermen who have gone forth for the finest of all sponges, have been able to keep busy at their earthy and watery industry for many unbroken years.

Varieties

Four kinds of sponges grow in our Gulf waters, the finest being the "Sheepswool," or "Wool" sponge, which is com-pact and tough in texture, with its strength and toughness depending upon the depth of water in which it has grown. The "second best" is the "Yellow," the third, the "Grass," and the poorest in commercial value, the "Wire" or "Velvet." The best and the least however are equally dark grey in color after the gurry has been removed, and attain their lighter and pleasanter commercial hue only after bleach-ing in a solution, often of simple potash.

XXIII. THE SHIPYARD

I must go down to the seas again, to the lonely sea and
    the sky,
And all I ask is a tall ship and a star to steer her by. . . .
               —MASEFIELD

Modern trap boat in the making at Kennebunkport
Maine

A DRIZZLE of foggy rain was falling across the sandy shipyard, drawing up its silvery meshes occasionally to let a sad
ray of washed-out sunlight touch the frame of the little trapboat — where two men worked face to face across the new
side planking — and then dropped back again to soften the
lines of the picture once more. There was nothing though
to shut out the sound of the hammers as they rang out and
echoed along the village street, tapping their way along the
side of the boat, doing double duty as they forced the planks
into place and then nailed them fast. Peace and industry

271

seemed wedded together here at the side of the salty river. Kennebunkport had once been a famous shipbuilding center, but now there was but a small yard, a small launching dock and a small drydock where fewer and smaller boats were made, and yet boats sturdy enough to go to the Banks for fishing in bad weather. So, this drizzly morning only three men were visible in the shipyard, but they went cheerily about their work, showing the whole world how work can bring out the best and the happiest in a man, in spite of rain.

A boat to ride the seas. That such a structure, which must be watertight and strong enough to ride the oceans of the world at their worst, should have been made by "rule of thumb" or "by guess and by say-so" seems contrary to reason, but so were the old ships made, according to venerable shipbuilders still busy at their craft. After all, it is not so hard to understand after one has watched a ship being put together, for one is then convinced that rule of thumb means most careful attention to the individual needs of each article worked upon, and understanding of natural variations and a conscientious disregard of anything which smacks of generalization and common denominator, that curse of modern living. Each board and plank which went into a boat and each treenail or "trunnel" which held it in place, had its own edges and surfaces, and few indeed were exactly like any others. Water tightness and balance and all of the other things which the sea demands of a boat were assured therefore, not in spite of the old rule of thumb, but because of it.

When the drizzle came to an end, two or three neighbors dropped across the road to the old yard to pass the time of day, and although the ship wrights were engrossed with their work one would have thought the whole job was just a social way of passing the time. The greater the difficulties of the work, the kindlier the tones of the two men who worked face to face became, and there was always time to shout an answer to a loiterer or a passer-by. The little trapboat, destined for fishing in deep waters, might be said to be standing there in its undies, for barring the few top planks which had already been fitted into the waiting groove in the stem, there was nothing more than a skeleton frame, partly covered by a small wooden awning of rough boards over the stern end. The task of the morning was to get those planks to fit so closely against the frames or ribs and hug each other so closely that each two should become as one. The men's heads were perhaps one foot apart, yet their voices rang out loudly above the hammer strokes:

"How's that goin', Freddie?"

"Good." The first three planks had slipped into place with little trouble but the fourth one was acting up, refusing to snuggle.

"How's that, Freddie?"

Quite seriously: "I could crawl through, Ralph."

"How's it now, Freddie?"

"There's an eighth of an inch, Ralph, sternward," came the answer from a few inches away, but over the planking. More hammering and urging.

"I got a strain on it now, Freddie," and the hammer came down with short quick strokes. "How's it now?"

"It's slippin', Ralph. Good! " A few more strokes and then a cry rang out louder than those which had come before, which seemed to say "Wooden wood," but was actually "Wood on wood, Ralph, wood'n wood." The plank had gone home against its neighbor at last.

"She sets all right does she, Freddie?"

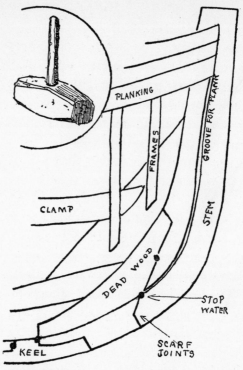

The parts that never show. Wooden maul

Slowly the planking grew downward over the ribs. Later it would cover also the view of the long clamp, and the deadwood tightly scarfed into the stem, with its two heavy "stop waters" or wooden pegs driven into the scarfing seam to check any possible passage of water. The stern build was braced by a great naturally curved wooden knee, and its ribs had grown shorter and of a rounder curve after they passed the sternpost which was mortised into the huge keelson log below. Strutting out for a short distance beyond the sternpost, the keel and its load the keelson, ended abruptly, waiting for the coming of the propellor and its shaft and the

274

rudder. From stem to stern each pair of ribs had its own reinforcing block, and where the engine was to stand, heavier blocks had been set as "engine beds." There was not much to launch yet, but the structural form was about finished. Freddie and Ralph would see a good many more winters before they gave up shipbuilding, but on a street across the town an old man, who had finished his shipbuilding days, told a sketchy story of his early life in this same town.

Master Builder Warner

Today he is spoken of lovingly as "Old Man Warner" but in 1873 when he came to town from Prince Edward's Isle, he was a young and vigorous workman for the busy shipyard. His frame is large, his manner and voice kind, his hearing hard, but the old days drifted back to him in answer to questions or through thought connection, as casually and disconnectedly as vanished days should. "Masts? Those were good days when we got those into place. If the masts were small they'd lay on the wharf, but if they were big, they'd lay in the water 'longside. Then old Sam would get his hoss and hook him on, and he'd drive clean up to the center of town hauling that mast till it reached where it had to be. 'Go on, Sam, go on,' old John Maitland would say, then he'd say, 'Now Sam, back her up, back her up,' and the great stick would begin to slide into place in the keelson. First there was the keel and the keelson on it. It was higher than my head where it went in. The first mast was made of four pieces of pine. They'd make a tunnel through 'em and drive in an iron to hold 'em together. Then the blacksmith would put iron bands on, eighteen inches apart. Put 'em on hot and let 'em get cold. Then the second mast would be made of one stick and settled down into the mast head. And the third one in that.

"The sails were made of hemp. They'd sow the flax and it'd grow so high," laying his hand on his hip, "and they'd cut it and tie it in sheaves, twelve sheaves to the shock. Then they'd break it on the bench, then they put it on the wheels, some were little and you sat to 'em, while others were that high. You know the kind the women walked the floor to all day. Then they'd put it on the loom, it would take the woman and one of the girls two days just to put the strings through and over the rolls, and then they'd weave it for sails. After I came here they stopped using hemp and made different kinds of sails, a double top-sail, etc. . . ."

Mr. Warner insisted upon standing up although he was stiff and slow in his movements. He remembered suddenly that what he had told me of sails had been remembered from his days on Prince Edward's Isle, and then we remembered together that what had happened there had happened in this country also a few years before. Then he told of having to adapt himself to the ways of "The States." "There wasn't any Christmas here, or holidays or Sundays, when I came in 1873, and we worked nights too. At night we'd go out to the river and shovel mud for ballast and then nail the boards down. When the ship got to New York they'd heave it out and put in the cargo. The first ship I worked on here was the *St. John Smith* and she went to New York and I never heard of her again. All the other boats I heard about, but I never heard of her." It was as though a mother at the end of a long life had been counting over her many children and had lost one strand of living, and that her firstborn.

"Once I shipped on a boat to New York with a crew and it took us sixteen days to get there. Sunday morning when we hove to we were just over Newfoundland. We never knew why.

"You remember that long house down by the river that is used for a boathouse now? That was the old riggin' loft. We used to make real boats here. They're makin' play boats now. Why, the bowsprits used to run almost up to the street. There were sixty men working all the time. If you lost your work in one place the other shipyard man would put his hand on your shoulder and say: 'Come work for me.' They were always looking for men. There were men all around here and they didn't have any courthouse or any policemen or any jails. If a man and me had trouble we'd go out behind the barn and fight it out. In my country we had a religion that was different from that around here in those days. There was no Christmas here. When I told the Boss I wouldn't be there workin' on Christmas Day he didn't say anything. The day after Christmas when I went down in the morning we were all waiting in a line and the Boss handed out the tools and told 'em all what to work at but me. So I says: 'Just fix up my bill for the four days you owe me.' So I took it to Mr. ———. He lived in Kennebunk and wore a high silk hat and he says: 'William, what's this for?' And I says, 'I always go to church on Christmas night and so we drove over.' He picked up his silk hat and says: 'Come with me,' and he took the bill to the Boss and says: 'As long as there's work in this shipyard you give it to William. I'm paying the men here.' "

One knows as he looks and listens to William today that it was his steady rule-of-thumb thoroughness which made him, in time, master of the shipyard.

277

OF THE EARTH EARTHY

In this same Maine village in the middle of the 1700s, the ship-to-be called out many ingenious ways of preparing the material of which it was to be built. Here are a few of the interesting ones:

> Ship Building. Deckplank, the wales and other thick work used in the hulls being whip-sawed by hand over a pit 30 feet in length and 4 feet wide in the ground. Square stick was rolled over this, one workman upon it above, one in pit with crape protecting his eyes from sawdust, the plank was sawed. (Apparently crepe was the sheerest of the woven materials at that time.) The keel was first laid, canted on its side. Stem and stern then mortised in, the whole shored up and raised, and the frames built piece by piece usually being carried up on the workmen's shoulders. Split poles, styled "ribbons," were laid and secured on the frames for shaping the bow and stern. Copper spikes were so seldom used in the early time that children searched for them among the chips. The resident blacksmith produced the ironwork, even some chain plates that secured the shrouds. Bars of iron heated in forge, divided into strips, cut into short lengths, pointed and headed, as spikes.
>
> Steam-box: Large iron kettle beneath its middle part from which steam of boiling water entered the long box working pliable the plank within it in an hour's time, and suitable for using at the bends of the ship. Water for this steam-box was brought by a boy from a spring.
>
> Oakum for caulking was produced by cutting up old junk, (old rope) which was then spun and rolled into balls for use. Seams pitched from a kettle of boiling substance near by.
>
> Working day in shipyard from sunrise to sunset.

Here we have another description with its own points of helpfulness:

278

THE SHIPYARD

Blocks set close to water's edge in shipyard, at proper inclination for launching (la'nchin'). Keel is laid on this, generally on top of false keel. Keel dowelled together for length, and grooved on both sides. Stern must have strongest timber, backed by the apron and the sternson, all bolted together, and secured by a knee. Then the sternpost of solid oak is mortised into the keel, and strengthened by an inner post. Backbone now ready for ribs. At each end of keel the space too limited for framing, called the deadwood. Floor timbers with alternate short or long arms, next let into keel at right angles, from floor rise the futtocks which make the frame and shape. Next lay down the keelson — stout timbers running from stem to stern, bolted over the keel, with two or four keelsons, bolted through floor and futtocks. Ceiling goes up the sides from the keelson. . . .

The caulking was done by driving oakum with caulking irons, or reaming irons, between the seams of the deck and the outer planking and then covering it with pitch, which made all watertight. The caulking job might be done by men who made that their special craft, and a New Englander of 1763 got his pay in barter, two gallons of tar "for Calking and Baying a Skiff,"— not only water-tight but proven so by launching in the bay. "The caulkin' kept out the water and the sheathin' kept out the worms."

Wood 'n Wood

The blacksmith might be needed here and there on an old boat, but it was wood which carried men about the seas and around the world as far as a ship could go. The "ship's knee" which had been placed in the stern of the new trapboat was a sturdy brace which could be used at many angles. Sailors, as well as farmers, had to know their wood, and which trees

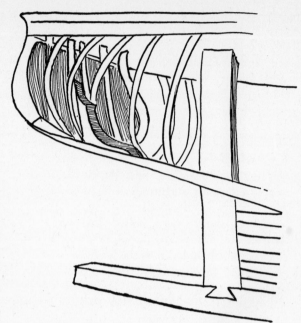

The keel, stern post and ship's knee in the sternbuild

would behave best under certain circumstances. Many knees were made of oak, than which there is no harder wood, but hackmatack was the only wood for the knee beneath the decks. There are three roots to the hackmatack, and when two of these were cut out the remaining one made the perfect bracket or support. Ship builders hunted for crooked trees for their boat frames or ribs, and were careful not to lessen their strength by cutting against the grain. Whole sledloads of knees would be teamed in from the country by the farmers to the shipyards, and gladly were they received. Steaming of the great planks, as we have already seen, was another way of easing strain on wood as well as shaping them to their destined berth.

THE SHIPYARD

Timbers were sometimes left in salt water to preserve them until they could be used. We are told too that hulls of some of the new ships made during the 1700s in New England, were seasoned with salt, "which was thrust through the air streaks of the inner ceiling, and between the frames, with sticks, by men and boys." Stop-blocks prevented this salt from escaping into the bilge and dissolving there. The trunnels, or long wooden pegs which fastened plank and timber together, were rived out of cross sections of blocks of oak trees, and shaped with their sides smoothed into eight even planes, right in the shipyard. Made in this shape they could not turn or slip in their sockets, nor fail their captain when the waves were high. Made of wood too were the gaff and boom, the pulley blocks of two or more folds, and the wooden shives within the pulleys; great wooden blocks were used for hoisting the mast to "step it into place"; the helm or "hel-em" was of wood, and there was the oaken fid about a foot long, or one made of "linkum vitae" as old seamen call the lignum vitae.

"You can't git linkum vitae any more for a fid to make a hitch in a rope, nor for nothin' else much," Henry Williams "from down Maine way" told the visitors to the four-masted schooner on which he was first mate, and which was docked in Southern waters. "They's a parcel of things you can't do nowadays that you could use to do." And now two years later comes the latest landlubber infringement on the habits of the "salts," at least the lake sailors, the legal prohibition against the use of the ancient and honorable sea terms "starboard" and "larboard" or "port," and the substitution of the unsalted "right and left." One can almost hear First Mate Williams telling the sea and the sky what he thinks of this helpful suggestion from shore, on matters nautical. But as he sorrowed over the lack of linkum vitae there came from below deck the voices of the East Indian crew which was loading lumber, and their working song came drifting up:

> Blow the man down, Bullie,
> Blow the man down.

Then the answer:

> Hey, hey, blow the man down.
> He's from old—Boston Towne.

"That there's the bo'sen first. He calls out to the Ab-ies and the OSs, and they answers him with each heave of the lumber. Why, the Ab-ies is the able-bodied seamen, and the OSs is the ordinary unskilled workmen."

There was also the "camel" of wood. In old Nantucket harbor when a ship was sighted they fired up for steam to take the floating drydock, or "camel" out to the entrance of the harbor, if the incoming boat needed to be helped across the bar and had signalled in. This was moved out, sunken, the vessel towed within, water was pumped from the camel which later arose carrying the ship, then propelled itself and the ship over the bar.

Although wood is supposed to float, it was often found necessary to lash pine to oak to keep the former from sinking.

The Launching

So exactly does the shipbuilder know his boat in the building that he paints the waterline on it before it is launched — and it never fails to tally with the line of the wet. No matter how many boats have previously been made in a shipyard, the day of a launching is always an exciting one. Just how will that carefully constructed body take the water, and will she set high and proud or low and squatty and off line? Here is what an old writer has to say on the subject from a practical standpoint. Because he begins with the laying of the keel we find that the machinery for the launching has been in mind from the first.

Lay keel. Large bed logs laid in ground ten feet apart from 30 to 40 feet in length, and extending one after another at right angles with the keel on either side. Keep stretched upon blocking built up some four feet high from the ground so the ship carpenter may stand under the vessel to drive treenails and bore for bilge bolts. Therefore the blocking is in pyramidal form. When frames of ship's floor are laid they are shored up from the bed logs on either side, and with added supports between these logs and thus remain through the period of framing, ceiling the inside and planking the outside, and until the day of the launching approaches, when heavy planks five inches are also blocked up beneath the vessel each side of the keel. The upper part of the plank is smooth (sometimes made so by a slight fire of shavings to remove previous marks of use). Then smeared with grease. Then a sixteen-inch "bilge timber" is laid on each of the running planks and also bearing directly on the bilge of the ship, and beneath which and on the upper surface of the bilge timber the wooden wedges are driven, which in the process of launching, slightly lift the vessel, when the blocking beneath keel is driven out of place, cob by cob (the cob work is the boarding beneath the keel) until the ship rests upon its bilges alone, and this great weight with the slippery surface of the running plank and bilge timbers, and felling of the few shores and props causes the hull to start, carrying with it usually the bilge timbers, the heads of which arise out of the turmoil of the waters.

OF THE EARTH EARTHY

Surely that last phrase will repay us for any breathlessness which may have come from the lack of punctuation marks, for one can readily visualize that "turmoil of the waters," when the great hull suddenly leaves the land and makes her maiden bow to the sea. Here a modern adds a few more facts to this great occasion: "The bilge-way is a grooved plank greased with tallow and black lead. The blocks are on top of the 'ways' and well wedged with wedges driven in with a maul. Since the keel rests on the blocking you got to cut out the blocking and just as soon as the last one goes you got to back out quick, for away she goes. Sometimes they served, in a tin cup, a tumbler of rum with two of water and often some molasses.

"Once at a la'nchin' a girl got so excited that she jumped over a spar and her big petticoats flew out and she gasped out: 'If any of you young men saw my ankles I shall go and destroy myself.'"

Once launched, the boat was brought back to the wharf to have its mast and spars, its rigging and its sails added and the whole made shipshape. This was done, as they said in New Jersey, by the "ship's Tailor."

The Mast

We have already learned that the mast was a matter of four pieces of pine to the man who worked in the second half of the 1800s, but it was not until Isaac Harris of Boston, who was living during the war of 1812, thought of this idea, that the mast was aught but a sturdy pine tree, peeled and stood up by itself to stand the strain of wind and weather, cannon-balls and lightning. The passing of the great forests of pine made this new method a necessity, but the Norwegian pine still supplied some of our sailing vessels with single tree masts.

THE SHIPYARD

The English kings never forgot, until the very eve of the Revolution, to stipulate in each new land charter that all white pine should be marked and left for the King's Navy and touched by the settler only under a heavy penalty. Many a cove on lake and river carries the name of the old days of mast cutting and "rolling" into the water for conveying to a shipyard. On Lake Champlain there is an old "Rolling Banks," and near Portsmouth, New Hampshire, on the bank of the Piscataqua, there is "Mast Cove." An old sea captain tells of the handling of these great trees as though they were simple toys. "Take four yellow pine sticks fifteen inches square, round 'em up, and make your mast. Then put a strap around the center and hist it up above the deck. Then lower it until it strikes the keelson. Yes'm, an old horse raised the derrick, and traveled quite a space too, for the length of the mast." This lowering was "stepping it in." A mast might stand sixty feet above the deck and twenty-five feet below it.

Our First Boats

There may have been other boats built in this country before these of which we have early record, for men were here long before 1607, but at that time the expedition led by Georges and Popham to make the first settlement in Maine, needed either to replace a lost vessel or wanted to augment their fleet, for they built them a boat on our shores. With this claim given credence, the long-standing claim of New York City that it had the first shipyard in the country, has to take second place. Adrian Block after reaching the waters of Long Island and giving his name to Block Island, lost his ship, his only one, and was forced to spend the winter of 1614 on Manna-hatta while a new one was being made and outfitted in the new land without any shipyard conveniences. Quite appropriately he called this new boat the *Onrust,* meaning unrest. His shipyard is believed to have been at about 39 Broadway.

Massachusetts has this list of pioneer shipyards all nicely worked out for us with the number and type of boats built through those earliest years:

1628-9	Large barque at Salem
1631	Winthrop on his Medford farm launched *Blessing of the Bay* which was built of locust wood. A nice note, this, of farms producing their own boat woods.
1632	Two others at Medford
1636	One boat at Marblehead
1640	A Ship at Salem
1642	Three ships at Boston
	One at Dorchester
	Another at Salem
1643	One boat at Gloucester

The commonest type for those days was the "ketch" which was considered a large ship. It was a two-masted vessel, square-rigged on both masts with a tall mainmast at about the center and a short aftermast. In 1626 the *Sparrowhawk* sailed out of England and, apparently like so many other ships of those days, landed by luck rather than by seamanship. The *Sparrowhawk* sailed into a small inlet of Cape Cod, and did it so badly that she was damaged on the bar and had her planks started. This was in 1627. She was repaired, but then a storm cast her ashore on the eastern shore of the harbor where she became a hopeless wreck. Humans and cargo being removed she was soon completely covered over with sand, so that in time the newly raised dune came to be

THE SHIPYARD

"the Old Ship." One hundred and fifty-five years later, or in 1782, the sands of time shifted enough to reveal the ship through its covering of dune sand. Eighty-one years more, or in 1863, the boat attracted attention again and Amos Otis, antiquary of Yarmouth, examined her and found that she lay rather below the surface of the meadow which had formed about her after the closing of the original inlet, and over which the sand had drifted.

Investigation brought to light that the boat was well built of oak which was not in the least decayed, even the corners of the timbers being as sharp as when they had first been hewn. The iron, alas, was a thing of the past and left nothing behind it but stains in the earth where it had died. Here again we see the apparently soft and yielding outlasting the seemingly solid, making some students believe that iron tools may have been in use among some of the ancients who accomplished such amazing feats — as we think — without them. The repairs which had been made after the first landing on the inlet bar — in an improvised shipyard — were still visible in such ways as the splitting of the treenails with a chisel, so that wedges might be driven into them to make impossible their loss. Decks and bows were gone, but in the hold there were beef and mutton bones, soles of shoes, a metallic box and a pipe bowl. The ship had been perhaps of seventy tons burden. The midship section was described as a decided semicircle, the stern having a remarkable length of deadwood, like our modern steamers which are made for speed. It was found from the old *Sparrowhawk* that what was supposed to be a modern way of piecing up or building the ribs, was known in the early 1600s, for they showed here in her sides. The keel showed but one step for a mast, but it is thought probable that a small mast with a lateen sail must have been mounted at the stern, making the common rig of the old ketch of that time. Two years after its last discovery the old vessel was raised, and finally came to rest on a more friendly bar, the basement of Pilgrim Hall at Plymouth.

"The better to fish the anchor," some of the early boats left the forward rails open.

The Dugout and Bitterhead

Far from being the product of the shipyard, the old dugout has yet had too great an importance in the life of the country to go entirely unmentioned when we are on the subject of boats. The Indians stood in awe of the winged ships which sailed majestically into their coves and lives, but they were past-masters in the art of gouging out a tree and shaping it into a boat, and showed the white man how to do it. Someone has said that in the 1500s the Indians first soaked the side of the log with gin and then added fire to soften the wood for gouging. Was any beverage which they may have made from their grains and flavored with juniper, enough like the white man's "firewater" to burn freely? These dugouts were hollowed in any way which was easiest for the man who was going to use it. Some found whacking out the hollow with an ax the easiest way; some burned the log along one side and finished the gouging with an adz; some had great curved iron shaves for the work, some used stones as the redmen had taught them. One of the longest of these dugouts was called the "piroque" and was hollowed from a poplar tree and measured often sixty feet in length. Dugouts are still being made and still being used in the Southern States, their shapes varying.

288

*From Tennessee to Maine the old flatboats play
Noah's Ark for modern flood victims*

The name "flatboat" covered a multitude of boat styles.
There was the ferry-boat with its wooden aprons at the ends
to raise and lower as a gangplank as they approached and left
the shores, and its rail-fence along the side, and its only pro-
pelling power the long hooked pole which was slid along a
wire cable stretched across the stream. There was the bateau
for carrying cargoes, a broad and very long boat lying close
to the surface of the water all around and propelled by river-
men who walked from the front of the bateau to the rear,

289

pushing against a long pole resting against their padded shoulders. West Virginia called her broad flatboat the "bitter-head," and toted her salt and iron and other cargoes for long distances on them. If Noah were on earth today he would feel very much at home among our floods, and probably greatly approve these crude low boats which in many cases have been the most practical ones for rescuing stranded refugees. From Down East to Down South they have been pressed into service and saved many lives within the last year or two.

Jottings

Since a study of the famous old figureheads of our American ships would lead us away from industries and into the arts, it must suffice here to say that sometimes there stood in the shipyards a small building where these glorious and daring runners-before were hacked and hewn into being, and where the sternboards' ornamentations received the strokes of the carver's knife and chisel.

Our first seamen had to depend largely upon the tides and the winds for their locomotion, so it is no wonder that our first steamboat, built by John Fitch in 1804 and sent up the Delaware as far as Burlington, caused great wonder and much talk. One can judge of the comments at that time by a remark made by an old sailing vessel captain of today:

"A man has to know how to handle a boat and be ready for anything that turns up at sea, when he's on a sailing vessel with no power. Any man that can hold a paint pot and brush can get a job on a steamer."

THE SHIPYARD

A young seaman on the old yacht which was once the pride and joy of P. T. Barnum, but which now carries thousands of bananas from Cuba to a chain of stores in the South, having been through three hurricanes the fall before, said in answer to questions: "No, there's no reason in being scared when you're at sea, because you've just got to work as hard as you can to get through, and if that work don't do it, nothing will."

XXIV. SAIL AND RIGGING LOFTS

He drew vp the sayles and came with a quarter winde
to haue the vauntage of the Sonne.

A "palm" of rawhide, pigskin and steel,
— the sailmaker's thimble

Floor and Dress

SURELY no dance floor could have been smoother than the
floors of the old rigging and sail lofts of the sailing days, in
fact, those who swung themselves in the mazes of old
"Money Musk" rarely had for their merrymaking, floors
half so good as did the sailmakers. Their floors were waxed
and rubbed smooth so that the heavy sails of duck might be
hauled about easily in the making, and no parlor floor ever
shone with greater cleanliness. Upon these smooth clean surfaces the sail patterns were drawn with white chalk and yards
of canvas were laid out for cutting. The sailmakers themselves
wore white clothes to aid in the general cleanliness of the
work, and their shoes were white and soft, to save wear on
the perfect floors. While we are speaking of wearing apparel
we might mention the famous "palms" which the sail-
makers wore, and still wear, on their sewing hand, in place
of a thimble. This palm was a strap of rawhide sewed together

at the back and fitted to slip over the hand and cover the palm. There was a broadening at one point to allow room for a thumb opening, and then exactly in the center of the palm there was a raised mound of pigskin into which was inset a flat disk of steel, corrugated to catch the needle for each hard thrust. Sewing on heavy canvas is not an easy task for most people, but never does one find a sailorman who confesses to anything but great enjoyment and ease in the work. It is worth visiting a port where the old sailing vessels still tie up, to see the seamen at their sewing, patching a torn hole, mending long rents, or fastening new rope along the edges of the sails.

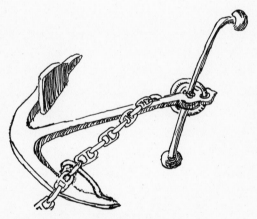

From either the blacksmith's shop or the "chaundler's."

Some of the old sail and rigging lofts still catch the eye along our shorelines, generally because of their great length. The reason for this length was obvious, for "one suit of sails," as they said in the 1600s, covered a vast amount of flat space and a ship must have more than one suit with which to go traveling. The old meaning of "rig" was to "dress," and we have already seen that in New Jersey the rigger of a vessel was the "ship's Tailor." It is a nice old expression "to rig a ship" for it meant quite a personal service to something which had grown personal in the mind of its builders, a ship never being "It" but always "She."

The men who did this rigging had a different craft from that of the boatwright, ship joiner, or "ship carpenter and joiner," and could not begin their work until the actual construction was over and the hull launched in the water. In a large shipyard there would be the riggers and sail-makers close by ready to take on their part of the work at once, within the yard itself, so that no time was lost between the acts; but while the old crew of workers had known planks and nails and knees, the new crew knew ropes and canvas, blocks and tackle, and whatever must be added. At this point the "ship chaundler's shop" did its part in supplying necessary equipment, for there could be found pulleys, oars, anchors, casks, buckets, capstans, lanterns, pumps, blocks and tackle, rope and "hel-ums," or helms. Sometimes the rigging loft and the sail loft were near the shipyard, but not of it. In New York City in 1762 there was, on Cart and Horse Street, a "rigging loft" in full swing on the main floor, while up above in the "sail loft" the making of sails went on. Later this "Old Rigging Loft" was know as "The Rigging House" at 120 William Street.

To stand on the deck of one of the old sailing vessels and look up at the great masts towering so far above, to realize how small that deck must seem when hundreds of miles all

about produce no single sail on the horizon, and to know
that not only the trip but the lives of men depend upon the
make of the sail and the rope, the blocks and the tackle and
the handling of them all, gives one an added interest in the
little old lofts where miles of sails and miles of rope have been
tailored to fit their respective ships.

Rigging and Shroud

"Them old linkum vitae fids now, some men used to take
'em to make a hitch," said an old captain as he showed his
visitors how each joint of spliced rope was carefully covered
with canvas. "But me now, I likes a marline spike to make
a good marline hitch when I'm makin' the seizin' on the
standin' riggin'." The marline spike of iron is about fourteen
or fifteen inches long and well pointed and used for separating the strands of rope when splicing is going on. Landlubbers
know it generally as that convenient weapon which, according to fiction, seems always to be lying handy on the deck
for cracking open men's heads. "Rope riggin' was the kind
when I was a boy, but wire riggin's the kind now. It's wound
round the rope and we call it 'seizin', and if you're goin' to
draw it tight enough for bindin', you make a marline hitch
or loop, so, and then poke the marline through and draw it
tight." Then later:

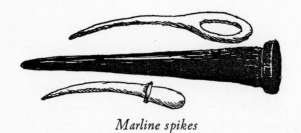

Marline spikes

295

"That there's a luff ta'kle. When the sail is set and you want to take up more, it's the jig you want. But the luff now, it's this a'way. You got two small blocks and ta'kle but they aint heavy enough, so you take two more and connect by tyin' the rope across, and you got four blocks connected."

Block showing revolving shives and lashing rope.
Maine coast

In 1777 and earlier, the rigging of the ship was "the sails and tackling" so that the two parts of the work, dealing with canvas and rope were closely interwoven. To a landlubber the terms and names used in these old lofts are badly intermixed and confusing, but to the sailor there was no confusion. He started with a "suit of sails," and knew each one coming and going, from the fore sails to the aft sails and then to the mizzen. It mattered not to him that "tackle" and "tackling" and "rigging" and "shroud" all meant rope and rope arrangement, or rope fitted and running through pulleys, or that "rigging" was "tackle" and "tackle" sometimes meant "a machine for raising or lowering heavy weights, or that again the "rigging" included the duck sails. These seamen were themselves "sail-loosers, sail furlers and sail trimmers" when they went to sea, but underneath their tarpaulins they were just hard-working men who knew that if they did not know all there was to know about those sails and riggings, there was always the marline spike lying handy on the deck to assist their memories.

How the rope rigging or shrouds or tackling were made must be discovered in the old-fashioned rope-walk of those early days.

XXV. THE ROPEWALK

~~~~~~

Just picture a cordage mill with the sky for a roof,
the ground for its floor, and equipped with crude hand-
made machinery from blocks and wooden sticks . . .

The Columbian Crew

~~~~~~

That Long, Long Walk

"THE old Gloucester ropewalk reached from the site of the
old windmill where the tavern now stands, almost to the
Cut Bridge and the Old Pump. It was finally cut up and used
in different places. One part was taken on a raft across the
harbor and made into a dwelling at Rocky Neck; another
part became a blacksmith shop, and the endpart was turned
into a stable. I remember the sign that used to hang on that
old stable; it was in very crude printing with the Ss all turned
the wrong way and it read HORSES BAITED AND
CARPETS BEAT. I don't remember where the rest of
the old walk went, but you can see that they were long old
affairs.

"At the end of the walk was a large wheel turned by a boy
—somewhere around eight to twelve years old—with a crank.
At the end of the crank shaft there was a hook. Around this
hook the hemp was caught after a ropewalker had wound it
many times about his body, enough of it to go all the way to
the end of the long walk. The walker moved backward and
paid out the hemp slowly in front of him as he went, while
the boy kept the hook turning and so twisted the hemp. At
the end of the walk the hemp was hooked onto something
there to hold it in twist. Two or three twists must be made
and then all laid together to form the big rope."

THE ROPEWALK

There, one might say, was the whole story of early American rope-making in a nutshell. Gloucester was one of the many Atlantic seaport towns which made its own rope for its seafaring boats and captains. The usual ropewalk, extending on and on far beyond the limits of any ordinary mill or shop or factory, was made in this lengthy form for a very good purpose. Rope to be strong and evenly wound must not be allowed to turn corners or even bulge around curves, since at once one side of it becomes stretched to make those curves, while the other shortens itself up to wait while the big outer edge is coming around. A woman who sews knows that she gets a puckered seam if she holds her two pieces of cloth folded back over her finger for convenience in placing the stitches. A company of soldiers knows that in a pivot swing, the man at the center must keep turning in just one spot while the rest swing about him. A child knows this same truth when he "snaps the whip." With rope the idea is the same, and the ropemaker contrived to have as few turns as possible in his rope length. A ropewalk might be as wide as twenty-five feet, although they were generally narrower, but some of them stretched for more than a quarter of a mile out into the fields; some measured 1200 feet and there is one still in operation in Philadelphia which is 2200 feet long. The first ropewalks had no roofs over them, for a shed a quarter of a mile long would have been quite an undertaking for a beginning industry in those beginning days, but if one but planned the spinning of the hemp on fair days, the walker could get along very well with sun and sky. In time, of course, the sheds began to appear and later the sides were enclosed so that the spinning could go forward regardless of the weather.

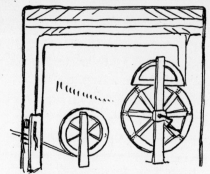

Early type of ropewalk wheel

Early Ropewalks

Joseph and Philip Veren had a ropewalk in Salem, Massa-chusetts, in 1635. The next one recorded was at Boston in 1641, the occasion for it being the building of the ship *Trial,* a one hundred and sixty ton vessel. One John Harrison had been asked to come to America because he was a skilled rope-maker at home in Salisbury, England. He had his home on Purchase Street and set up his "rope field" ten feet and ten inches wide, at the foot of Summer Street. Here was no covered way for the walkers but a series of posts fixed in the open fields and enough of them to permit the making of the largest size ropes. He had been assured the monopoly of the rope industry for twenty-one years, but, shortly, along came John Heyman who "set up posts" with intent to use them, claiming that he too had a license to make rope. Harrison's insistence upon his rights finally brought the revocation of Heyman's license and Harrison had the field to himself. In 1662 we see John Heyman busy at his own ropewalk in Charlestown.

"There are several rope-makers who have large and curious ropewalks, especially one Joseph Wilcox," some one wrote of Philadelphia in 1696.

THE ROPEWALK

New York's first ropewalk was built in 1718 and located on Broadway "opposite the Old Common," which would lead us to believe that New York had been leaving the building of ships to other seaport towns, also that old Broadway must have been rather comically bedecked with her mighty rows of posts in the heart of the town. Being of wood, and draughty places, these old ropewalks in time became nuisances because of the frequent fires which started in them, and in many towns were delegated to spots more remote from the center of things.

Norfork, Virginia, had had a ropewalk for sometime before 1777 because at that time James Woodie was presenting his bill to the House of Delegates for working fifty-four days to hire wagons and superintend the removal of the implements of the ropewalk works from that town to Warwick, the same State. By 1794 Virginia and Maryland were leading the country in the rope industry.

Rope for the "Flying Cloud"

It mattered not whether it were North or South, the need for rope was felt equally wherever ships set out to sea, wherever men toted large burdens, or animals dragged heavy weights, or workers went down into wells, or climbed to high spots. Especially was it necessary that a seaport should have its ropemakers, for sea captains not only had need of much and many ropes but must plan and oversee the exact quality of the rope which they knew their ships would require under every strain and circumstance. No kinking rope for them, which would disturb its "lay" and thus reduce its strength; no rope too large for their blocks and pulleys which would soon show resulting wear.

All rope was made by hand until the 1890s but today most of it is made by machinery. Four ropewalks remain in the country, and their owners, although they have installed little cars which run on narrow tracks to carry the ropemakers on their long way, insist that only in the long ropewalk and by hand can large rope be well made. They like their "walk laid rope." One of these is the Fitler ropewalk which has been busy in Philadelphia since 1804, ever since a ropemaker named Kurtz planted his posts in the "Northern Liberties." Just as the hemp slivers were bound together into rope, so were new generations of the family drawn into the old business, giving the country another of those inherited sequences where one family has carried on from one century into and through the next. The office of this firm was in one spot for one hundred years lacking three months, before it decided to try a new spot. Beverley, New Jersey, has a ropewalk longer than the one in Philadelphia which makes an approach to the half-mile mark, and is called the longest walk in the world. At Boston there is the ropewalk at the Navy Yard, built in 1834 and turning out rope the following year. Here, for sixty-three years, rope had been spun by hand, and one may say by foot, the change to machinery coming only in 1898. By 1810 there were altogether one hundred and seventy-three ropewalks in the country, and one still on Broadway in New York City.

THE ROPEWALK

Rope — From What

Rope could be made of almost any fibre or material which could be twisted. The one requirement was that the vegetable substance have a flexible and tenacious fibre. When it was hemp which was used, its grade depended largely upon what part of the plant was taken, the center producing the finest grade which has a silk-like sheen and is pale, almost white in color; the second grade from next the center is heavier and darker than the first; while the outside of the stem is more brittle, browner and of a coarser quality. Each grade how-ever had its place and usefulness. Hemp and flax were used oftenest in early rope-making, although as early as 1610 the newly arriving Virginians had found "silk grass for cordage" and in 1612 discovered that the common water flag of the marshes, when boiled, would yield an integument remarkable for the strength of its texture as well as length, which would make both fine linen and stout and enduring cordage. "Bulrush" was another word for this common flag of the marshes, and from the bulrush came the "junci," the substance used in making rope, which in turn became eased off into "junk." In time the worn-out remnants of old rope took on this name of "junk," which is probably why we apply the same word to all sorts of trash. "Junci" was so legitimate a term in the 1700s that they still called the kind of land which abounded in bulrushes "juncous."

Six Careful Steps to Rope

Roughly, the steps in rope-making may be given as follows:

Hackling	Tarring
Spinning	Forming the Strand
Winding on Bobbins	Laying the Rope

but even when we know this much we find that, as in all industries, there were local and individual ways of taking each of these steps — which is of course the reason that the study of old customs and ways of work is so worth while. The standardized methods of today will yield little of individuality to future generations — but probably they will not care at all, for individual ingenuity will have become a joke of the primitive years.

The word "cordage" covers a multitude of things, for under its banner we find string, cord, line, rope, hausers and cables, all cordage because they are made of twisted fibres. The processes for their manufacture were nevertheless much the same.

The Hackling

The word "hetchelling" is a common one still, in New England, and means the first treatment which flax underwent from our ancestors, after it had left the field and was to be prepared for spinning and weaving into cordage. Sadly enough there really is no such word, although it has appeared often in print. On the other hand the word "hatcheling" has been correct for many centuries, with "hackling" coming along as a close synonym, but shadowed by the incorrect "heckling." Apparently our forebears loved their Es better than their As. We thus find that the hemp must first be broken or hackled to separate the unwanted from the wanted parts, and to lay it in long loose threads called "slivers." The implement on which this was accomplished was a simple board with pointed iron teeth inserted in it about an inch apart, across which the hemp was drawn back and forth until its fibres had been made to lie evenly side by side, and the too coarse parts removed. The bundle of hemp caught together after it had been punished on the sharp needles, was a "strick."

Spinning, Tarring, and Reeling

Now we come to that surprising person, the rope walker and spinner, who spent his life walking backward instead of foreward with the rest of mankind, and not on a tightrope but upon the good hard earth. Some of these walkers simply had a rope-lathe which they fastened into place on a post for the making of the season's rope. In 1847 a Southern planter jotted down in his daily journal that "two of the negroes fixed up the rope lathe and made rope for half a day," showing that the process was not too difficult to undertake for a few hours' work. Rope is still being made casually in the Tennessee mountains. Without benefit of shelter, a post, a warping block, wheel, warping hooks and plenty of land made up the better part of the whole crude outfit. An old writer put it thus: "Posts large enough to permit the making of the largest sizes of rope were fixed in the ground in the open fields, and upon these the cords were suspended and the ropes made."

At the head or fore-end of the walk stood a large wheel; some said that it looked like a spinning wheel, others like the heavy wooden wheel used overhead in an ox-sling, and others saw it still differently. It has a hand crank for turning, generally by a boy but later by horsepower. The larger the wheel the greater the power, of course. One of the old wheels had a band passing around the periphery and over the semi-circle above it, in which was placed a number of wheels, the pivots of which ended on the far side in a small hook. Now the spinner gets ready for his walk. He takes the stricks of hackled hemp and wraps them about his waist in a thick eight-inch belt, with the bights in front and the ends crossed

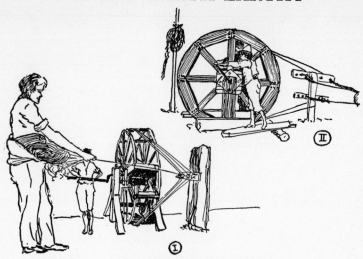

*They are still making rope from the waist, in
foreign lands*
Courtesy Columbia Rope Company

over behind him. First he draws from his hempen belt enough
fibres to form the size of rope which is desired, bends them in
the middle and fastens the bight upon a rotating hook.
Instantly the twisting begins and the spinner starts walking
backward while with his left hand he draws from the front
of his belt with an even regularity, always the same quantity
of fibres to add to those which are already being twisted. In
fact the twisting yarn draws after it other fibres. His right
hand, covered with a woolen cloth to protect the forefinger,
seizes the fibres and compresses them so as to keep the yarn
of uniform size.

Along with this spinner was probably another, going likewise his backward way, for there could be as many spinners
as there were hooks on the axes so that several lengths of yarn
could be spinning at the same time. Quite as important as
the uniform feeding of the fibre was the constancy of the

turning wheel; and the turn in the yarn was determined by
the rate at which the spinner walked. Since a ropewalk was
of such length it stands to reason that some sort of support
would be needed for the growing yarn, and so "bearers" extended from the posts, or wall if such there were, over which
the twist was passed. The end was finally reached and then
various things might happen, according to local habit or the
need of the hour. Thus:

"Two or more spinners might be going down the walk
at the same time and at the end they joined their yarns
together, each then beginning a new yarn, and returning to
the other end where the second spinner again took his yarn
off the whirl and joined it to the end of the first spinner's
yarn, so that it continued on the reel. When a sufficient
number of yarns were spun, they were wound from one reel
to another, passing between the two through hot tar, and
were then ready to be twisted into ropes. This old process
was used until the 1820s, when horsepower was employed
for the wheel."

Some one else says: "When the length of yarn is finished,
it is either passed to one side upon the bearers to await a
finishing process or wound upon a reel and put aside until
wanted. If it is to be tarred it is done now. A number of yarns,
two or three hundred, are laid together in parallel order, and
passed through a boiler of hot tar. As it becomes saturated,
the bundle of yarns is drawn through a hole — a 'grip' —
which presses the tar into the yarn, and removes the surplus."

Again: "When the thread is spun to the planned length
the spinner cries out to another, who immediately takes it
off the hook and gives it to a third person and then attaches
his own fibres to the same hook. In the meantime the first
spinner keeps fast hold of the end of his yarn, to prevent its

untwisting or doubling, and as it is wound on the reel (at the head of the walk) proceeds up the walk, keeping the yarn of an equal tension."

At the Navy Yard in the old days of "walk laid" rope, they, at this point, bound together the ends of the spun yarn and wound it on bobbins, tarred it, and set it away for several months to be sure that it was properly aged before it was put into rope form. They found that a good spinner could in a ten-hour day spin about 13,000 yards of yarn from eighty pounds of hemp.

No rope was thought fit to go to sea unless it had been tarred, but today some kinds of rope are not tarred at all, and considered quite as durable. One of the things about rope which reminds one that it was once a living thing, is the way it wears upon itself through an internal friction, its strands in imperceptible motion, constantly rubbing against other strands, and causing a slow but eventual destruction. Saturated with tar before the strands were laid together, this friction was lessened and became harmless.

Forming the Strand

Slivers of hemp were spun into yarn
Yarn was twisted into strands
Strands were laid into the hawser
Three hawsers formed a cable

Terms designating the same process and the same equipment, varied sometimes in different sections of the country, but the process of twisting the thin yarn into a firmer strand and then into the ropes for different purposes were practically the same everywhere. In general, cordage had, and has, three strands, or "gin," and until the rope grew to the size of an inch and a half it was "laid" through the use of the spinning wheel, in the "twisting and laying walk." The "hither" ends of the yarn were fastened to separate whirl-hooks, or "whorls," while the "remote" ends were hooked to the "loper," a swivel. So that the intertwining should not proceed too rapidly for the good of the strand, there was a "top" which was interposed which had two or more notches terminating at the apex, as well as a handle or "staff."

At the head of the laying and twisting walk was the "tackle board," made of two stout timbers stood vertical in the ground with a strong board across them in which was a horizontal line of three holes for the reception of winches and forelock hooks. At the far end of the walk was the "sledge" whose breastboard was similarly equipped with holes and hooks. When the desired number of yarns had been affixed to the hooks, front and rear, the sledge was drawn back. This started the twisting at both ends but in opposite directions. Naturally a contraction of the yarn would set in which would drag the sledge toward the tackleboard. From one fourth to one third of the original length was diminished in this process, but what was lost in length was gained in strength, for the yarn was all there still although in a different arrangement.

The word "hard" designated the twist which was given the yarns and when this was sufficient the new strand was complete. It is worth noticing that before the Revolution the word "strand" still had to do only with the edges of the sea, while "cord" and "line" and "string" filled the bill in the vocabulary of the ropemaker.

Laying the Rope

Although the strand might need two or three hundred threads of yarn to form it, we now come to the magic three of this industry, in the "laying" of the rope proper. To the middle hook of the tackle board the three strands were attached, and each was laid into one of the three grooves of a cone-shaped piece of wood — which we have already met as the "top" — which receded from the twisting hook as the rope was formed. This was the simple "laying" or "first lay," and brought the strands into the formation of a "hawser laid" rope. In the "shroud hawser-laid" rope we find the "second lay" in which four strands are twisted around a corepiece placed in the center to make a more solid rope. The "third lay" was also called the "cable laid" and was three finished ropes twisted or laid together to form a cable. By some the word "laying" was applied only to the making of small rope, while "closing" was used for larger or cable size rope.

Twist and Lay

Not just any old rope would do for just any old task, for sea captains and well-diggers and trawlers all had different uses for their rope and began to make their individual needs known to the ropemakers. It became a matter of how to twist and lay rope for countless industries and uses and the ropemaker who could meet these demands was the man who put his cordage on the map for years ahead.

In order to keep the fibres as nearly as possible parrallel in the finished process, yarn, strand and hawser were all twisted in certain directions. The yarn was spun to the right. The strand was formed to the left. The hawser or rope was again laid to the right, while the cable, composed of three "right lay ropes" was laid to the left. There must be care also in how the rope was coiled and how it was left to stand; in other words, rope was a something not dead but almost as alive as a willow stick which, after being severed from the tree and left to die, takes root and springs into leaf at every opportunity. The wise seaman or oildriller did not leave his rope in too hot a sun or even in an unventilated storage place, but gave it ventilation as he would have to his pet dog. Many years had passed though before these little points had been learned about rope. It was learned too that "plain laid" rope uncoiled counter-clockwise, while "cable laid" and "left hand lay" rope uncoiled clockwise. Above all it was gradually learned that rope must not be allowed to kink, for kinking "disturbed" the rope and confused its "lay," and if persisted in could easily cut the whole rope in two. Far better to take no chances and keep the coil of hard-earned rope on a flat base with its end drawn up through the center of the coil. It is rather a jolly thought that although the present day often insists upon steel cables, the heart of these must still be made of hemp, for nothing has ever been found so capable of mooring a vessel as the vegetable, blue-flowered growth.

Block and tackle and knot

Ropes and Ropes

The simplest twist of all is that of two strands which the sailmaker uses for thread. Ropes have ranged in size from three-sixteenths of an inch, to the newly achieved three-foot hawser on the ship *Queen Mary*. The farmer needed his single-yarn binder twine, as much as the skipper needed his hawser for the anchor, and there was need for towing ropes

—painters—for lobster marline, trawlers' lines, lariat ropes for the cowboy, and great ropes for placing caissons, and for working in mines and wells. Fisher needs there were a'plenty for deep-sea lines and hand lead lines, not to mention shrouds of the sailing vessels and ropes beyond computation which kept them all afloat. In the smallest farmhouse or cabin, rope had its place, and when freshly washed clothes could be taken off the bleaching greens and pinned to a rope line to blow in the clean pure winds, the housewife had indeed obtained a boon. Before ropes were made available in isolated homes, the leather thong or whang was worked overtime, but so far as is known was never twisted into rope in this country as was done in Egypt.

It is always well to know the ropes.

XXVI. TAR KILN AND PITCH POT

Tar water is of a nature so mild and proportioned
to the human constitution, as to warm without heating,
to cheer but not inebriate.

BISHOP BERKELEY

Each to His Own Method

THE handy-man and the tinkerer, the mechanic and the
shopman, all had those same six mechanical powers for
effecting all of the different sorts of work to which any of
them might apply themselves. If the pulley would not accomplish it perhaps the lever would, and there were always
the four remaining resources, the inclined plane, the wheel
and axle, the screw and the humble wedge. For the man who
worked even more closely with the earth, there was a similarly
limited number of methods of refining the various earth
substances, and these methods become familiar to us as we
trace a path through the old out-of-door industries. The
leech-tub is conspicuous when we are working for soap and
potash; we have already become acquainted with the burning of limestone and iron and shall see charcoal undergoing
the same process; the kiln and the sun and the air are the
agents of such substances as tobacco, hops and peat which
must be dried; brick gives us the need for baking; paints and
numberless other things had to be ground; and boiling and
distillation are resorted to for salt and tar and turpentine and
other makings. The earthy products then could generally
be made to yield their riches if they were leeched, burned,
boiled, dried, baked, distilled, or ground.

The versatility of the pine tree is as famous as that of some

313

men. For instance, just one of its varieties, the pitch pine, can produce from its gum such a wide range of useful products as turpentine, rosin, tar, and pitch.

Georgia's Home-made Tar

In the making of tar and pitch we find two of these processes being used, the smothered burning of the pitch-pine to obtain tar, and the subsequent boiling down of the tar to obtain the pitch. An old Georgian who spent his boyhood on a plantation remembers that his people made their own tar and did it with very little trouble. He says:

"We had a big board with a shallow groove cut in it a little way in from the edge, and an outlet on one side. They took a big iron pot and turned it upside down on the board with its edges inside of the groove. Inside, the pot was filled with split lightwood splinters — we always called it 'light'ood.' They'd set fire to these and they'd flare up and burn hard, they were so rich with juice, and in a little while you'd see the hot liquid tar begin to run down and out into the groove and then slowly creep around to the outlet, where it would drop down into another pot set to catch it. When they made it this way it was just for small home uses, but when they made a business of it of course they had regular kilns.

"It was used for several things. It was a sure cure for 'boy's ground itch,' but you had to mix it with grease if you didn't want to take off the skin, Ground itch? Why, that came from wading in water after rain, some worm it was. They used to use it too mixed with grease to save your hair, and the darkies smeared it on the hogs to rid them of lice. Some folks made a salve of it for sores, or you could drink a little in water for your health.

"Sometimes they made tar out of the stumps of dead pines

that had been used for something else and were saturated with rosin. They'd sweat out the tar. Pitch is the next thing. Tar is thick liquid, and when this is done down there'll be some resin-oil and the rest will be pitch. Pitch is harder than tar. It's to naval stores — you know, turpentine and rosin — what black molasses is to the sugar industry."

The Tar Kiln

It is evident then that tar is nothing but the natural gum of the pine tree forced out of the wood by heat so closely confined that it became a smother. So simple a process it was that wherever the pine tree grew, there some tar might be found in the making. New England was not too particular about having the pitch pine for her tar making, but used pines of whatever sort, according to her early historians. New Hampshire's method in the 1700s was to stand the wood upright in piles and cover it completely with sod dug from the base of the pile. At the top a hole was left open and the fire started, causing the melting tar to flow out at the bottom into the circular trench in which stones and bricks had been laid as a gutter. From this gutter the tar was led to barrels sunk in the ground near by.

Less crudity and more tar were obtained after 1800 by using clay to form a circular floor with a declivity toward, and an opening at, the center. From this center opening a pipe was buried under the ground which led two feet beyond the circumference of the floor, where it conveyed the liquid tar to sunken barrels set to catch it. Upon the clay floor the dry pine wood, split into pieces, was piled, and the whole structure covered with earth thrown on in great shovelfuls, all except the hole at the top where the fire was to be kindled. After the kindling even this hole was covered, but in order to temper the heat and keep it at the right power to keep the tar flowing out through the bottom, the tar burner knew exactly how to thrust in his long pole here and there to let in air where it was needed.

The Tar Heel State

North Carolina became such a tar-burning State that the name "Tar Heel" was given it. It was said that so much tar floated away as waste into her streams, that the folks walking barefoot just naturally gathered it upon their heels for permanent wear. But for all of her years of burning tar the methods have not needed to be changed to any extent. Tar burners still keep busy splitting up long ten-foot pitch-pine wood into "splinters" that you can hold in your hand, they dig their shallow circular basins into which it will be piled, but now it seems best to lay the wood horizontally instead of vertically, and always with the inner ends slanting downward to the centre of the pit. The pile when completed is generally about as high again as the workmen who have built it. Some kind of a surrounding board structure is then built a foot or so back from the circumference of the pile so that earth can be banked against it and all air cut off from the base.

For a full week the workmen must divide the task of constant watchfulness lest a flame get started and the whole mass be consumed down to ashes. So they keep throwing on more and more earth wherever a weakness begins to appear. During this time the tar is running out from a central outlet to flow into an underground wooden trough which carries the stream finally into the open where it falls into the vats or barrels stuck in the ground. As much as seven or eight barrels should be produced from a kiln of this size, and "kiln" is the word which is applied to this pile of wood and earth, and the tar must be dipped by hand from the vat with a long-handled dipper and started down another trough to the barrel in which the tar will be kept or sold, and this trough-end will diminish until it is exactly the size of the bunghole into which the tar will finally pass.

Making tar in the "Tar Heel" State, from the pitch pine to the barrel

Pitch from Tar

When William Bartram, the son of the great naturalist, visited the wonders of Florida in 1776, he found, west of Mobile, "three vast iron pots or kettles, each of many hundred gallons content, for boiling tar into pitch." In Carolina about the same time they were using the earth itself for a kettle for making pitch, digging large holes near the tar kilns and lining them with a thick coat of clay. Into this they led a quantity of tar and simply set it on fire, letting it flame up and evaporate for a long enough time to turn the mass into pitch. When this process was finished, they "lade" the pitch into barrels and took the next lot and so on until they had completed the output of the kiln.

Pitch is the solid after-product of tar, and is of a darker color —"pitch black." Our first thought of its usefulness is for calking seams in boats, and North Carolina has a memento which she cherishes. "Blackbeard" Teach was a famous pirate of around 1709, and had his home on the Pasquotank. On Bath Creek, what is believed to be the round brick foundation for a huge kettle, still stands, and it is thought that it was there that Blackbeard Teach boiled his tar for calking those vessels of his which meant bounty and escape and life or death to him. He had plenty of pines for his "light'ood," plenty of privacy, and probably plenty of pitch. He did not use the great oven after 1718 for at that time some unromantic person caught him and cut off his head.

This open-air way of letting flames dart skyhigh during the tar-to-pitch process, seems to have affected the nerves of some folks, for a group of Philadelphians who had a habit of "boyling" tar on the public wharf were told by the city council to change their habits and play their dangerous game far from wharves, and at least twenty feet from any building or haystack.

Never a Covered Wagon on a northern trail, nor a Conestoga Wagon on a more southern one, but had hanging beneath its body the necessary tar-pot. This was generally made of a piece of hollowed tree about a foot long, and fitted with a wooden cover which could never come entirely off, since it slid up and down on the great leather loop of strap with which the pot was fastened to the under crossbars, and which was fastened to the inside of the pot. In the center of the cover was a hole in which the long tar stick stayed when it was not on active duty on a wheel hub. Since these wheels were sometimes between seven and eight feet high — for the taking of humps and rocks with the greatest possible ease — it is natural that they should need much greasing on a long journey. The tallow in the tar-pot was what those wheels wanted and needed, but the tar came along too to keep the tallow from running away.

Wooden tarpot which hung beneath a Conestoga wago, Pennsylvania

One lonely old woman in New York who is biding her time to go to heaven, is sure that there is a hell for some of us, for she has found the recipe for tar and brimstone in the Bible.

XXVII. LIGHTHOUSES

~~~~~~

Mariners and others interested in having knowledge of anything wrong with any aid to nagivation in the St. Johns River District are requested to give prompt information to the superintendent of lighthouses at Charleston, South Carolina.

~~~~~~

Life Savers

UNDER the comprehensive title SUN, MOON AND TIDES, the above notice is carried daily in coastal Southern newspapers, being perhaps the most earthy and elemental notice in the whole sheet, for it savors of life's verities. In the same column and under the heading ST. JOHNS BAR, three full stories are told, each in but two or three words, stories having to do both with the high seas and the hearts of women and men on shore, and they are, "Passed In" and "Passed Out" and "Vessels in Port." Behind all of this careful pronouncement regarding the ships at sea, stand tall, impressive, and unfailing, those watch towers and guardians of both Davy Jones and the sailorman, the Lighthouse.

Lest some complain that keeping a lighthouse was not indulging in one of our early industries, it may be well to recall that an industry was "habitual diligence in any employment, either bodily or mental," and surely no industry of the first two centuries in this land called for more of sinew and earnest thought than that of "keeping the light" in one of the early established lighthouses. Today, along with many other buildings of the past, some of these tireless-eyed guardians are being put up for sale to the highest bidder. It behooves us therefore to take notice of them while they still

LIGHTHOUSES

stand in their old familiar lines and proportions, and before they become whatever Tom, Dick and Harry may choose to make them. Some of the large and ancient ones will probably live on as mementoes of simpler days of lighting the waves and pointing the way, even though they are superseded by modern electrical automatons, but some will go, are already gone.

Mount Desert Rock, Maine
Stamford Harbor
Tybee, entrance Savannah river, Georgia
Montauk Point, Long Island

The *Boston Sunday Globe* carried an editorial in September, 1934, which tells the tale of the old lighthouse as poignantly as may be:

> The abandonment of nine coastal lighthouses in Maine is the snapping of another strand in the frayed hempen hawser which tethers the vessel of New England's life to a mooring in salt water. The motor car competes with coastal steamer, our fishing schooners, their sail areas cut down and their bowsprits sawed off, are turned into motor craft; even in Summer a coasting schooner is now a rare sight, and the square-riggers vanished long since. Thus vanishes also a type of man, bred by conflict with elemental nature, who once gave his color to the life of Yankeedom. Mechanism may replace human labor, an automatic gas flame may light a wave-swept rock as reliably as a man-tended beacon, but it fades the color out of the marine painting as well as out of the human portrait.

OF THE EARTH EARTHY

Surely no words could better tell the loss which accompanies so many of our gains, but at least we can learn and remember those means by which life's canvas was so valiantly colored for and by our forebears, before it is too late. Isolation may well be called the great outstanding fact of the life of an early lighthouse keeper, for even if he were not settled on an island offshore, he was apt to be high up on a point of land where few passers-by could be hailed on the way to store or wharf. Faithful care of the light was the first item in the light-keeper's creed, and aid to the shipwrecked perhaps the second, for while care of those who had been wrecked was not his required job and he received no extra pay for it, it became often his desire and accomplishment. Old records have preserved some of these acts of heroism carried on at the foot of the great lighthouses, but doubtless there were thousands which were never recorded in writing. No man would be a lighthouse keeper who was made of lesser stuff than the best which was vouchsafed to the make-up and calibre of mankind.

There are many cases of lone keepers being badly hurt and yet keeping their lights trimmed and burning; and all were constantly mounting spiral staircases of endless steps and replenishing the oil, with their chief reward an easy conscience or the sight of a ship being kept away from treacherous rocks beneath pounding breakers. The probability is that the storms of the 1600s were no more severe than those of the 1900s and we may read with joy the following report turned in by W. W. Roff a dozen years ago from the Alaskan Coast. It might easily have been the story of an ancestor but proves that, given a chance to meet Nature squarely head-on, men can still measure up. The Mendenhall Bar Lights were apparently scattered through the harbor rather than all in one lighthouse.

> The severe cold weather caused me no end of trouble keeping the lights burning during the last quarter. At one time it was as low as 16 degrees below zero, and a severe Taku wind blowing. Chimneys broke almost as rapidly as I could replace them, and at one time all four lights were out for 24 hours before I could reach and relight them. At this time the bar was unnavigable and I tended lights over the ice on creepers, carrying oil in this way by pack saddle on my back. At one time the ice was from 1½ to 2 feet thick and very high tides caused it to break the floes, which, with the strong tide in the channel, made tending lights difficult and danger-ous. At one time my boat was swamped, and I lost a case of oil and nearly perished by freezing. It seems a miracle that any of the light towers are left standing. I have watched big floes strike them; they would sway and crack but yet stand.

From the other extremity of the country comes this report from the keeper of the post lights on the St. Johns River in Florida in 1912:

> I arrived at the light at 9:30 A. M. I took the lamp out, and as I went to blow it out it exploded and knocked me off the light (twenty-two feet), and I did not know anything until 12 M. When I came to I found the lamp gone. I crawled back to the boat two hundred and fifty feet, got another lamp and put it on the beacon and lit it. Then came home (eight miles). Injury, broken leg just above the ankle and severe bruised shin and arm and lick on head.

OF THE EARTH EARTHY

One of the first concerns of the newly formed Federal Government was the safety of men and ships at sea, for during the first session of the new Congress meeting in 1789, the work of erecting and maintaining lighthouses was provided for. It goes without saying that before this or from the early 1600s until the last quarter of the 1700s there had been lighthouses devised and cared for by the Colonies themselves, for the Atlantic coast had a way with it sometimes which would have done credit to the oddly named Pacific. It was natural then that as soon as the Colonies were joined together under one national head, these earlier lighthouses should have been passed over to it. Massachusetts led the Colonies in the erection of lighthouses, having six to her credit at the forming of the new Congress, built and located as follows:

1716	Boston	1771	Cape Ann
1746	Brant Point	1784	Nantucket
1768	Plymouth	1788	Newburyport

New England's other lighthouses of this period were:

1749	Beavertail, Rhode Island
1759	New London, Connecticut
1771	Portsmouth, New Hampshire

For the middle Colonies:

1764	Sandy Hook, New Jersey
1765	Cape Henlopen, Delaware

For the South:

1767	Charleston, South Carolina

Boston Light 1716

Many of these are still active, or if not active, still standing.

Light for the New Country

It is claimed that Cape Henry lighthouse was the first erected in the United States, and while this may be misleading to the casual reader and those who know of earlier ones, the claim is still probably correct, for it was built in 1791, two years after the words "united states" had been tied together to mean something to the world. The lighthouse at Portland Head, Maine, and the one at Tybee, Georgia, were erected in the same year, and may claim a like honor.

Lighthouses seem to grow in dozens, for one dozen sprang up before colonial days were ended, and another dozen

OF THE EARTH EARTHY

appeared before the close of the century, and among the later ones we find the South getting her share at last.

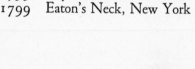

1791	Portland Head, Maine
1791	Cape Henry, Virginia
1791	Tybee, Georgia
1795	Sequin, Maine
1796	Bald Head, North Carolina
1797	Montauk Point, Long Island
1798	Baker's Island, Massachusetts
1798	Cape Hatteras, North Carolina
1798	Cape Cod, Massachusetts
1798	Ocracoke, North Carolina
1799	Gay Head, Massachusetts
1799	Eaton's Neck, New York

"Hatteras' Blinkin' Eye, worst light in the world."
Original 1798. Replaced 1870

LIGHTHOUSES

The first decade of the 1800s saw fifteen lighthouses erected, the second decade, twelve, while within the next half decade there were twenty-six more established, showing that we cherished our brothers at sea and the ships which they mastered.

Naturally the Atlantic coast was furnished with lights a good two hundred years before there were any on the Pacific coast — the first there being in 1854 — and it was still later that Alaska had warning beacons set up.

Cape Florida Light

Lighthouse Personalities

Some of the old lighthouses have, figuratively, outshone others through their more strategic positions, their location at historic points or through their length of service. Boston Light is famous as the grandparent of them all and after two hundred and twenty-one years is still in commission. The Cape Henry lighthouse, while still standing, has handed her arduous duties over to a youngster built in 1887, but she will continue to be the old familiar landmark for sailors and be saved for future generations. As it happens, it was at this spot that the first Virginia settlers of Jamestown landed, after being driven off their prescribed course by a mighty storm, and the old lighthouse will remain as a monument to this arrival on April 26, 1607. The State of Maine could hardly carry on without the light at Portland Head. Old for that section of the country although not built until 1827, the Cape Florida Light below Biscayne Bay, is counted one of the chief figures in lighthouse history even though it no longer functions; its keeper of the light in 1836 was killed by the Indians. Old Tybee at the entrance of the Savannah River in Georgia, and Cape Romain in South Carolina — the latter now a leaning tower — stand high in notable service. Secondary towers were erected along inter-island waterways and at the mouths of quiet harbors, so that there are many old lighthouses now outstanding because of more than a hundred years of lighting the waves.

Visibility for a great distance was the first concern in designing our lighthouses, just as it was for those first beacon-tenders in past ages when a structure was built high enough to hold a bonfire at its top which could be seen far out at sea. But visibility was not enough, for the seamen must not only be able to see the light by night but the tower by day and seeing it, recognize it as standing at a certain known spot. This called for personality again, some distinctive sign or dress to make it unique. Shape and height and thickness all entered into this effort at personality, and color and the way that color was applied. The Light on Anastasia Island, off

LIGHTHOUSES

St. Augustine, wears spiral curves of black and white; Cape Henry's young escort is striped vertically in black and white; Montauk is white above and dark below; Henlopen Light was white below and dark above, and Old Ocracoke runs white as far up as the light. Some wear red.

Personality and individuality appeared also in the light itself. When night came on and the light, rather than contour and coloring, took over the task of warning, the mariners watched for the frequency and intervals between flashes, or watched to see whether there were any flashes at all. When Old Hatteras Light was relieved by the new "Blinking Eye," that "graveyard of the Atlantic" off Virginia had a new note to be set down in the mariners' primers.

1. Ocracoke Island, Pamlico Sound,
North Carolina 1798
11. Henlopen Light, at Lewes, Delaware, which
"went into the sea" a short time ago. Built 1765

Simple Lights

The first lighthouses were of stone or brick and their height depended upon where they stood, on a high cliff or a lowland. One step beyond the raised bonfire on a high frame, they

329

were all equipped with some sort of lantern holding at least one lamp. These lamps used wicks and some sort of oil, either that of the whale, or from pressed plant seeds, or good home-made lard oil. The sides of the lanterns were glass panes or "lights" which were gradually increased in number to make more of a sparkle; and then in time came the idea of a rubbed-up metal reflector. Kerosene and coal oil made a step ahead and from the former was developed the incandescent oil vapor light which gave a white glowing heat. The incandescent oil vapor lamp placed within a carefully designed lens of great size was the most powerful light known until the coming of electricity, and is retained in some of the lighthouses.

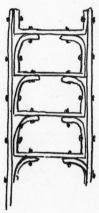

Iron ladder which was the last lap on the trip to the light, at Henlopen. Rescued and preserved

It was the eventual understanding that great lenses — large enough to hold several men standing up—which would gather and concentrate the rays from the lamp within, would send rays out over the sea in a powerful beam, which brought us our first long-distance aid. Those who lived near a flashing lighthouse know the almost lifelike nature which they seem to possess, and this regular flashing of a great eye was accomplished by the revolving of the entire lens which was regulated by a clockwork arrangement with heavy weights hanging from it. It was the winding of these heavy weights every few hours which kept the light-keeper's nose close to the grindstone, for if the well-known and watched-for flash should lag or vary, the individuality of the lighthouse might be mistaken by those who were steering by it and the mariner be literally "all at sea" as to his whereabouts. There had to be also the perfect cleansing of the lantern's lenses, oil in full measure, and plenty of leg power for climbing those spiral stairs.

Cape Henry Light. Original

Cape Henry

Standing as she does on the landing spot of the first English settlers, on April 26, 1607, because she is perhaps the first of our national lighthouses, because the shifting dunes which surround her give her a mystery quite her own, and because she has beauty of line, old Cape Henry standing on her point in Chesapeake Bay deserves some special attention. More than a light, she is a monument, watching at the cradle of the nation, as far as the English speaking people are concerned. Fortunately the study of its history has been made easy because of the work done by various historical societies of Virginia, one of which now holds from the Government the deed to the old lighthouse. In 1789 Virginia gave the site for the lighthouse and in 1791 the Government erected the tower. It is of red sandstone supposedly brought from the Rappahannock and stands eighty feet high. The keeper's cottage stood not far away at the end of a curving path and near by was also the oil cellar which had been provided for in the contract for the building, but both of these marks are now gone. During its ninety years of service its old-fashioned lamps with their crude reflectors used the different fuel oils as they came along, fish oil, sperm oil, lard, and kerosene. In 1862 the lamp had three wicks, each with its own oil pump, and although this lamp was destroyed early in the Civil War, the light was restored in 1863 under guard.

One hears tales of much greater antiquity for some of our old lighthouses than Government records show, and so there are some who claim that Old Cape Henry was built in 1690, while in Florida others claim that the Anastasia light off St. Augustine is much older than the Government allows and that it replaced an ancient lighthouse of the Spanish. Tradition may be quite as safe as Government findings in some cases, and yet when claims are made for the purpose of boosting local business it is not difficult to detect and discard them. There may have been beacons burning to aid the boys at sea which are now quite forgotten, and tradition regarding them would be quite as welcome and valuable as the most dignified official guarantees.

XXVIII. THE CHARCOAL PITS

Coal Meant Charcoal

TO MANY of our forefathers, mined coal was entirely unknown, to some it was only a name, and to the majority of them "coal" was a homemade affair made by burning and charring wood in a home-made coalpit. A kind fate had decreed that this home-made coal should make a hotter fire than that which was dug from the ground, and so everything was well, with a wood fire burning on the hearth or in stoves when they came along and charcoal burning in the shop forges where great heat was needed for many of the handcrafts. Mined coal came in time, but while it was considered a convenience by some blacksmiths, many preferred their own hotter charcoal, and for fuel in the home used wood for many years more. Thus when our grandfathers spoke of "coal" they meant the kind which grew in their coal-pits where their felled trees had been stacked, after deadening by "girdling" perhaps, and buried in sod and left to smudge and char for a few days.

Woods for Making Coal

Some of the Southern States avoided pine wood when trees were being chosen for making into charcoal, and the harder woods like oak were marked instead. In New Jersey they used pine for charcoal-making and found that one and a half cords of that wood would make eighty bushels of good charcoal. In Florida, too, pine was in favor, the trees being belted — the bark cut in a girdle around the trunk to die — making good "cole wood." To the man who looked with discouragement upon his great forests which must be cleared before he could get "new ground" for planting, the charcoal

333

burners in his vicinity were a godsend, for he could give his wood away for the asking, saving only that kind which was best for fences.

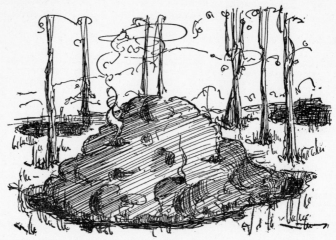

Charcoal pit covered with earth to smother flame,
Bayard, Florida

Florida Charcoal

Pernell Smith is a negro charcoal burner near Bayard, who lives in a low old farmhouse beneath one of those Florida trees whose ordinary branches are greater than the trunks of most trees elsewhere. One turns off the highway into a grassy road to reach the house and passes beneath the giant arms of the live-oak to do so. Just a "little fur piece" along the grassy road brings one to the charcoal pit which is Pernell's business office and factory. Here his charcoal kiln rises like a monster anthill and close by are marks of other coal-pits which show now as great blackened disks on the ground among the trees.

"My father used to take two or three weeks to burn a kiln, for he used sod. Before he died he learned from other charcoal burners to cover the stacked wood with pine-straw"—to a

334

THE CHARCOAL PITS

Northerner this is pine needles — "and then put the black charcoal dust or soil on top of that. He piled the logs different too. They were big tree trunks and he'd just roll them up against each other until he had a long ridge or moundlike. I always cut my wood into four-foot sticks and stack them standing up toward the middle with a yard space left under in the middle for the fire. After that is going good and the stack measures about twelve feet across I put on the pine straw and the black dirt and smother the whole mass."

As we stood talking together of his work, thin yellowish smoke was seeping up the sides here and there, which Pernell reported meant that all was well within and the job progressing as it should. "There now, you see that blue smoke coming through over there? That means the fire's getting ready to break out." He grasped the shovel and began to pound on the side of the mound, then shoveled up earth from the encircling trench and threw it over the leak. Wherever the blue smoke appeared he was there with his shovel.

"It's generally finished anytime from thirty-six to forty-eight hours, and I have to get up four or five times every night, when I'm burning, to look at it and see that it isn't breaking out. If it got going it would burn the whole pile up and I'd lose all my wood. Sometimes I have to poke it some to stir it and start a good draught. When it's done I rake off the dirt and there lays all the big black chunks to sell. The little pieces that have broke off I rake off to one side to use for covering. I always keep the two kilns ready. One burning makes about ten bushels at ten cents a bushel, but I only get about $6.00 for it 'cause I have to buy my wood." Here is certainly ambition on a farm which does not produce its own timber.

OF THE EARTH EARTHY

A New Hampshire Charcoal Pit

When George Mayo, who lived in East Alstead, New Hampshire, was a little boy about 1850 he had his eyes open for what was going on about him, and as an old man loved to recall the simple devices which his neighbors had for carrying life on simply. The following is reprinted from *Candle Days,* with change of names:

When I was a boy and going to No. 8 school — it used to stand up in Eb's pasture—I always loved to slip away after school and go upon Messer Hill and watch Harvey Taylor the blacksmith at his coal-pit, when that time came round. He went up once a year and took his food along and a cover to sleep under and didn't come down until the fire was out. You see charcoal made a hotter fire than wood, and the fire on his forge had to be hot. First of all Harvey would dig away a lot of sod, then he'd set the wood up on end like an Indian's tepee, with a hole in the center for a draught; short pieces there were at first, only two or three feet, but getting longer for the outside of the stack as it grew bigger. When the stack was done, it was high as Harvey himself and about twelve feet across the base. Then he built his fire right under the little stack in the middle and it would smoulder for three or four days. With the sod he had dug up first, he would cover the whole stack; and this and the earth he used kept the fire from breaking out into a blaze. Poor old fellow, he got almighty tired of watching that fire before those days were done with, for he had to watch night and day that the air didn't get through the covering and send his whole stack up in flames. The slow heat charred the whole stack, you see. I forgot to say that right in front, he left a little opening to see through so he could watch the fire. It was that hole that I liked to peek into. No, the wood did not have to be very big, even those pieces on the outside were not a foot through. Some made their pits long and narrow and boarded up the sides, but Harvey didn't, and I liked his good old way the best.

The underlying principle in this process of charcoal burning was, that if the supply of air is limited only the more volatile ingredients of the wood will burn away, and the greater part of the carbon remain.

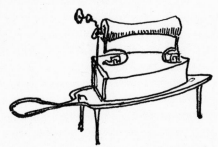

Polishing-iron filled with charcoal through twisting rear door. New Castle, Delaware

Uses

Since charcoal burns with neither smoke nor flame it became a useful fuel for those rooms which had no fireplaces or other means of heating. One old New England hotel had holes cut in the walls between the bedrooms close to the floor so that a brazier or charcoal burner might be set in them and lend their heat to both rooms. Thus down a long corridor, each chamber would have two stoves. The old brazier was like an iron pail or bucket fitted with a perforated iron cover.

Polishing irons for laundry work were heated with charcoal, a little door at one end opening for the refilling.

For two centuries charcoal may be said to have been the fuel for manufacturing processes, and we will soon find that that iron made in the "charcoal era" was far superior to that made later with coal or coke. Even roadmakers became

337

charcoal-minded. The *Cleveland Herald* in 1840 carried this story:

> Charcoal Road: Timber from six to eighteen inches through cut into lengths twenty-four feet long, piled lengthwise in the center of the road about five feet high, being five feet wide at bottom and two at top, then covered with straw and earth in the manner of coal pits. The earth required to cover the pile taken from either side, leaves two good sized ditches, and the timber, although not split, is easily charred; and when charred, the earth is removed to the side of the ditches, the coal raked down to a width of fifteen feet, leaving it two feet thick at the center and one at the sides, and the road is completed. Through the winter and spring while nearby sections of corduroy road were felloe deep in mud and nearly half-axle tree deep where the logs were broken, the new road had no mud at all, and was like hard washed sand with no ruts.

Down at Key West lived Panther Key John, a Florida charcoal burner who used to burn his charcoal and sell it from his own boat along shore. When we learn that he lived to be one hundred and twenty years old and carried on his trade until the end, it would seem that charcoal might be an aid to longevity.

Fifty coke ovens in a row at Low Moor

THE CHARCOAL PITS

Coke and Coal

It was coke which finally superseded charcoal for use in the old iron furnaces and all those others which had used the latter exclusively as the pioneer heating power. A very early definition of coke is that it was cinders made of pitcoal; a later one was that it was "mineral coal charred"; while a man who saw the change from charcoal to coke take place in the old iron mines, says it is "coal burned out and down to carbon."

It is said that the first coal was discovered in 1817 and while not accepted as a fuel was yet used somewhat on blacksmith forges, but in Chesterfield County, at Midlothian, Virginia, coal mines were discovered and worked before 1730, these being probably the oldest in the country.

XXIX. THE PEAT BOG

Those that are first cut vp are called Turffes of the vpper part, and such as are taken downward, are called Peates. —NORDEN, 1607

Here Too

OUT of Ireland where words have a sweetness and ring quite their own, comes the expression "peat winning." To "cut" sod for burning would, to an American, be strange enough in all truth, but to "win" peat from bog and lowland would be something quite different, and possible only in a land where elves and leprecauns dwell in fern and loveapple shade. We have all read of the peat bogs of Ireland, but many of us have never known that our ancestors cut or "won" peat right here in America and kept themselves warm with it through stiff New England winters.

In Coldbrook, New Hampshire, there was David Noyes who burned peat which he had cut on his own farm. His granddaughter describes the place in a certain field which she remembers as having been pointed out to her as the place of peat, when she was a small child. "There was a great hollow about an eighth of a mile long and not very wide, and above this rose a little hill, and then over the peak there was good firm ground." This peat bog was used productively through the middle of the 1800s. On Salisbury Plain in England they were burning "peet" until 1840 and perhaps longer. In Ireland they still burn peat.

"Peat is a species of turf used for fire," says an old definition, and then goes on to explain that turf is a clod covered with grass, and most necessary to a "horse-courser" for

340

racing purposes. In this way we see that the turf which went into peat-making or winning, was the same old turf or "grass-ground" with which we are all familiar but having a swamp base.

Composition

The composition and make-up of peat is, roughly, decayed vegetation found in the form of a bog or morass, marsh or common swamp, where the water is fairly still but not stagnant, and the earth stratum beneath it impervious to drainage. This means that the vegetation is always mainly aquatic, made up of reeds and rushes and moss grown through the years. Given these attributes the process of disintegration and decomposition of the turf sets in through molds and fungi, and moist atmospheric oxidation. As this continues, the sedges and reeds become waterlogged and sink to the bottom forming the underlayer of a mass which will in time grow to a considerable thickness. As the weight increases with the added deposits the mass becomes compressed and carbonized, but for all of this a moist atmosphere is essential.

The peat of one bog might appear very different from that of another, some of it being a light pale yellow and looking like compressed hay with all of the original plant formation remaining visible; the peat of another bog might be a solid mass of dark brown substance, looking like blackish clay, while still wet, and, when dry, like coal in which the original wood texture still shows plainly. Peat is also "kin" to bog-iron, for the latter was found in our early peat ponds or bogs.

Tools and Muscles

"Winning turf" was surely done not by art or play — the usual ways of winning — but by good honest conquest, for

the wrenching of peat from the earth brought forth resistance
and called for plenty of muscle on the part of the winner. It
called too for a special tool of good handwrought iron which
would cut and not break under strain. These peat-cutters
varied in style so greatly that it would seem that if one were
well fitted for the work, the others could hardly be so.

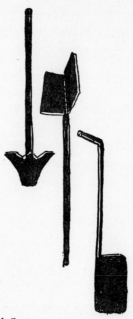

Three different peat-cutter designs

One was like a butcher's cleaver, with a long slender
handle which turned at sudden right angle away from the
plane of the spade-end; one looked like a trident for spear-
ing brook fish, with three points turned upward and the
narrow straight end turned downward for cutting. Ireland's
peat cutter had two planes at right angles to each other to
cut bottom and one side of a sod at the same time; this was
called a "slane." At old Monroe Tavern in Lexington,

THE PEAT BOG

Massachusetts, built in the 1690s, peat was the usual chimneyplace fuel, and it was the task of the chore boy to see that there was never less than two bushels handy to the hearth at all hours of the day and night.

As a general method of cutting peat, there is first the shallow foot-deep trench formed by cutting out chunks of bog a foot deep and three or four feet long. When one long layer has been removed, another is dug from the same trench, and if the deposit be at all solid, steps are formed in it, while the digging goes lower and lower. When the water is reached the work still goes on, but with longer handled cutters. Once removed from their ancient bed, the sods are drained in the open, and then stacked so that the air can circulate between them for their complete drying. After they have been turned frequently all sides about, they become dry enough to be used as fuel, and are known as "dug peat."

Peat burning is among our really obsolete practices (although The Depression brought it back for the few ingenious) and the very thought of burning earthy clods calls today for a stretch of the imagination for most of us; and yet, the burning of peat for warmth is no stranger than the burning of coal, which likewise has been formed of decayed vegetation slipped beneath the surface of the earth, and after eons of time comes back to us as stone fuel. It must be the dampness and original sogginess of the peat which has made its burning seem anomalous.

It is good to know that we may add to the accounting of ingenuity of our forefathers, the productiveness of supposedly worthless swamp-lands to keep a fire roaring up the family lum. Undoubtedly many log cabins, riverbank cave homes, and even less crude dwellings in our first settlements used the sod or peat roof. The Scotch spoke of "casting divots"

or "paring turf" to roof their homes, and when peeved were
known to say of the peevee, "I often wish there was a het
peat down his throat."

XXX. THE IRON WORKES

With many a stiff thwack, many a bang,
Hard crab-tree and old iron rang.
                                    —BUTLER

Early Bog Iron
IT WAS not necessary to go mining for iron ore when the
first settlers began to need iron for their daily living, for in
bogs, sometimes peat bogs, scattered all over the Eastern part
of the country, ore was awaiting them. It all seems quite too
simple to be true, but this much needed bog ore was usually
found loose on the bottom of ponds in from two to twenty
feet of water, where a man equipped with tongs similar to
those used in gathering oysters, might rake up for himself
from a half to two tons of ore a day. The nice part about it
all was that within twenty-five years these bogs, no matter
how thoroughly they had been raked, would reproduce their
ore for another gathering. Large ponds sometimes yield from
one to six hundred tons a year, with swamps or bogs, doing
proportionately well. It must have been a great lark when one
of our forefathers went out fishing on a rainy day, and pulled
up iron ore on his fishook and found that he had a new farm
product which could be turned to good account on his home-
made forge. Surely this was a land of promise.

These bogs or "brittles" were found in limestone valleys
in New England; and a man's meadow might have strips of
iron-stone, called "sledges," from which our great sledge
hammers get their name. For many years the iron for the
building of ships came from England, but the iron needs of

the run-of-mill New Englanders were supplied by seaboard ponds, swamps, and iron-bearing springs.

A West Virginia flatiron made on a home forge

To be Exact

Here we have the simple facts behind these handy supplies for home needs:

> Seaboard ponds deposited large quantities of oxide or sesquioxide of iron. This mingled with vegetable mould and combining with water partially solidified into spongy bog iron ore, or crystallized into a more compact hydrate. This would yield twenty-five percent or more of crude iron. Sea shells furnished a flux which easily fused it and when mixed with silicious ores the product was fairly good metal for castings.

At the base of it all were the soluble iron salts, and it was upon them that the vegetable decay in the water acted, percolating through the deposits until the water emerged and the air caused a decomposition of the iron solution and spread itself as reddish "sludge" along the shores of the meadows. In Maryland the river Patapsco was first named "Bolus" by Captain John Smith in 1608, because along its banks he found a red clay resembling "bole armoniac" which, interpreted, means earth, plus a bitter salt, made of urine, salt soot, etc., which combination was very valuable.

As in the study of salt, so we find in that of iron, that no

product of the earth is ever entirely independent of all the
others if it is to be developed and refined. Salt could be produced in quantity only when it had fuel in quantity somewhere near, and as if a wise Providence had planned it all
carefully, oils and gases were soon discovered in the same
neighborhood. If iron were to be produced for man's use it
must be taken from the ground and made liquid, and this
could be done only where there was an abundant supply of
fuel close at hand. Think of the surprise of the man who
found in his hillside layers of iron, lime, and coal. It was
estimated that a bog-iron furnace could be run through one
season's blast, on from eighteen to twenty thousand acres of
timber to be turned into charcoal, because wood, like iron ore
had the knack of reproducing itself in a cycle of years, a sort
of rotation of crops and cuttings making it possible to keep
some of the timber always at the right size for using. Water
power became a necessity for a furnace or forge, and this
was rarely far off.

Primitive Processes

Back in the 1600s the ways of turning out iron were naturally crude, and yet the ironworkers of those days caught a way
of work which persisted, in essence at least, for two succeeding centuries. Perhaps the simplest way to present old iron
working is to let each process, in its own shelter, speak for
itself.

THE FURNACE. The terms "furnace" and "forge" are
used interchangeably often, but the real furnace was the place
for smelting the rough ore or iron, melting and separating it
from the foreign substances in the rock; while the forge had
to do with shaping the smelted ore into forms. However, we
act with the Romans, and call them by whichever name the

Old Roaring Run furnace of the early 1800s.
Maurice Langhorne

local folks preferred. One old furnace had a hearthstone with the sides rounded up in an arch about a yard high and the rest of the furnace lined with brick. This furnace had a run or "tap" of iron of about eight tons every eighth day or "founday," and this amount was produced by twenty-four loads of charcoal. To every load of eleven quarters of coal

348

(charcoal) one "load of mine." Another old forge was an outdoor hearth upon which the ore was piled directly and melted by the heat of the charcoal or wood piled with it. Soon some one thought of an idea to hasten the process and great "leathern lungs" or bellows, were made and swung between tree trunks or green posts, their pipes connected with the bottom of the "forge" (this time). The "trompe" came next in line of improvement, and this was a pipe filled with "water and air" to form a draught. The "cotolan" forge introduced the openings in the construction which were really flues through which a draught might pass to keep the fire at an even temper. The "cold blast" was worked out by applying water power to the great bellows. With the coming of the flue we approach the later furnace which was a more permanent structure of huge granitelike sandstone blocks, with an opening at the top through which the ore and limestone and charcoal were poured to burn together for the elimination of impurities. From an opening at the bottom the fluid ore was run. At first the wood was placed at the bottom of the furnace in order to burn up through the rock ore placed just above it, while the limestone was placed on top so that it would melt and, running down through the ore, act as a flux. Later they were mixed in together as the quickest way for all to function. When the ore was ready to be tapped it was run out into sand molds to form "pig iron." Anyone who has ever seen an old sow nursing a line of twelve little newborns all laid out in an even row at right angles to her feeding apparatus, will see the reason for calling iron which was run into one long sand trough with numberless straight channels running off on each side, "pig iron." The term "tupelo" was used in South Carolina about 1785 to denote a small furnace for melting small quantities of metal and "drove by horse or from the main blast." This may have been a corruption of "cupola" which was the name given elsewhere to the vault or hopper directly above the fire.

THE BLOOMERY. The word "bloom" was not an inappropriate one for the flowering iron as it flamed into radiance, and so a mass of crude iron undergoing its first hammering was given that name. In 1777 a "bloom" was an iron bar, the result of the first steps in iron making, and the form from which all wrought iron would develop. In the bloomery, then, at the bloom forge we see the crude iron, now cleared of its old earthy companions, being worked directly without passing through any form of casting. The bloomer-man of the late 1600s had fitted up a foot-blast or treadle and could make one little bloom, or less than a hundredweight a day.

THE PUDDLING POOL. Puddling was converting iron which had been cast, back into a state of malleability where it could be handwrought — the shingling and welding of manufactured iron into plates and rods and bars. An old puddling pool still remains at old Demarest Landing on the Hackensack River in New Jersey.

THE FORGE. The blacksmiths tell us that today's iron cannot compare in quality with the iron of fifty years ago. One reason is that the old iron made with charcoal was benefitted in some way which was lost when the "charcoal era" passed. "It won't take hard handlin' and it rusts bad," and it was the great amount of "handlin' " which the old iron received which gave it much of its power to bend but not break. The forge proper did no smelting and therefore the blooms or bars of iron which came to it had to be reheated before they could be worked upon; it was then hammered and "squeezed" to be made of the proper purity to be called first class. It was probably not until another century had passed that the trip-hammer was brought into play for the making of new blooms. This old trip-hammer was one of the simplest and yet most ingenious of the old workadays' implements. A woman described it thus:

"We were tramping along a Southern country road with not a sight of man or his work anywhere about us, when gradually we became conscious of some rhythmic regularity which seemed to come from up above our heads, behind the roadside growth. So we clambered up the bank and went over the ten-rail snake fence and still saw nobody. But not far away something was moving and as we went closer we saw that a great pole was moving up and down like a seesaw. It was one of the old trip-hammers pounding cornmeal. The pole seesawed across the crotch of a crooked stump and at one end had a heavy wooden block fastened to it, and at the other a smallish wooden box. Beneath the block stood a gum hollowed out to hold the grain. Then there was a hollowed tree length resting on a wall which brought the water from a brook up to a height to fall into the box. We watched it at work. The box slowly filled until it could hold no more and then the weight of the water carried it down toward the ground. When this happened the block at the other end of course went up. Then by this time the box had emptied and come up again and so the block had nothing to do but come down, and with a crash it went into the center of the hollowed gum, pounding the corn there into smaller and smaller bits. Later we heard that this was called a 'plumping mill' in that section." So also power came to the old forges. After the smelting furnaces began to form their hot molten metal into pig iron, the cooled bars were still sent to the forge to be beaten into a purer state before going out into the world as "marchantable goods."

THE ROLLING MILL. Here were heavy steel rollers through which heated metal was passed to be made into sheets, or rolls, or various desired shapes. In Massachusetts the rolling mills were mostly busy rolling nail-roads from which spikes and nails of all sorts were later worked out by hand by the man who bought them and took them home for rainy-day work, because no machinery for making nails was available for nail-making until 1783 and it was long after that date before nails became easily procurable. Rolling mills were generally run by the huge outdoor wooden mill wheel standing under or over a brook's flow.

THE SLITTING MILL. The name tells the story, for here the sheet iron was slit into bars sometimes so small that it was used in cotton cards. Here they rolled iron as well, for part of their work was making hoops for barrels and casks. The following picture gives us real information:

> Slitting and rolling mills, a new invention of the 1600s, containing eighteen bushels of mixed, roasted and broken ore. The fire was at its height in about ten weeks, and a hearth of good stone would last forty foundays or weeks, during which it never went out. The hearth was never used a second time. The forge had two hammers, one the finery and one the chafery. At first the metal was brought into a state of blooms and anconies. A bloom was a foursquare mass two feet long, prepared by beating a loop or mass of metal weighing about three hundredweight, with iron sledges upon an iron plate, and afterward with the forge hammers worked by water. This was called "shingling the loop." After two or more heats at the finery, the mass was brought to the ancony,

the middle of which was a square bar of the desired size, and the two ends rough square lumps. At the chafery the bar was completed by reducing the ends to uniform size with the middle portion. Three loads of wood coal made a ton of iron at the finery, and one load of small coals at the chafery. One man and one boy at the finery made two tons of iron per week. Two men at the chafery made five or six tons a week. Both finery and chafery were open hearths covered with heaps of coals, blown by bellows in the same way as the furnace, but not so large.

The sow trough lead from the smelting furnaces to the moulds. The pig was any of the moulds in this pig-bed. The sow and pigs received two heats at the finery and three at the chafery. A heavy square mass was a "half bloom"; a bar with two knobs was a bloom. The greater end was the "mocket head" and the lesser the "ancony end." At the fourth heat the mocket head reduced, at the fifth heat the ancony end came to the state of a bar.

MAGNETIC SEPARATOR. One of the ingenious ways of separating ore from its encumbrances was used on the Ausable River in Northern New York about 1810, and was called a magnetic separator. In shape it was like a hogshead open at the ends, with many horseshoe magnets inside to catch the ore as it was shoveled in at one end to run down and out at the other. Another way was to have sieves which were "jogged" up and down by hand, but by 1835 a way was found to separate the ore by water, and the old ways were eventually abandoned.

"Time was when any man who could raise means to start a forge fire on his own account, could work it with advantage and profit. You mined on the surface, just backed the team into holes and carried it away. Pretty soon you might see some flame coming out the top of the old furnace, then you would throw in some more charcoal, and when it was time to tap it, you'd blow the horn for the hands to come and help." It was all quite casual.

Iron furnace, Pompton, New Jersey
Where iron was made in Burlington, New Jersey

Chronology

Since bogs and swamps which produced iron ore were scattered rather widely throughout the early Colonies it is natural that there should have been many ironworkers and colliers at an early date. It is therefore impossible to give credit to all who pioneered in this important industry in their respective localities, but a few men were outstanding enough to warrant special mention, while some others have been remembered through early notes or traditional lore.

1585   Iron discovered in North Carolina

THE IRON WORKES

1609   According to archives of the Spaniard Don Ma-
guel, an attempt to manufacture iron in
Virginia and machinery erected.

In a letter, Sir Thomas Dale speaks of a
"goodly iron mine at the head of the Falls
in the Powhatan... on the Pembroke
side."

1619   The popular belief has been that the first iron
works in the country were those erected on
Falling Creek, Virginia. Some of the old
building is still standing a few miles outside of Richmond. In 1608 samples of ore
were sent to England and eleven years later
John Berkely and twenty others, nearly all
skilled workmen, arrived to work the iron
mine. Soon established, they were in 1622
massacred, with the exception of a boy,
probably Berkely's son. The next year Englishmen came to erect a bloomery at the
same site but gave up the attempt because
of the expense. In 1712 George Sandys
chose the above spot because of its ideal
combination of ore, water and wood. Here,
two and a half centuries after the massacre,
slag from the first iron making was found.
A claim is made for a bog iron furnace near
the Tuckahoe River in New Jersey at
about this date, but who could have been
playing around that section at that time,
even for game, is not mentioned.

1630   Thomas Hudson had the first New England
bog iron workes at Lynn, Massachusetts.

1637   The Bay Colony granted to Abraham Shaw one
half of any "coles or yron stone wch shall
bee found in any common ground wch is
in the countrye's disposing."

1639   Brent's Forge, in St. Marys County, Maryland.

1643   The first successful iron works in New England was erected by John Winthrope, Junior, and ten others, banded together under the title, "Company of Undertakers for the Iron Works." This was near Lynn and the Saugus river. From near-by bog ore, eight tons of iron a week were produced, and a forge was later installed for its refining.

1646   A forge at Braintree, Massachusetts.

1652   A forge at Taunton, Massachusetts.

1655   At New Haven, Connecticut, an iron mill erected by John Winthrope, Jr. and Stephen Goodyear at the southern end of Saltonstall pond. Ore brought from North Haven, or Bogmine Wharf by water.

1679   Iron workes at Shrewsbury, New Jersey, Colonel Lewis Morris.

1696   Iron-stone or "Oar" found in Philadelphia.

1600s   Welsh settlers were mining iron in Iron Hill, near New Castle, Delaware.

Old Speedwell Iron Work, Morristown, New Jersey. Called also the birthplace of the electric telegraph

THE IRON WORKES

The new century saw Maryland setting up her first furnaces in 1715 about three miles above the later Havre de Grace on the Susquehanna, where remnants of the early works are still discernible with the old blast furnace which was run by water power during the 1780s. Pennsylvania had her first furnace, according to some authorities, at Colebrooke Dale in 1715 with the famous Anthony Morris and friend James Lewis as owners. Others claim the first one for Thomas Rutter who built a furnace on Manatawny creek in 1718. The second one which was built on Durham creek in 1727 seems to stand undisputed. Then came Peter Grubb's great iron mines at Cornwall "ore hills" or "ore banks," a few miles south of Lebanon, New Jersey, and his Hopewell furnaces, and all owned by Peter himself until his death in 1754. The Elizabeth furnace of Baron Henry William Stiegel a few miles from his handmade town of Manheim, was active during the 1760s and part of the 1770s, and a plant for casting iron was added which gave us the much sought-after fire-backs of quaint design. Up in Moodna, New York, a furnace appeared in the 1740s; Passaic County in the Jerseys was busy with iron in the 1760s; Ethan Allen was working in a blast furnace in Vermont in 1762; Cedar Springs, South Carolina, had her iron works during the Revolution and the Queensboro furnace was turning out cannon for the war, at West Point at the same time. In Virginia the Jerdonne family, or "Jordans," had already begun its interest in iron works before the middle of the century, so that it appears that America was a land of iron to be had almost for the asking.

The Iron of Virginia

The deep folds of the Alleghany Mountains stretching lazily caty-cornered across Virginia are proving today that even a

mine and its furnaces and forges may become places of beauty
if only man will keep hands off for a few decades and give
Nature her chance again. Back in the 1700s men were
pressing slowly west through the Old Dominion, and
glimpsing along the faces of the deep-sided gorges, those
touches of rust color and burnt sienna where iron ore had
been exposed through erosion. Quick were these pioneers to
grasp at this means of gaining wealth, and iron mines became
established in large number, especially in Alleghany County,
where they ran their day to be abandoned later not for want
of ore but through the exigencies of changing conditions and
easier production elsewhere. Today they stand not as ex-
amples of failure but of an early and vast energy and progressiveness on the part of our forebears who ventured into
unknown gorges gutted with limestone caves where snarling
cat and hungry bear were at home.

*Old Cedar Run furnace near Grahams' Forge,
Virginia. 1832*

In spite of the supposed unloveliness and grime of these
old mine centers, the names which the countryside furnished
for them were sweet and fair, and they became Longdale,

THE IRON WORKES

Low Moor, Roaring Run, Double Ridge, Iron Gate, Rich Patch, and all were situated on such interesting places as Horse Mountain, Potts Valley, Iron Mountain, Sweet Springs, Clifton Forge and others equally appealing. Some mine owners chose to honor their wives and daughters and called their furnaces the "Dolly Ann," the "Bess," the "Jane," or the "Lucy Salina." The "Jane" has almost passed from memory but the negroes still remember the "Loose-Alene." In one twenty-mile area eight furnaces were working at the same time.

Old stone building at abandoned Longdale furnace

The Longdale furnace was the oldest large one in the State, and stands today, Nature-rescued, with its old buildings fast falling to ruin, but guarding its precious old steam engine of ancient vintage. The Jordan family which went to these parts in 1823 were responsible not only for Longdale but for several other ore property developments in the county. It was in 1794 however that perhaps the first furnace of all was constructed and this was at the Iron Gate where the Jackson River had worn away the mountain and exposed great mineral wealth, on land granted to Robert Gillespie by King George III in the 1770s. Within this narrow gate, between the great rainbow arches of whitish sandstone and close to the river's edge, some one, possibly Gillespie himself, established an iron furnace, setting it up against the great cliffs and sending outbuildings as far as the great rocks in the river to find permanent and easy foundations. Most of the rocks used in the furnace proper were smoothly faced by hand and cut into great oblong blocks. Over the opening at the top a little house was set, to which the oxen made their way along the side of the cliff to dump the ore. An arched opening toward the river gives strength to the structure and shows what looks like a "pair of stairs" coming down from above and going back into unseen recesses out of sight, the receding iron sides of the firebox and immense solid blocks of tremendous width. Within this great hopper, thus stepped back, the burning of the ore took place. At the left bottom a shallow opening still remains to show where the tapping was done when the burning was finished.

The ore was mined from the mountain above and at first brought down by oxen, but later loaded into little cars and run down a steep track by a rope twisted about a drum. At this mine the ore was not found in large lumps, the largest being only about three and a half feet at the base and tapering toward the top and measuring about one ton, but its quality was said to be of the supremely best. When the Jordans took over the running of this mine a nest of buildings sprang up a few hundred feet up the Jackson at the turn of its sharp elbow, and a great man-high stoned tunnel made a short-cut behind the point of land where water was brought through to the stone-walled race which followed close to the river's bank. Here arose three refineries, a chafery, a run-out fire, two hammers which were worked by water-wheel and turned out one hundred and thirty bars a year. The frontispiece of this book shows the remnants of the house-topped furnace, the casting house at its feet, and the ruins of another building.

When the iron was ready for shipment it was loaded on to old bateaux which rode low in the water, and sent down the river to Lynchburg. Men supplemented the force of the river when necessary, by using long poles against well padded shoulders, as they walked from front to back of the boat with tireless regularity. A rough log-house sheltered them aboard their ship and a pile of earth made their hearthstone, and great and many were the adventures of those splendid trips. Arrived at Lynchburg the bars which had come out of the bowels of Iron Gate went into a rolling mill where they were passed beneath great rollers to provide wheel tires, and later, new-fangled rails to carry people about in cars.

It was the old "forge" or furnace, up under the cliff just around the corner of the mountain, which finally gave Clifton Forge its name. Mined on both walls of the gorge, the iron took men high up above the running river, and into places which could not stand the strain of their picks and hammers and one day a wall gave way, and now an old opening is pointed out where lie buried the skeletons of two men and a mule. Even the old forge had its tragedies, for within it not long ago a bandit shot his captives in the place where once colliers had burnt rock, and was himself shot. Back in the old tunnel, tramps now find shelter against cold nights and squat about their campfires with the rock moun-

Clifton Forge furnace in Iron Gate today.
See frontispiece for yesterday

tain hanging far out above their heads. Sometimes a weird light burns close to the ground down the gorge, but an old man says calmly: "I've been seein' that light for forty years when I was out coon huntin' at night. It's nothin' but the gas comin' out of the ground — once in a while it goes out somebody has to light it again and then the young fellars all think they've found somethin'. But speakin' of lights,

362

you ought to been around here when old Low Moor mine was workin'. The word would come that they were goin' to tap or run a cast that night, and everybody'd drive over to see. The sky would be bright red all over. Funny that was too, because the iron itself was dead white heat. They'd cart off the slag too in iron cars that they run in under, and dump it over the side. The molten stuff, it looked like thick cream. They did three casts in twenty-four hours. Did you ever hear that the furnace-flue dust that settled up around the top of the furnaces was a kind of zinc and killed insects? Sort of a bug death."

*The better type of mill-worker's house at
Low Moor, Virginia*

Here and there through Virginia one sees the remains of these old mines and furnaces. There will show a bit of fine old wall, or a tree growing up through the old furnace top, or there will be a nestling of low red cottages left in a snug valley where the miners once lived. Sometimes it is a cellar hole or a half-filled cave entrance among gray sandstone and gory, red-smirched rock, which will give the clue. Each man-made scar is compensated for with some still more ancient mark of loveliness, until one seeks rather than avoids the old mining centers knowing that wherever iron ore was found, there too must be found the rough and alluring elements without which it could not have been formed. Of all these ancient mines of this section none can compete in beauty with that of Clifton Forge, where its great rainbow background of sandstone is visible for miles through the gaps, and the giant devil's-slide plunges down the gorgeside between massive upright slabs of weather-worn rock, marking not only the faithful old stone furnace but the very ages themselves.

Run-of-the-mill red cottage for the other workmen

XXXI. THE FOUNDER'S FOUNDRY

~~~~~~

"The Pot calls the Kettle black."

~~~~~~

Old Steepel Bell of New England

"Bells, Bells, Bells."

THE oldest of all the shops in London stands in the White-chapel Road, on ground used for the making of bells in an unbroken succession of years since 1570. Silver-tongued, brassy-voiced, broken-toned, harsh or sweet, the bells of the world have been ringing out for centuries. The Spaniards brought us our first bells and hung them in their missions to summon the Indians and themselves to prayer. Two of these old bells have been found, and stand in the rooms of the Florida Historical Society at Jacksonville, one dated 1709, the other 1758 and bearing on one side the words, "Santa Maria" and on the other side "ORAPRONOBIS" in one long line. In Louisville, Georgia, there hangs in the center of the old slave market an old American bell which was cast in New Orleans by the American-French in 1772, and decorated with French inscriptions and Frenchy medallions. In Philadelphia in 1713, William Hill, the Beadle of the town, "lately in a heat broke his bell," but where that bell was made we do not know.

It was Paul Revere — who may be classed with Benjamin Franklin and Thomas Jefferson for a vast versatility — who became our earliest well-known maker of lovely bells, bells which soon after 1792 began to lure the desires of those little towns which had started building their white-"steepeled" and white-spired Meeting-houses. Many a house of worship was built without its bell tower and made to wait for years before money could be found for a "Paul Revere bell" since a spire would have to be raised. Paul and his son divided the honors in this bell-making business and their foundry was at the lower end of Foster Street near Lynn Street, now known as the Boston Causeway.

When our forefathers had learned the almanac by heart and were forced to turn to the wordbooks for reading, they found there that to "found" was "to cast brass and so forth into bells," and it is for this reason that we give bells first place here. The Latin "fundere" means simply, to cast, without specifying the metal, and gives us that wider range which includes the great number of small country foundries in which many things were cast besides bells.

Bell Tower, State Capitol grounds,
Richmond, 1824

While they were not usual in this country, we too had our early companiles, or bell towers. One of the loveliest, and sturdiest because it is still with us, stands in Capitol Square, Richmond. It has a red brick, square base and an open-work cupola of wood painted white in which the bell is visible. It has a fine flavor of the artistic past when architecture was somehow easily made beautiful. It grew from the following legislative enactment of March 1824:

367

OF THE EARTH EARTHY

That the Executive be, and they are hereby authorized to have the house, commonly called the Barracks, now standing on the southwest corner of the capitol square, sold at public auction, and to have a small two-storied house, with a cupola for a bell, not exceeding twenty feet square, erected, for the accomodation of the guard stationed for the protection of the Capitol, on or near the site of the said barracks!

Certain present-day records tell us that it replaces a wooden tower from which had pealed forth the call to colors for the regular and volunteer troops for the earlier protection of the city, and this gives us an earlier date for a Virginian bell tower which apparently stood close to the old barracks which were demolished. Although the two old structures may have been combined in the one new one of 1824 which was to "accommodate the guard," the now old Bell Tower is thought of today only in connection with its bell, which sounded its tocsin until the end of the War Between the States.

"Bell-metal" from which many of the early bells were made was an alloy of copper and tin; some think of it as a mingling of almost any kinds of metals which happened to be handy. Although one of the English Kings' pet activities was chartering copper mines to their newly settled children in the American wilderness — that their own pockets might be better filled — we were getting our first copper and brass in the 1600s from Wales, in sheets to be worked up into needed domestic vessels. By the end of the 1600s we were casting some of the brass in New England foundries, the Jackson family being the most conspicuous at this work; when Jonathan Jackson died in 1737 he seems to have left everything but bells to his credit, there being door knockers, candlesticks, brass basins, various kinds of table ware, brass-headed hearth dogs, and pots and kettles, all made on American soil. It was from Holland and England, though, that most of this hollow-ware was brought. To be sure, a London brazier was working beneath his sign near the old Market Slip in New York City in the 1740s and by 1780 little old Manhattan had her own Kip and Montague "founding in brass." Brass was an alloy of copper and zinc, both to be found in this country.

It may safely be said, however, that iron was "run of the mill" in the majority of foundries.

Founder Men

At Cold Spring on the Hudson, back in 1820, the men who worked in the foundry were awakened in the morning by the blowing of a horn through the streets, and by six o'clock were at their work. At six-thirty they stopped to eat their breakfast and at seven sharp were back at work again. At noon the horn blew again and the afternoon stint was from one until six. Who would want a Founders' Day in those times? It was the coming of anthracite coal which made the casting of iron easily possible, and in 1826 when Seth Boyden of Newark, New Jersey, discovered a way to cast iron which was as good as that which had been previously imported, our dependence upon England for malleable iron was ended. A usefulness was now found for some of the iron which was not good enough for "bar iron" upon which there would be great strain — this was cast into hollow-ware.

There are a few outstanding names in connection with our first foundries, the knowing of which will constitute at least a beginning knowledge of an industry which has been called by some "the foundation of our American industries." We have already met Thomas Hudson of Lynn, Massachusetts, who, about 1630 discovered bog iron ore near the Saugus River and set up the first New England iron works. Hudson's name is generally overshadowed or even forgotten for the better known one of Joseph Jenks, who came from England about a decade later and set up a foundry close by, winning perpetual national fame by casting our first iron pot in 1642. It was a little pot, holding only a quart, but great in publicity for its caster. Jenks was however a real "iron master" and received backing for his work from Governor Winthrop and the Colonial Assembly, for in 1646 he received one of the first patents granted in the country, and it was for improving sawmills and scythes, and to this was added another for "making the engines for mills to go by water." Of course we know by now that the iron which came from such an early forge would be "charcoal iron" which was the best possible kind, but this charcoal fuel led once to a rather summary closing of our first foundry, because the ready-made coal pile was such a temptation to the neighbors that they stole it in the dead of night. Apparently Jenks got more "coal," for in 1652 he cast the dies for our first coin, the old "Pine Tree Shilling," with "Massachusetts" and a pine tree in bas relief on one side and "N. E. Anno 1652" and the coin value on the reverse. This famous casting established a mint in Boston Towne of "forme flatt." Jenks also had a foundry in Rhode Island and his old home built in 1655 is still standing.

Jenks is called the first founder to work in brass and iron on this continent. He made the first models, and the first castings from them, and these included tools and implements and chimney hearth wares. He died in 1683. In one way he was more fortunate than a neighbor who started his business in Braintree that same year that the first patent was granted. This was the Dr. Child who made a gallant attempt to be useful through his iron craft but after turning out tons of pots and mortars and other household needs, was cut off in the midst of what his fellow-men called his sins, and prevented from pushing a glass works and a black lead mill because of his religious toleration.

To Taunton from Wales came the Leonard family in the 1680s to be known in this country for seven generations as ironmakers. Their foundry was at the Raynham of today, and from the fifth generation came Eliphalet, in 1775, destined to make the first bar of American steel. Pennsylvania took her place as a leading iron colony in the 1700s. We have already met Thomas Rutter here, and into his family married a young man by the name of Potts. This marriage was to mean much to the country's iron industry, for the Potts foundry became the core of a town known as Pottsylvania, later as Pottsgrove and finally as Pottstown where the foundry still exists. Potts had a son who followed him as a founder and he in turn had iron-making sons. Historic Valley Forge was named for the early forge of the Potts.

Besides Baron Stiegel's artistic iron firebacks, already mentioned, there was also his unique "Iron Bible" a strange six-sided iron box of a stove which was set through the wall close to the fireplace, burned small twigs, had no pipe, and was decorated with scenes cast from Biblical literature. Stiegel came out of Germany in 1750 and only two years later was party to another fortunate marriage in the iron world, by winning the fair hand of Elizabeth Huber whose father was a successful iron man at Brickerville. Here in a few more years, Stiegel came into the possession of the Huber furnace and later we see the Elizabeth Furnace taking a conspicuous place. Actually an iron maker, Stiegel is of course better known for his beautiful glassware, almost the first to be so called in this country.

Primitive Molds

When Joseph Jenks and his contemporaries began their casting of iron their molds were formed of common clay. This was before 1650 and it was not until nearly ninety years later, that any change was made in the mold material. At Kingston there was an Englishman who had the startling idea of making molds of sand instead of clay, and Joseph Mallinson of Duxbury was using this type of sand mold in 1738. As in all of the industries, various names were used locally to express the same general tool or implement. In bell making there was "the stake surrounded with a solid brick-work perfectly round, five or six inches high, and of a diameter equal to that of a bell, and called a millstone." The lower part of the bell mold was the "core" and the upper, the "cape." The inner case was swathed with straw rope and a coat of loam. The fluid metal was poured in between the straw and allowed a slow cooling. It seems that there was great danger of explosions in this process, as flames would dart out of the vent holes; and so before 1826 complete loam mounds were packed in pits beneath the surface of the foundry floor to resist the pressure of the fluid metal.

Typical Old Foundry Still at Work

Standing right at the turn of the road where it crosses the bridge, overhung by tall maples and elms, well founded on its wall of rock, within murmur distance of Cold River which flows just below it, is the old Lufkin-Bragg foundry. It looks healthily shabby as it is approached head-on, but all of this is forgotten when its quaint sideview is glimpsed across the

THE FOUNDER'S FOUNDRY

Old Lufkin-Bragg foundry at Alstead,
New Hampshire

stony stream, showing its long low stature. It does not go back into the dim era of the ocean-front settlements, for this part of the country only became white-manned in the middle of the 1700s: it was built at about the beginning of the Civil War. For only two weeks out of the entire year is it now busy, two weeks which turn out spring plough points for farmers, but no one considers its usefulness past or its

373

life-span foredoomed. It is outstanding perhaps only because it is one of the few old iron foundries left on a country road-side, and because it is so typical of many which once flourished and have now either slipped into the passing brook or dropped so many shingles that the old stack is now peeping through at the sky.

One must step over the sill and down with the same careful step to enter the low door of this old foundry, and the window-panes show themselves a highway and refuge for captive flies and spiders which have crawled and fought there for decades. At the far end is the old stack of steel with its brick frame and support, measuring five or six feet. At the left of the stack a flight of intriguingly steep and risky steps mount and turn to mount still higher to reach the "charging door" which is located at the back of the stack and through which the alternate layers of old scrap iron and coke are thrown in for smelting. Incidentally this high door has a fine hand-wrought handle. When the iron has been melted by the heat of the coke, it escapes from the stack through a hole in the form of a glowing liquid, and whenever it is necessary to stop it, a clay ball is set against the opening and the flow stops at once.

The Flasks

It will be necessary now to look into the preparation which has already been made for the reception of this molten liquid. Down each side of the foundry room have been placed two rows of heavy wooden triangular box-like frames, called "flasks." These are of two separate parts fastened together with clamps, the top being the "cope" and the lower part the "nowel" or bottom-board. They are nine inches high, eighteen across the base of the triangle and twenty-eight along the sides. The founder must have them well dressed for the next step in casting; some one has had to hitch up the team and drive west to the big sand pits for the "molding sand" which is found only here in this section and drag it back the five miles. The sand is moistened and then tamped firmly into both bottom board and cope. Just behind the foundry the old pattern house used to stand. Here wooden patterns were cut and whittled, turned and smoothed and polished, to form a perfect impress for the mold sand. Whatever their shape, would be the shape of the finished article. This pattern was now pressed about half-way down into the sand of the nowell, and the tamping iron made to fill its every crevice and curve with the sand. Then the loose sand was carefully brushed off of the pattern and that in the nowell smoothed to lie level with the side uprights. Now the "parting sand" (which had been gathered in the brook and burned) was sprinkled over the molding sand so that after the cope had been pressed down over the pattern to get the top imprint and had rested there for ten minutes, it could be removed without making a fuss about it and leaving a rough and broken surface in the sand which would have occurred if the molding sand had had the last word. Finally, after the ten minutes when the two parts of the mold are clamped together, the cope is taken off, and of course there has been no explosion because the molding sand's properties have formed a "vented mold." If all has gone well this upper part of the flask will bear in its bosom the perfect impress of the top of the pattern, and when the pattern itself has been removed from the lower part and the two are clamped together again the full pattern mold will be perfected in their combined center.

The "sprue" is a wooden stick about six or seven inches long which is now run through a point in the flask to the inside hollow mold, when it is carefully pulled back, for it has formed the sprue-hole through which the liquid iron can reach its mold. "Sometimes the sprue has a sort of tin gate at the bottom, which carries the metal to the mold and this method is called the 'flat-gate,'" the founder's wife tells us, "and you've got to be very careful to pat back any sand that is stirred up by the sprue. Sometimes the iron just slips through by itself."

So, at last, we are ready to let the molten iron flow out of its low hole in the stack. Men with ladles catch the liquid and carry it quickly to each flask, fill the mold and go back for more, until the two long rows of waiting molds have been filled. After this the time is short before the setting has taken place and the finished article — this time a plough point — can be taken from the sandy molds and stand ready to begin its wrangle with one of earth's many floors.

First piece of cast iron made in America.
Joseph Jenks, Saugus 1642

Kettles and Such

While bells may have been the founders' first excuse for working, pots and kettles could not have been far behind. The first object cast in iron in America was not a bell, but

a one-quart pot. The country founder could cast almost anything needed by his neighbors and turned out iron gempans,
washbowls which were really highsided skillets with the
same kind of pointed handle, all sorts of hearth hardware,
endless varieties of frying pans and porringers and a good
many things which seem odd to be made of this heavy metal.
Firebacks are considered old if they were cast by the Baron
Stiegel works, but in the Pickering home at Salem, Massachusetts, built in 1660, there have been firebacks pre-
sumably since that date which were made in the earlier
works at Saugus.

It is the pot and the kettle which really take front place
in our first foundries and by some these two terms are used
interchangeably, although the kettle was officially a vessel
in which meat was boiled, and a pot was a vessel for boiling
or holding liquids. There was a verb, "to pot," which meant
to season meat. Iron and brass kettles were brought by many
of our first families and were considered a necessity for those
crossing the great divide. A single pot was made to serve
all sorts of purposes, and as an old Southerner put it: "To
kettle the daily hog and hominy and other fare, once a week
to boil the clothes, on occasion to boil salt water to evaporate
it for the salt." The Northerner adds "and for boiling maple
sap when the sugaring comes on in the spring and for brewing the 'spring dose,' and making boiled cider apple sass."
There is a part of Gloucester, Massachusetts, now called
Magnolia, which for many years was known as "Kettle
Cove." There when the first settlers came, it was found that
only one pot had crossed with them, and so this one had to
be borrowed all around the group, and was kept busy turning out hot fish chowders and well boiled clothes. One of the
"greatpots" was the "blubberpot" used in whaling circles

and it measured about three feet deep and a good four and a half feet across the opening. The country folks around Amherst, Massachusetts, and many elsewhere, fastened their large brass kettles to the ends of their sled or sleigh runners after a hard blizzard to break out the runner tracks for the man who would be coming on behind, thus "kettlin' the roads."

There was also the "Dutch Oven," which was a low inconsequential-looking iron pot, fitted with an iron cover which had a hollow running around it and an upturning edge so that it could be covered with hot coals: beneath were three iron feet which raised the pot to allow coals to come in under it as well, and so when it sat in the ashes on the hearth it was completely surrounded with heat.

Then there was the "porringer," a vessel for "spoonmeat," the "porridge pot" for porridge or broth made by boiling meat, and also the "potager," a porringer to eat broth in. All of this potage-porringe type of vessel was created for the control and absorption of meats and nowhere do we find a porringer specified for our porridge or modern cereal. "Pot luck" came to mean whatever happened to be simmering in the great pot hanging from its lugpole, crane or trammel, but the stranger at the door seems always to have been glad to partake of this economical "pot-luck." A "pot ball" was a dumpling. Whatever the kind of pot it might be, it was so much a precious possession that even after our founder men had begun to function, it was never omitted from a man's will.

The tea kettle had to be imported until about 1760, but at that time or shortly after, the first American iron tea kettle was cast at home, supposedly "founded" at Carver. Massachusetts. Since it was cast in clay we can be glad that it did not delay bringing this honor to its native land, by exploding in the mold. A copper tea kettle was made in Plymouth in 1702. Up until 1730, the forges for making bar iron outnumbered the furnaces turning out hollow-ware in the proportion of three to one.

State Potages

Each State seems to have had some special treat which grew in their great chimneyplace pots. Here are but two of them:

Virginia has her "Brunswick Stew" made of squirrel or chicken already cooked, in a pot with potatoes, tomatoes, corn, and lima beans thrown into the broth and left to simmer for several hours or until thick. South Carolina has her "Fish Stew" done in an iron pot. On the bottom is placed a layer of strips of fat meat (some of whose fat has been tryed out beforehand), then a layer of sliced potatoes, then a layer of fish cut into large blocks the right size for serving, then a layer of chopped onions, then salt and black — and some red — pepper. Then repeat this whole process over and over until the great iron pot is nearly full, when it will be filled the rest of the way with water and catsup. This is cooked for thirty minutes. Gravy is made and the fish served on slices of bread, and then . . . to bed to take pot-luck with dreams.

XXXII. PLOUGHSHARES

Of the Earth

SURELY nothing was more of the earth, earthy, than the plough which scratched and tilled, ditched and furrowed, to make a seed-bed for man's planting. Of course when one gets down to simple truths it is a bit foolish to claim this "earthiness" for some things more than for others, when behind all lies the versatile "Earth" itself as our main reservoir of material and power. In the case of the plough we have something made from trees and iron mines, which, as soon as it is hewn and melted and welded into form, goes back to the earth from which it came, to grovel and struggle there.

The plough of today, and for some decades back, is a direct product of the iron mine and the steel plant but for some of our forefathers the plough, upon which their daily food depended, never had a touch of metal, only wood straight from the forest. It has been said that the plough of the early American settler reflected the ploughs currently in use in England and Holland; this is hardly the whole truth, for many a New World plough was nothing but the crudest tree fork, the upper prong hooked to the beast which drew it and the lower sharpened to gouge the earth's surface, while the main branch stretched out some feet behind to be fitted with a crude upright of a handle for haphazard guiding, or was even pulled by hand. Such a plough is still to be seen in St. Augustine, Florida.

We seem never to be done repeating for our own remembrance the fact that regardless of the century, the pioneer settlers used the same crude methods in outfitting their daily lives, whether they took up their land in the 1600s or the 1800s, and that they continued these methods until their own progressiveness, or chance, brought the more advanced ones. North Carolina, whose soil is light and sandy, made one of her ploughs, not long ago, with the beam hewn from a five-foot log, the ploughshare nothing but a five-inch branch of the gum tree cut about sixteen inches long and sharpened to a pencil point, then fastened horizontally below the beam with two stout braces of wood; she made another with the same length and kind of beam, but driven through it was a heavy knife of steel, shaped on a home forge to a sharp front edge, and broadening to three quarters of an inch at the back. In the light soil the first plough ran along entirely satisfactorily, and where the ground was not full of roots, the steel blade of the second, set forward at a slight angle, cut the new ground to perfection.

Down East Ploughs

When a ready-made plough arrived from the Old World in the early 1600s, its owner immediately had a boom in personal importance. Massachusetts Bay Colony had thirty-seven ploughs in 1637, rather a goodly number for such a new section, and yet to prove that the number was scant in proportion to the need, we find some towns granting bounties to the men who brought them in, and see also their service eagerly begged for by the neighbors before planting time came round. This old "bull plough" was aptly named for it took eight or ten oxen to drag it along, with its great ten-foot beam of heavy wood, and its four-foot landside giving it a total length of a dozen feet. Men rode upon it to drive it into the earth, and others walked behind to hoe out those places which had been jumped. For at least two generations, and probably more, these Bay Colony farmers wrestled with this modern convenience of their time, clutching the slanting uprights which served as handles, and plunging doggedly ahead through underbrush and around boulders.

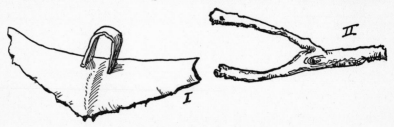

i. A unique Georgia plough
ii. Florida's ancient natural-growth plough

Southern Ploughs

We have had the plough census of the Bay Colony in 1637 and now Virginia gives her number for 1649 as one hundred and fifty. Like her sister Colonies she had both the imported English and the domestic tilling machines, the former costing one pound sterling and the latter a mere ten shillings. She had a way of referring to these machines as "the share and colter" until toward the end of the century, and had them drawn by oxen and cows geared with chains and yokes and hooks. Then came the moldboard, that invention of the Dutch mind. The South seems to have lagged behind the East and North in the use of the plough, and this was probably due to the fact that the greater physical energy of the latter peoples had begotten greater clearings in which a plough could be used, and also because more draught animals had been procured there.

To Augusta, Georgia, goes the palm for a most unique plough of solid iron, produced there in 1796. It is shaped like a bird with wings spread, and has a great iron hasp by which it could be drawn. It is not large, but must have needed much pressure to keep it in the earth.

General Plough Principals

We have already seen that the first plough attempt was the crooked stick, working on the principle of the double mold board and throwing the earth out on both sides. The next idea was to whack off one side of the stick to get the form of the single mold board which threw the earth on one side only. After this the plough became a wedge, the landside being parallel with the line of the plough's motion while the other side threw the furrow still to the right side and left it standing on edge. Finally the wedge was so twisted and shaped as to regularly throw the furrow completely over.

One of the things which was constantly striven for was the stream-lining of the plough, although that expression was far in the future. The first success in this idea was in getting straight lines from the sole to the top of the share and moldboard; the next in getting straight lines from the front to the back of same; then some one thought of laying down all lines on a plane surface, and still another of the importance of a center draft and the practical means of getting it by the inclination of the landside inward.

Its Parts

Perhaps a word as to the parts of the old ploughs may be worth while here. Today, without counting the bolts, our ploughs may have twenty-six pieces in their make-up, but in earlier times one spoke of "the plough and the plough-share" and enough was said. The "beam" was the backbone of the whole affair from which the share was suspended. At the fore-end of the beam was the clevis or clevice or draught iron to which the cow or horse or ox, or the six or eight of each which might be necessary, were fastened; at the other end was "the handle," or handles, upright sticks of wood by which the plodding plougher might attempt to guide his great landship. In some places, authorities tell us, it was not until the Revolution "the handle" made way for a pair of them, and then the beam was fastened to the left-hand one. A thousand years B.C. they were talking of the "colter." The coulter today is that little point of steel or fore-iron, the "sod cutter" or "bull tongue" which runs ahead of the point; as well as the pointed pieces of iron attached to the stripped standard for special after-ploughing or channeling. The "share" which was once the main part of the plough is now rarely spoken of, for in its place have come the "moldboard" and "point," separate but connected pieces. The moldboard is that part which catches the newly broken ground and with its smooth curved surface, turns the sod over bringing the under soil up into the sunlight. The point was once the sharpened part of the share and that which was subjected to the greatest wear and tear and had most often to be re-sharpened or bolstered with strips of iron, or replaced with a new welded point. The old "land-side" was of wood, a straight, smooth piece running along the other side of the plough from the share, a sort of guide for a straight furrow. The "standard" was the upright which connected the share with the beam, and today connects all of the parts at a central spot.

PLOUGHSHARES

Our Plough Inventors

One must remember always the influence which assisted us in our struggling advances. In the matter of ploughs, while we might go back to 1100 B.C. and the Egyptian ploughs, we will content ourselves by acknowledging help given by Holland, a Scotchman named Small, and an Englishman called Ransom. Holland turned the first furrow; Small improved the Dutch plough by making the greater portion of iron; and Ransom found a way in 1803 to case-harden and chill the point.

CHARLES NEWBOLD of Burlington, New Jersey, is called our pioneer plough builder, and while his invention was finished in 1780 it was not until 1797 that he procured his patent for it. His plough was our first cast-iron one with a mold board of an English cut but of one piece with the landside. It could be drawn by so few as two oxen, and left behind it so few "holidays" where the sod had not turned, that the usual follower of the plough, hoe in hand, could now be dispensed with. Newbold's very ingenuity was his undoing though, for the farmers were not going to be taken in by any wild-goose ideas, and have their soil "poisoned" by unheard-of iron plough shares, which must also make the weeds grow ranker. They refused to use the Newbold iron plough for years, and Newbold let plough improvement drop.

THOMAS JEFFERSON, along with his statesman duties, his architecture, and countless other interests, was also a scientific farmer and gave much thought to the improvement of the plough, writing at length on the subject in 1788, and doing practical work on it in 1793.

385

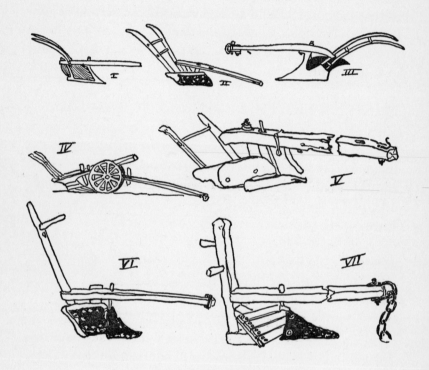

I. *Newbold plough* 1797
II. *Wooden share shod with iron*
III. *Jethro Wood plough*
IV. *The innovation of wheels*
V. *Common type of wooden plough*
VI. *A well shoe-ed mold board*
VII. *Mold board of small pieces to form a curve*

PLOUGHSHARES

JETHRO WOOD, a Scipio, New York, Quaker, had been much impressed by these writings of Jefferson's and started in to take up the work where Newbold had laid it down. By 1814 he had patented a plough all of cast iron except the beam and handles, his improvement over that of Newbold being that the workable parts were all made separately, so that worn ones could be replaced with little trouble and expense. This plough was intended for use in the eastern part of the country, and in 1839 when Wood died, it was in rather general use.

DANIEL WEBSTER in 1836 produced a huge, cumbersome plough which tilled the ground a foot deep or more. It had a four-foot landside, a bar and share forged together, a moldboard of wood covered with strips of iron, it measured eighteen inches at the heel of moldboard to the landside, and had a spread of twenty-seven inches. The share was fifteen inches wide.

JOHN DEERE, a Vermont blacksmith, decided as a young man to go west and in 1836 landed in Grand Detour, Illinois, to establish a new home for his growing family. Two days after his arrival he was at work in his new shop. Soon he came to realize that shoeing horses and repairing breaks would get him nowhere, and noticed that the covered-wagons were going through to the far western mountains rather than stopping on the rich prairie lands, because word had come back: "Pass up the prairie lands, for no plough will work after the first breaking." Near his own location much of the land was so sticky and gluey that ploughers had to carry paddles to keep their plough points clean enough to plough with.

OF THE EARTH EARTHY

*The John Deere "Self Polisher" made at
Grand Detour, Illinois, 1837*

Here apparently was a new need, a plough which could not only break up the prairie but cultivate it for second and many more crops. John Deere conceived the idea of a plough which would scour itself. He found a piece of an old broken mill-saw which had come originally from Sheffield, England, and with this set to work to make a ploughshare so smooth that it could indeed clean itself as it went along. Out of a log he cut and shaped a form over which he could pound out his steel in the needed curves, using a wooden beetle for the pounding lest the steel become dented in the process. The countryside became interested and watched young Deere at his forge and anvil, saw him carry the plough out day after day to test it in the ground, and saw him bring it back for further changes. One day he carried it to the flat boat on the Rock River, put it aboard and started poling to the other side to the farm of Lewis Crandel, where the soil was notoriously gluey. A crowd followed to laugh at him for attempting the impossible, but the test was a success, the ploughshare growing brighter and smoother with each sod turned.

PLOUGHSHARES

It is impossible to visualize this crucial test of the first steel share plough without sensing somewhat of the revolution in farming which it was to bring about. Our prairies have become the great granaries of the country and even of the world, and while the Eastern States with their lighter soils would have gone on quite unaffected by John Deere's work, the Western pioneer and his developments of the land would have written a very different story from the one which we read today. Friends remembering the great day in 1837, recall Deere's casual report of it:

"I cut the teeth off the mill-saw with a hand chisel. I cut a pattern out of paper for the moldboard and share. I laid the pattern on the saw and cut around it with a hand chisel, with the help of a striker and sledge. I then laid the piece on the fire of the forge and heated it, a little at a time, shaping it as best I could with the hand hammer." Another friend remembers that he said also: "After making the upright standards out of bar iron, I was ready for the wood parts. I went out to the timber, dug up a sapling, and used the crooks of the roots for handles. I shaped the beam out of a fence rail with an axe and a drawing knife. In this fashion I succeeded in constructing a very rough plough." One of the first three ploughs which John Deere made is still preserved in Moline, Illinois, the city which is called the "plough center" of the world. Every year of John Deere's life seems to justify the claim that in the making of their handwrought articles our ancestors were making splendidly handwrought specimens of themselves. A countrified "Vermonter," born in Rutland and raised in Middlebury, by loving his trade of blacksmith, daring the long, long journey to the Middle West, and having an eye open to the needs of the hour, became a man of unusual wealth and worth. Just a century ago his "first steel plough" had its simple but acclaimed test, and polished itself as it slipped along through the most notoriously gluey soil in the whole of America.

OTHER INVENTORS. While these men who have been mentioned at some length are outstanding in plough improvement, many others took part in its development, for between the ploughs of Newbold, 1797, and Jethro Wood, 1814, seventeen patents had been issued to other men. By 1880 the United States had granted 6686 patents for ploughs alone.

The Lufkin Plough

Typical of many tiny plough shops and foundries throughout the country were those of Charles M. Lufkin of Alstead, New Hampshire. Above Cold River, edging the highway where it turned to cross the bridge, and backed by its "pattern house," stood, and still stands, the foundry where the iron parts of the Lufkin ploughs were cast. A mile to the east, on the very crest of a land rise and, like its sister building, edging the common road, and standing very high above Warren Pond Brook which rushed headlong down through the valley, the ploughshop itself clung to the rocks. For so small a building there was much spaciousness. One went up and down narrow stairs to see all the wondrous new ploughs, and the stray burnished patterns made of wood and smooth enough to form a perfect impress in the casting sand and thus father the perfect castings which would follow in their footsteps. Here the ploughs were put together piece by piece.

In the fall of 1868 when New Hampshire held her State Fair at Nashua, a farm boy came bearing an invention which was to revolutionize ploughing in the hilly sections of his countryside. He was spoken of as "Ezra Lufkin's son from over to Acworth," and indeed was so, but the world was to know him later as Charles M. Lufkin, the inventor of the rigid landslide swivel plough. Charles seems to have been addicted to Fairs, for in 1893 we see him at the World's Fair in Chicago, taking first medal for his Alstead-made plough.

We have at least one plough in the country which is nearly two hundred and forty years old, one nearly one hundred and seventy-five years old, if tales be trustworthy, and both originating in Biddeford, Maine. Here and there the old ploughs pop up, some dated and some guessed at, while plough collections are becoming popular. They cover the wooden period, the time when iron straps came to strengthen the points, and iron plates the moldboards; they show the coming of the iron share and moldboard after some men had tried to shape the wooden one with many slender slats; they show the single upright for a handle, the cumbersome ten-foot beam, and practically all of the fine points which bespeak a day of slow attempt and honest ingenuity.

Says the Bible: "Thou shalt not plough with an ox and an ass together," "But," says the Southern Sharecropper, "we must."

And he does.

Cousining with the American plough was the great American reaper which revolutionized agriculture over a large part of the earth. Many a reaper was concocted to better the slow handscythe, sickle and reaping hook, until there grew up in the middle 1800s that famous "war of the reapers" among the various inventors who claimed the first model. Outstanding among these clever and ingenious men were Cyrus McCormick and his father, of Raphine, Virginia,

*Side by side, not twenty feet apart, the old
McCormick mill and shop still stand at
Raphine, Virginia, today*

the former producing in 1831 a reaper which was to grow in popularity and new attachments until it became the great reaper of the world. In the same decade which saw John Deere producing the first self-polishing plough, Cyrus McCormick in his tiny stone blacksmith shop under a slave cabin on his father's plantation, wrought and proved this awaited cousin of the plough which should garner where the latter had broken ground for the seed-beds of mankind. Each, given birth at a blacksmith's forge, was by pedigree and destined task, truly of the earth, earthy.

The little shop within the foundation walls of the old log slave cabin, where Cyrus McCormick gave his great harvester to the world

393

OF THE EARTH EARTHY

Simon N. Patten, who was the first dean of economists in our American colleges, used to say quietly and with a long, long look in his eyes: "Beyond anything else which I may have accomplished in my life I am proudest of the fact that as a young man I ploughed fifty acres of unbroken prairie land."

The little window above the old workbench where Cyrus and his father wrought, is closed

LIST OF ILLUSTRATIONS

LIST OF ILLUSTRATIONS

LIST OF ILLUSTRATIONS

397

LIST OF ILLUSTRATIONS

398

LIST OF ILLUSTRATIONS

LIST OF ILLUSTRATIONS

LIST OF ILLUSTRATIONS

LIST OF ILLUSTRATIONS

LIST OF ILLUSTRATIONS

403

LIST OF ILLUSTRATIONS

404

LIST OF ILLUSTRATIONS

405

LIST OF ILLUSTRATIONS

INDEX

407

INDEX

408

INDEX

INDEX

INDEX

INDEX

INDEX